INTRODUCTION TO
a Philosophy of Music

D0760148

INTRODUCTION TO
a Philosophy of Music

PETER KIVY

CLARENDON PRESS · OXFORD

OXFORD
UNIVERSITY PRESS

Great Clarendon Street, Oxford OX2 6DP

Oxford University Press is a department of the University of Oxford.
It furthers the University's objective of excellence in research, scholarship,
and education by publishing worldwide in

Oxford New York

Auckland Bangkok Buenos Aires Cape Town Chennai
Dar es Salaam Delhi Hong Kong Istanbul Karachi Kolkata
Kuala Lumpur Madrid Melbourne Mexico City Mumbai Nairobi
São Paulo Shanghai Singapore Taipei Tokyo Toronto

with an associated company in Berlin

Oxford is a registered trade mark of Oxford University Press
in the UK and in certain other countries

Published in the United States
by Oxford University Press Inc., New York

British Library Cataloguing in Publication Data

Data available

Library of Congress Cataloging in Publication Data
Kivy, Peter.
    Introduction to a philosophy of music / Peter Kivy.
        p. cm.
    Includes bibliographical references.
    1. Music—Philosophy and aesthetics.   I. Title.
ML3845 .K584 2002   781'.1—dc21   2001058833

ISBN 0–19–825047–9
ISBN 0–19–825048–7 (Pbk.)

10 9 8 7 6 5 4

Typeset in 10.75 / 14pt Dante by Graphicraft Limited, Hong Kong
Printed in Great Britain by Biddles Ltd., Guildford & King's Lynn

For my students:
   past, present, and future

PREFACE

When Peter Momtchiloff of Oxford University Press asked me to write an introductory volume on the philosophy of music, I imagined what he wanted was something for which the correct title would be: *An* Introduction to *the* Philosophy of Music. What I have written has a similar, but, however, importantly different title: Introduction to *a* Philosophy of Music. What does the difference amount to?

An introduction to the philosophy of anything, I take it, would be a volume written clearly and simply enough for no previous knowledge of the subject to be needed to understand it; a volume that would tell the reader about all the major issues in the field, and all the current positions on those issues that the author takes to be at least plausible enough to be worthy of consideration; a volume in which the author would stay more or less neutral regarding which position on any given issue might be the correct one. In other words, such a volume would be what is commonly called, in academic circles, a 'textbook': a survey of the field for the purpose of introducing the beginning student to it.

I did not wish to write a book like that, useful though such books might be. My model and inspiration, rather, was Bertrand Russell's perennial classic, *The Problems of Philosophy*—a book, I take it, that is an introduction to *a* philosophy, namely, the author's, as he understood philosophy at the time of its writing. In a perfectly straightforward sense, however, *The Problems of Philosophy* is, unlike a textbook of philosophy, *a work of philosophy* as well. And, to appropriate (or perhaps misappropriate) a concept that Russell himself made famous, the best way to be introduced to the subject of philosophy is not by description, which is the way a textbook does it, but by direct acquaintance with the practice of philosophy at its best, in real philosophical works that are accessible to the beginner. This is why so many introductory courses in philosophy will have as their texts not textbooks but such works as Plato's early dialogues, Descartes's *Meditations*, and similar 'accessible' masterpieces of the philosophical literature. So, without foolishly aspiring to the level of Plato, Descartes, or Russell, I intend this book to introduce the lay reader to *my* philosophy of music, not to *the* philosophy of music, *tout court*. Yet, in the perfectly straightforward sense in which Bertrand Russell's *Problems of Philosophy* is not merely an introduction to his philosophy but to philosophy *sans phrase*, my book, I hope, will introduce the reader to *the* philosophy of music, by acquaintance, by being as good an example of the philosophy of music, as it is currently practiced, as I can make it to be.

One more word, a word of warning, before I get down to business. This book, as I have said, is an introduction to *my* philosophy of music. Those views that oppose mine, on any given issue, I try to present informatively and fairly, but definitely not neutrally. I think I am right and my opponents wrong. So I am scarcely a disinterested spectator on the philosophical scene, and my fairness to my opponents should always be a subject of the reader's skepticism.

But, as much as I would like to convince my reader that I am right and others wrong, that is not my primary aim, which is, rather, to convince the reader that the questions raised in this book are interesting and important, to provoke the reader to pursue those questions further, and to show me mistaken in the end. It is a poor teacher who produces, or wishes to produce, sycophants, clones, or apathy.

This having been said, the pleasurable task now remains to me of thanking two people without whose support and help this project not only never would have been completed, but never would have been started in the first place.

It was Peter Momtchiloff who first proposed to me that I write an introduction to the philosophy of music, and I resisted the idea right from the start. I had always, in the past, turned down invitations to write introductions to *anything*, and this wasn't going to be an exception. But Peter was very persuasive, and, furthermore, Noel Carroll, who himself had been working on an introduction to aesthetics, started leaning on me as well. Together they constituted an irrestibible force, and I caved in. I'm not sorry. Writing this book has been a wonderful experience.

But my indebtedness to Messrs Momtchiloff and Carroll does not end here. Peter has been like the proverbial Rock of Gibralter in his support of my project, and has put up with my cantankerousness with all of the patience at his disposal—which is considerable. And Noel dropped a million other projects to read through the entire manuscript with his usual thoroughness, critical acumen, and generosity of spirit. I owe them both an enormous debt of gratitude for their help. But I owe them as well the assurance that whatever imperfections remain in this book are my responsibility alone.

Peter Kivy

Cape Cod
Summer 2001

CONTENTS

If you think that what I say is true, agree with me; if not, oppose it with every argument and take care that in my eagerness I do not deceive myself and you and, like a bee, leave my sting in you when I go.

Socrates (according to Plato), trans. G.M.A. Grube

CHAPTER I

Philosophy of . . .

If someone who doesn't know how to cook should buy a cookbook, she hardly expects, on opening it, to find the first chapter devoted to the question of what cooking *is*. Presumably, she already knows *that* much about the subject.

But it is quite likely that someone who buys a book called *Introduction to a Philosophy of Music* will not only not know what the philosophy of music is; she will not know what *philosophy* is either. So it seems not altogether inappropriate to begin with such a chapter as this. However, it is part of the nature of philosophy that to tell what philosophy *is* is itself a daunting task. It is itself a disputed question in the practice of philosophy, which immediately makes it look as if we are going around in a circle, since I will already be *doing* philosophy in trying to tell my reader what philosophy is.

Well, what of that? Perhaps the best way of learning what some subject is is to see it pursued. So in trying to give my reader a preliminary idea of what philosophy is I will not only be *telling*; I will be *showing*, by example, as it were, as well.

What *is* philosophy then? There are many ways of approaching the question. Here is one.

It is an obvious fact of English grammar that one can put the phrase 'philosophy of . . .' in front of all sorts of nouns. But it is also an obvious fact of *philosophy* that not every such combination constitutes a branch of the subject, as now practiced. Some of the currently recognized specialities in philosophy are the philosophy of science, the philosophy of history, the philosophy of art, the philosophy of education. But there is no philosophy of baseball or philosophy of sewage or philosophy of shoes. Why not? There's nothing wrong with the grammar.

Not only is there nothing wrong with the grammar, there are occasions on which such phrases as 'the philosophy of baseball,' or 'the philosophy of sewage,' or 'the philosophy of shoes' might well be heard, not uttered by philosophers, to be sure, but by other, perfectly qualified users of the English language. A sportswriter might be emboldened to describe 'Wee Willie' Keeler's well-known description of his practice, 'Hit 'em where they ain't,' as encapsulating his 'philosophy of baseball,' and we would all know what was meant, even the philosophers, in spite of it nevertheless being true, at least at the present time, that there is no philosophy of baseball taught in our colleges and universities, along with the philosophy of art and the philosophy of history and the rest. Is it possible that we might get a handle on what philosophy is by taking a look at what it might mean, for example, to say of Keeler's 'Hit 'em where they ain't' that it is his philosophy of baseball, even though, in fact, there *is* no philosophy of baseball? Let's see.

A number of things might strike one about 'Hit 'em where they ain't' as advice to an aspiring baseball-player. First of all, it's really a useless bit of advice after all. If a player should go to baseball camp to learn how to be a good hitter, he wants practical advice about where to place his feet, how to swing the bat, what he is now doing wrong in these departments, and so forth. If all the batting coach could offer was 'Hit 'em where they ain't,' he wouldn't be much use. It seems a vacuous truism.

Second, a precept like 'Hit 'em where they ain't' strikes us as something we would tend to preface with 'needless to say.' It is so *obvious* that the point of batting is to 'Hit 'em where they ain't' that it is tacitly assumed: 'it goes without saying.'

Third, however, vacuous though it might seem to be, on first reflection, 'Hit 'em where they ain't,' if reflected upon more fully, may seem ultimately to cast explanatory light on all of the things the batting coach has been telling the aspiring hitter. They are all now seen as *being to that end*. It all at once becomes clear 'what it's all about.' In other words, 'Hit 'em where they ain't' seems to be a very *basic* characterization of baseball: an ultimate principle, so to speak; the ultimate justification for everything else the batting coach tells the hitter. So it would appear to be the case that in calling 'Hit 'em where they ain't' Keeler's 'philosophy of baseball,' we are according it the status of a foundational axiom: something from which everything else follows. It is so basic it hardly needs stating; but stating it brings a form of enlightenment we would not have had were it to have been left, as it normally is, unspoken.

Of course there might be other 'philosophies' of baseball as well. Perhaps 'A good defense is the best offense' is the infield coach's 'philosophy of baseball.' Again, it is not much use in teaching the third baseman how to protect the line or the second baseman how to avoid the runner's slide in turning a double play. And these latter skills are what the infielders look to their coach to impart. 'A good defense is the best offense' is a mere platitude from the point of view of practice: a truism that hardly requires stating. But, like 'Hit 'em where they ain't,' it can be seen, when brought to light, as a basic premise from which all else follows. It may become the infielders' 'Liberté, egalité, fraternité.' It makes *them* see 'what it's all about.' 'A good defense is the best offense' may become in that way the infielders' 'philosophy of baseball.'

So it begins to look as if those uninitiated into the mysteries of 'philosophy' nevertheless know how to apply the word in a way quite understandable to competent users of the language, including the philosophers. There is no reason even for philosophers to think they are *mis*applying the word. Furthermore, it is reasonable to suppose that at least part of the meaning or connotation of the word 'philosophy' carries over from the discipline of philosophy to ordinary life and ordinary usage, or vice versa. So it is also reasonable to suppose that we can learn something about the word's meaning or connotation by extrapolating either from philosophy to ordinary life and usage or from ordinary life and usage to philosophy. And, since it is the discipline of philosophy I am trying to explain to people who don't know what *it* is, but *are* competent users of the English language, and do know what it means to say that Keeler's 'philosophy of baseball' is 'Hit 'em where they ain't,' it is from ordinary life and usage that I hope to get a hint, and give a hint, about the discipline of philosophy.

'Hit 'em where they ain't,' Keeler's 'philosophy of baseball,' has in common with many basic statements in the discipline of philosophy the seeming vacuousness, the feeling that 'this goes without saying,' and, for all of that, the enlightening effect that comes with subsequent reflection. Furthermore, it has in common the nature of being a basic truth, a foundational axiom: that from which the other precepts and principles of the practice or discipline follow.

Consider an example. In the philosophy of morals, more commonly called 'moral philosophy' or 'ethics,' there is a widely held theory that says that those actions are morally right actions that have, overall, the best total consequences. The theory, not surprisingly, is known as 'consequantialism.' But its basic premise seems every bit as vacuous a truism, initially, as 'Hit 'em where they ain't.' In effect, all it seems to say is: 'Do what will turn out to be best.' Do I need a *philosopher* to tell me *this*? As well, like 'Hit 'em where they ain't,' it would seem to 'go without saying'; hardly to require explicit statement at all. *Of course* it is the point of moral reflection to tell us what we should do to make things turn out for the best. That is an underlying assumption too obvious to require uttering out loud.

However, some sustained reflection on the consequentialist first principle may lead one to a degree of illumination: may lead one to reach moral conclusions one might not have reached otherwise. Lying is wrong, we have all been taught; and we have been taught, too, not to cause pain to others—two moral precepts as obvious as the consequentialist one. But what to do when telling the truth will cause pain to others and lying will prevent it? *Both* alternatives seem wrong *and* right. The consequentialist first principle suggests to us how to solve this moral dilemma. We must choose the alternative that will produce the best consequences all around. We must calculate the consequences of lying, and of telling the truth, and choose the alternative producing the best, or the least bad.

Thus the consequentialist first principle, those actions are morally right that, overall, have the best consequences as compared to the alternatives, vacuous though it may seem at first, and hardly worth making explicit, turns out to be a foundational principle in the philosophy of morality, from which other principles can be derived, and which casts broad illumination on our moral practices. It is in these respects that it resembles 'Hit 'em where they ain't', and 'Hit 'em where they ain't' resembles it.

But, just as there are other 'philosophies of baseball' besides Keeler's, there are other philosophies of morality besides consequentialism. That, however, need not detain us. For they will all have precepts and principles with more or less the same characteristics of seeming vacuousness, the absence of need even to be explicitly stated, and the ultimate power to illuminate crucial aspects of what they underlie. These characteristics may not explain what philosophy really is, or why it is, but they do seem partly to characterize what philosophy contains: what it is like. And the recognition of this, even though we may not be fully aware of it, is why, I think, we refer to precepts like 'Hit 'em where they ain't' and 'A good defense is the best offense' as 'philosophies of baseball.'

An important caveat, however, must now be entered. I am not saying that the philosophy of *anything* consists *merely* in these foundational precepts and principles about which I have been speaking. Any philosophy worth the name consists of a great deal more than that: and principally of complex systems of arguments and inferences. For it is characteristic of philosophy, at least as it is practiced in English-speaking countries today, and as it has been practiced, all over Europe, since antiquity, that claims are not made without reasons to back them up, *or* without reasons why we should not expect them to be backed up. In a word, the philosophy of *any-thing* is a *system* of thought of which the foundational statements I have been talking about are a prominent and essential part.

The reader may now fairly ask, however, why, if 'Hit 'em where they ain't' and 'A good defense is the best offense' are like founda-tional statements in recognized areas of philosophy, there really *isn't* a philosophy of baseball, properly so-called, as there is a philosophy of morality or a philosophy of science? If there are 'philosophical' precepts and principles in baseball, why are they only 'philosophy' in an attenuated sense. Why is the philosophy of baseball not a part of the curriculum in my university? If there are 'philosophical' precepts in the practice of baseball, doesn't it follow that there *is* a 'philo-sophy' of baseball? What *more* is needed to turn the 'philosophy' of baseball metaphorically so-called into the *philosophy* of baseball properly so-called: philosophy in the literal sense of the word?

To begin to answer this question, I will revert to something I said at the very beginning of this chapter. I said, it will be recalled, that one can obviously join any noun to the phrase 'philosophy of . . .' with grammatical correctness. But, I added, it is also an obvious fact of *philosophy*, at least obvious to *philosophers*, that not every such combination constitutes a branch of the subject, *as it is now practiced*. I added that qualification then, and underscore it now to convey an important truth about philosophy: what can be a philosophical practice in the literal sense, and what cannot, is not fixed forever. The philosophy of something may be philosophy in one period and cease to be in another. The philosophy of something else may never have been philosophy but may come to be now or in the future.

To instance a particularly relevant case in point, it is not stretching a point too far to say that Plato (427–347 BC) had a 'philosophy of gymnastics' that, in his most famous work, *The Republic*, formed a part of both a philosophy of education and a philosophy of the state, which is to say, a political philosophy. Why did Plato have a philosophy of gymnastics, and why is such a thing no longer a part of *our* philosophical practice?

It appears to me that the answer must have something to do with the role that gymnastics, and other athletic pursuits, played in the lives of the Athenian citizens, in Plato's time, and the role they play—or, rather, *fail* to play—in our lives and times. In a word, they were an integral part of the very being of the Athenian citizenry, seen by Plato not merely as an entertainment or a relaxing pastime, but as a builder of moral character. Our educators sometimes pay lip service to that idea—'a sound mind in a sound body' they say in the catalogue—but we know better: we know perfectly well that they do not mean it; that 'sports' are a profession for their participants and an entertainment for the rest of us. There can be no philosophy of *that* except in the attenuated sense in which Keeler had a 'philosophy' of baseball.

A practice or discipline or body of knowledge, then, seems to become 'eligible' (if that is the right word) for philosophy, properly so-called, when it becomes for us a way of life; when it cuts so deeply into our natures as human beings that we are impelled to explore and reveal its innermost workings.

If what I have said so far is close to the truth, then we can say that philosophical theories and analyses tend to consist, on first reflection, of, among other things, vacuous truisms that hardly need stating, but that, on further reflection, and developed into systems of assertions and inferences, come to be seen as foundational beliefs, casting light on the superstructure they support. Such foundational beliefs, apparent platitudes, occur in all manner of human practices, witness Keeler's 'Hit 'em where they ain't.' But they begin to become the philosophy *of* some human practice when that practice is seen as deeply implicated in our lives, even to the extent of helping to define us as human beings. And that is why there is, at the present time, a philosophy of science, a philosophy of art, a philosophy of morality, but not a philosophy of baseball.

We can now ask, with some understanding of what we are asking, What about the philosophy of music?

The philosophy of music, if there is such a practice or discipline, would consist, in part, of the same kinds of foundational axioms, and inferences from them, as any other subject susceptible of a philosophical study in the first place. But *is* it susceptible of such a philosophical study? Or is it, like Keeler's philosophy of baseball, merely a 'philosophy' in a jocular, half-humorous way? In other words: Does music strike deep enough into human bedrock that, like morality or science, it can be seen as partially defining our lives? Before I try to answer that question a slight detour is required.

Since about the middle of the eighteenth century, we have come to see literature, drama, painting, sculpture, dance, architecture, and music as all belonging to the same group of practices that we call, in English, the 'fine arts.' But it was not always thus. Plato did not group all of these together. Music and the visual arts he considered 'crafts,' like shoemaking or pottery—*techne* in Greek, from which we get words like 'technique' and 'technical.' Poetry, on the other hand, including drama, he classed with prophecy as an 'inspirational' practice.

So for Plato music fell under the philosophy of craft; in this case the craft of representation or 'mimesis.' And he had a philosophy of music, therefore, by implication, since he had a philosophy of craft, and music was one.

But, because music played such an important part in the lives of the ancient Athenians, and in their education, music, as a craft, was given special attention by Plato: very close scrutiny. So it is fair to say that Plato not only had a philosophy of music because he had a philosophy of craft, and music was one. He had, as well, what can with some justification be called a more or less separate 'philosophy of music.' (We shall have occasion to look at some aspects of it in the next chapter.)

When the modern system of the arts was formulated, in the eighteenth century, with music among them, music had a philosophy, since the fine arts had a philosophy, much in the same way that it had a philosophy for Plato, since it was a craft, and craft had a philosophy. But in at least one very important respect, the place of music in philosophy was very different in the eighteenth century from what it was in the work of Plato. It had, in effect, fallen from grace, and was considered worthy of only scant attention. It was, by universal consent, the 'lowest' of the fine arts and was treated by philosophers accordingly.

Since the eighteenth century music has had a spotty history in the works of the philosophers. From time to time a philosopher of the first rank has taken a particular interest in it. More often than not it has been given but a casual nod in passing. It has, by and large, hung on by its fingernails just because it *is* a fine art and fine art has a philosophy.

Until a short time ago, it remained true that, with few exceptions, those who wrote on the philosophy of art wrote little on the art of music (and when they did, with little real musical knowledge). Indeed, I cannot imagine a publisher even thinking about commissioning an introduction to the philosophy of music until almost the day before yesterday. But now music has emerged from its philosophical obscurity and, not gained, but *re*gained its rightful place. Why and how?

Well, if it is the case, as I have suggested, that a human practice becomes subject to a philosophy when it becomes a way of human life, deeply implicated in how we define ourselves as human beings, then it must be the case that, in the last twenty or thirty years, or, at least, in the fairly recent past, music has achieved such a status. But that doesn't sound right. Surely music, like art itself, stretches back into the dim prehistory of the race, and spreads itself over the entire globe. In other words, there never *has* been, *anywhere*, a culture without its music; and that music penetrates to our blood and bones hardly, I think, needs argument.

We might usefully compare the philosophy of music, in the present regard, to the philosophy of science. The philosophy of science really does illustrate and support the claim that a practice or discipline becomes a potential subject of a philosophy when it becomes a major and fundamental part of our lives. For the philosophy of science has indeed emerged in lock step with the emergence of science itself as a major player in our lives.

But music shows no such history as that of the growth of natural science. What I think it shows is not, so to speak, a 'participation history' but a 'recognition history.' As science has grown, and its practical applications, so also has grown its participation in our lives. Music, however, has always been there. What has not been there is the recognition of the fact. Thus, we must revise somewhat our claim that for a practice to become susceptible of a philosophy it must become part of our lives. What *also* must happen is that it be realized, *recognized*, that it has become so, or, as in the case of music, *that it has been so all along.*

But it may well be asked whether there is anything to back up my claim that the recent re-emergence of music as a subject of sustained philosophical inquiry is the result of what I have called a 'recognition history.' I think there is.

It was natural enough that, when music ceased to be seen as a craft, in the middle of the eighteenth century, and came, somewhat gradually to be sure, to be seen as one of the fine arts, there should be an increased interest shown it on the part of an educated public that might heretofore have looked down on it as not worthy of serious notice by 'gentlemen of quality.' Indeed, a sign of music's new reputation in 'arts and letters' was the publication, in the last quarter of the eighteenth century, of the first real history of the subject, by the great English musician and scholar Dr Charles Burney (1726–1814).

This interest in the history of music, and its place in our lives and culture, began to accelerate towards the middle of the nineteenth century, with the development of the academic disciplines of historical and ethno-musicology: that is to say, academic disciplines devoted solely to the history of Western music, and the systematic study of non-Western musical traditions. The growth of musicology in our own times has been more rapid still, and its increasing concern with the relation of music to other human practices a notable development. It is, I therefore suggest, the musicologists who have, in the last half of the twentieth century, prepared the ground for the re-emergence of philosophy of music as a discipline in its own right, liberated from the philosophy of art as a whole, of which, until recently, it had been for a very long time but a minor appendage. It is historical musicology and ethno-musicology that have made us keenly aware of what has always been so: that music is a deep and abiding force in the human family, no matter when or where that family has flourished. Were it not for the musicologists, I don't think the ensuing pages would have been possible.

By dint of the musicologists, then, music has gained its recognition; and in virtue of that recognition it takes its place among the 'philosophies of . . .'. So, with this slight detour concluded, let us now take stock of what we have so far learned.

The kinds of precepts and propositions we tend to call 'philosophical,' outside the philosopher's study or classroom, tend to have the following three features: they seem, on first reflection, to be vacuous truisms; they seem to be so obvious they tend to remain unstated; on more considered reflection they come to be seen as casting light on, as explanatory of, the practice or discipline for which they are the (frequently) unspoken foundations.

Such precepts, isolated and unsystematic, can occur anywhere, as, for example, in what we only half-seriously call a 'philosophy of baseball.' But where they occur as part of a true 'philosophy of . . .' is where they deal with some practice or discipline that lies at the heart of our consciousness, of our lives as human beings. And when they do occur there, they form a system of inferences and arguments, not merely a loose collection of precepts or aphorisms, like 'Hit 'em where they ain't' or 'The best offense is a good defense.' That is why we mean it with full seriousness, not merely half-seriously, when we refer to a philosophy of science, a philosophy of morality, or, as we have now come to see, a philosophy of music. A philosophy of music, then, will be a system of precepts and propositions, perhaps, on first reflection, vacuous truisms not worthy of being made explicit, but, on reflection, richly illuminating of the practice they underlie, a practice that as far back as we can trace it has been at the center of our lives and helped to define us as human beings. And with that having been said, it is high time for me to get on to *my* philosophy of music.

But let no reader be lulled into believing that he or she has really learned, in these brief introductory remarks, the true nature of philosophy. At best I have given the reader some idea of what it looks like, not what it *is*. To do the latter would be to undertake a far different project from the present one, a project I could not myself undertake.

Indeed, I freely confess that I do not myself *know* what philosophy is. Should the reader, on that account, put this book down and read no further? After all, he or she might reason, here is someone who has written a book on the philosophy of music and now admits he does not know what philosophy is. In other words, he literally does not know what he is talking about. How can we place any confidence in what such a person says about the philosophy of music (or the philosophy of anything else)?

But such a decision to reject outright what follows in my book would be quite unwarranted by the argument given. The philosophy of anything is a *practice*. Like all other practices, one need not have a philosophy of *it* to know how to do it. To know what philosophy *is* is to have a philosophy of philosophy, just as to know, in a philosophical way, what piano playing is is to have a philosophy of piano playing. Furthermore, if it seems obvious to you, as it does to me, that you don't have to have a philosophy of piano playing or, more generally, a philosophy of the performing arts to know how to play the piano, it should seem obvious to you, as it does to me, that you needn't have a philosophy of philosophy to *do*, to know how to *practice*, philosophy. To appropriate a distinction made famous by the late English philosopher Gilbert Ryle, being able to do philosophy is a matter of knowing *how* . . . , knowing what philosophy is is a matter of knowing *that* . . . One needn't have the latter knowledge to have the former.

So have no fear. Though I don't know what philosophy is, do not have a philosophy of philosophy, I still know how to *do* philosophy. And the philosophy of music is what I shall now proceed to do.

In any event, as I said at the outset, there *is* another way to teach what philosophy is than by giving a philosophy of philosophy. It is simply to make the learner *acquainted* with what philosophy is by presenting him or her with a philosophy of. . . . In other words, one can impart to others an idea of what philosophy is by *showing* rather than by *telling*. What now follows is an introduction to the philosophy of music. *It* is philosophy. What better way to tell you what a giraffe is than to show you a giraffe? One giraffe is worth 1,000 words.

CHAPTER 2

A Little History

The oldest and most continuously reiterated precept in the philosophy of music, sometimes merely amounting to a simple expression of faith, other times reaching the level of sophisticated theory, is that there is a special connection between music and the human emotions, beyond the connection there might be supposed between emotions and any other of the fine arts. It stretches back into the mists of time, has its first philosophical embodiment in Plato's *Republic,* and is already present in the myth of Orpheus, singer of songs, whose music could subdue the savage beasts, and even the lord of the underworld himself. The philosophy of music begins with Plato's account of music and the emotions. It is there that it is logical for us to begin our study.

A great deal is known about ancient Greek theories of music in Plato's time. But little, if indeed anything, really, is known about what Greek 'music' sounded like. Because we can't listen to ancient Greek music, the way we can, for example, now, even to the music of the Middle Ages, it is very difficult to have any confidence that we know exactly what Plato was saying about what our translators customarily render as 'music.' We quite literally don't know *what* he was talking *about*.

The reader is forewarned, therefore, that what I say here about Plato's theory of music and the emotions, as well as what I say about his great student Aristotle (384–322 BC) in the same regard, may well be completely wide of the mark. Nevertheless, we do know what later ages *took* Plato and Aristotle to be saying, which is what influenced *their* accounts of music and the emotions, up to our own day. And that, after all, is more important for *our* purposes than what Plato and Aristotle really may have meant.

Music, in Plato's and Aristotle's time, was mainly vocal melody with words, accompanied by a stringed instrument such as the lyre. Whether the accompaniment was 'polyphonic,' whether, that is, it consisted of notes other than those of the melody, seems doubtful. In other words, the accompanying instrument or instruments simply played more or less the same notes as the vocal melody. This is known as 'monody,' or 'monodic' music.

The music of which I am speaking was constructed on seven 'modes' or scales, each consisting in a distinct, fixed sequence of intervals, giving it a distinct sound quality as well as, the Greeks thought, a distinct 'ethos' or mood: each mode, in other words, was associated with a different emotion (or range of emotions). (You can get an idea of what a 'mode' is like by playing on the white keys of a piano the notes from D to D, which is the modern version of the 'Dorian' mode, or the notes from F to F, the modern version of the 'Lydian.')

It was Plato's view, as expressed in Book III of the *Republic*, that a melody composed in one mode would arouse in hearers emotions or states of character appropriate to that mode, melodies composed in another mode emotions or states of character appropriate to that one, and so on. He thought, for example, that there was a mode (unnamed) whose melodies could instill courage and warlike emotions in men. Furthermore, he thought this was the result of that mode's being an imitation or representation of the tones and accents, the cries and shouts, apparently, of brave, warlike men. In other words, Plato can be taken, and was, by many, to have claimed that, in general, melodies have the power to arouse emotions in listeners by imitating or representing the manner in which people express them in their speech and exclamations. This notion, as we shall see in a moment, re-emerged in the sixteenth century, and set in motion a train of speculation concerning the relation of music to the emotions that has endured unbroken to the present day.

Aristotle too endorsed the notion of an intimate relation between music and the emotions. Indeed, in his *Politics*, Book VIII, Chapter 5, he made the intriguing suggestion that music represents not the physical expression of human emotions but the human emotions *themselves*, and that men's souls move, emotively, in sympathy with these representations.

How musical sound can imitate or represent emotions, Aristotle, unfortunately, never made clear. And, as the Platonic theory that it imitates or represents the sounds of human expressive utterances is more easily grasped, and more plausible to boot, it was the theory that had the greater influence, as enticing (as we shall see) to the modern sensibility as Aristotle's more daring proposal is (if, indeed, we understand it correctly).

To tell the story I have to tell I must now skip nearly 2,000 years, to the close of the sixteenth century. This is not because the intervening period is barren of speculation concerning music and the emotions. But there *is* a special continuity to the story that begins with Plato and Aristotle, and picks up with the revival of their emotive theories of music in the late Renaissance. It is that continuous story that is most germane to our project and, therefore, most profitably pursued.

In the city of Florence, towards the close of the sixteenth century, a group of the nobility, calling itself the *Camerata*, in collaboration with some of the city's most talented poets, composers, and theoreticians, attempted what they took to be the revival of Greek tragic performance, which they had come to believe, on the authority of Aristotle's *Poetics*, was a sung, *musical* performance. In the process, they invented the art form we know now as 'opera.'

What is of particular interest to the philosopher of music is the theoretical underpinning of this new artistic enterprise. In essence, what the members of the *Camerata* and their associates espoused was a version of Plato's theory, outlined just now. They argued that the power of music to arouse the human emotions lay in the representations, by melody, of the human speaking voice when expressing the various emotions. Thus the composer, if he wished to arouse joy in his listeners, must write a melody representing the tones and accents of a person expressing joy in her speech, if melancholy, the tones and accents of melancholy speech, and so on. (It was assumed, from the start, that the arousal of these emotions was a good thing for music to do.)

At this point it would perhaps be useful to introduce a bit of terminology. Let us say that the *Camerata* produced an analysis of how music can be *expressive* of the human emotions. It was expressive of sadness in virtue of arousing sadness in listeners, expressive of joy in virtue of arousing joy in listeners, and so on. Throughout this book I shall refer to such theories as 'arousal' theories of musical expressiveness. Further, I shall also describe them as 'dispositional' theories, because, according to them, music 'possesses' emotive properties as 'dispositions' to arouse emotions in listeners, the same way that opium has the dispositional property of putting people to sleep.

Throughout the history of speculation with regard to musical expressiveness, various mechanisms have been suggested by proponents of the arousal theory for how music manages to do the arousing. The members of the *Camerata* had what I shall call a 'sympathy' mechanism. They believed, that is to say, that, because music represents the speaking voice of an agent expressing an emotion —remember, this was a recipe for how composers should write music for characters in a drama!—we, the listeners, are aroused to that emotion by 'identifying' (in imagination) with that agent and thereby feeling the emotion the agent is represented as expressing (and which, naturally enough, we assume he or she is feeling as well). I shall call this, simply, the 'sympathy' theory of emotive arousal.

We can, then, with our new terminology in place, summarize the *Camerata*'s theory of musical expressiveness. It is an arousal theory, and a dispositional theory of musical expressiveness; a sympathy theory of musical arousal.

With the *Camerata*'s theory so described, an interesting point emerges. There really are *two* projects here: the analysis of what we are saying when we describe music in expressive terms—sad, happy, and the like—and the analysis of what we are saying when we say that we are deeply, emotionally moved by music. The arousal and dispositional theories tell us the former; the sympathy theory the latter. Now it so happens that in the writings of the *Camerata* both projects reduce to the same thing: the arousal of what I shall call, from now on, the 'garden-variety emotions,' which is to say, the common, ordinary, basic emotions in the human repertory: joy, melancholy, anger, fear, love, and a few others of that kind. But such a conflation of the two projects is not the only way to proceed. As we shall see later, not only is it not necessary to think that, when we say music is expressive of the garden-variety emotions, and when we say it is deeply moving, we are saying the same thing: it is not advisable either. In fact, the best way to represent what is happening is to provide quite a *different* explanation for how music is expressive of the garden-variety emotions, and for how it can (at times) be a deeply moving experience to listen to it.

For quite a long time arousal theories of musical expressiveness and of music's capacity to move us emotionally prevailed; and the sympathy theory was frequently appealed to as the mechanism for the arousal. But in the middle of the seventeenth century there was an important development that at least provided an alternative to the sympathy theory as an explanation for how music could be thought of as arousing the garden-variety emotions. This was the publication, in 1649, of *The Passions of the Soul*, by the great mathematician and philosopher René Descartes (1596–1650). In this highly influential work on what we would call today the 'physiological psychology' of the emotions, Descartes proposed that each of what he considered the six basic emotions, or passions, wonder, love, hatred, desire, joy, and sadness, was directly caused to be experienced by a particular motion of the so-called vital spirits, *esprits animaux* in the original French edition. Descartes conceived of the nerves as a pathway of tiny pipes—essentially a plumbing system in miniature—through which the vital spirits, a subtle and volatile fluid medium, flowed, connecting the brain with the limbs and senses of the body. This fluid medium was supposed by Descartes to have a particular way of configuring itself, each such configuration capable of arousing one or other of the six basic emotions. Thus, for example, a person who perceived a threat to her safety would have stimulated in her nervous system the configuration of the vital spirits capable of inciting her to fear; and fear is what she would experience.

The Cartesian psychology and physiology of the emotions were quickly adopted by many music theorists, who speculated that the motion of musical sound might directly excite the vital spirits, thereby arousing the listener's emotions. Thus, it was thought that, if a composer wished, say, to write sad music, what he had to do was to write music whose general configuration resembled the configuration of the vital spirits appropriate to the arousal of that emotion. By this means music could, it was thought, be expressive of all the basic emotions. All the composer needed to know was what the basic motions of the vital spirits were, appropriate to the basic emotions, as explained in Descartes's book , and write music to match those motions. This theory came to be known as the 'doctrine of the affections,' *Affektenlehre,* in Germany, where it was most conspicuous, and was assiduously adhered to, in compositional practice, by many of the most famous composers who flourished between 1675 and 1750, including Georg Frideric Handel (1685–1759) and Johann Sebastian Bach (1685–1750).

Of course no one today believes in Descartes's vital spirits or the psychology based on them. But theories that ascribe to music power over the physiological mechanisms of the human body that are supposed to be directly responsible for the arousal of the emotions still crop up, and have been around ever since Descartes's pioneering venture into the physiology and psychology of the emotions. Thus, we can put the 'physiological' theory of how music might arouse the garden-variety emotions alongside the sympathy theory, as a perennial possibility.

The arousal, dispositional theory of musical expressiveness, joined with the arousal, dispositional theory of how music moves us emotionally, remained in place from the time of the *Camerata* to the first years of the nineteenth century: a period of over 200 years. Sometimes the sympathy theory, sometimes the physiological theory, in its more or less Cartesian form, was the driving engine. But the general outline, whether sympathy or physiology was appealed to, remained constant.

The first major break with this 200-year stasis was, all in all, a momentous occurrence in the philosophy of music: the publication, in 1819, of *The World as Will and Idea*, the major work of the influential German philosopher Arthur Schopenhauer (1788–1860). Schopenhauer's *magnum opus* was, essentially, a theory of *everything*, in the grand old manner of philosophical speculation no longer thought productive or respectable. But that his cosmic pretensions are not now taken very seriously does not mean he did not have enlightening things to say on many of the particular topics that fell under his gaze. In particular, his account of music, and its place in the system of the fine arts, has been sympathetically received by many philosophers and musical theorists of a philosophical bent. Shorn of its cumbersome metaphysical underpinning, Schopenhauer's philosophy of music makes a good deal of sense: at least, it points the theory of musical expressiveness in a new and fruitful direction.

For reasons that are unnecessary to go into here, Schopenhauer thought of the universe—ultimate reality, if you like—on the model of a striving, cosmic human will. Music, he thought, was pre-eminent among the fine arts because it reflected or represented this cosmic will more directly than any of the others could do. Indeed, he sometimes called music a 'direct copy' of the will.

This conclusion was of moment for the philosophy of music, first, because Schopenhauer elevated music from the rather lowly status it occupied in the eyes of the eighteenth-century philosophers to the status of the fine art above all others. Indeed, music was anointed *the* Romantic art *par excellence*, as the nineteenth century was *the* Romantic century.

Furthermore, Schopenhauer broke the stranglehold that the arousal theory had had on the phenomenon of musical expressiveness for over two centuries. For, in making music a representation of the will, Schopenhauer suggested at the same time that it might be a representation of the human emotions as well. The emotions music is expressive of were moved, at a stroke, *from* the listener, and into the *music*, the place where most contemporary philosophers think they belong. (If that move was what Aristotle had in mind, in his elusive remarks in the *Politics*, it was finally, at long last, taken up again.)

As well, Schopenhauer explicitly separated the fact of expressiveness from music's power emotionally to move the listener. In other words, Schopenhauer was saying that music is expressive of the emotions in virtue of its representational power, but not emotionally moving in arousing whatever emotion or emotions it represented. This conclusion has been welcome to some, including myself, but not, as we shall see, to others.

All in all, then, Schopenhauer instituted a revolution in our philosophical thinking about music in general, and about the relation of music to the emotions in particular. He, so to speak, put pure instrumental music on the philosophical map, lifting it from the level of a 'pleasant' art to a deeply significant one. And he pointed the theory of musical expressiveness in what seems to most of us to be the right direction, putting the emotion music is heard to be expressive of into the music, as perceived property of *it*. To be sure, he envisioned only one way to do this: to think of expressive properties as representational properties. Contemporary philosophical analysis has discerned *another*, more plausible way. But that remains for the next chapter to reveal.

Schopenhauer's revolution in the theory of the musical emotions was one of two revolutions the nineteenth century produced in that regard. The second came in 1854, in the form of a little book by the Viennese musician and music critic Eduard Hanslick (1825–1904). It was first translated into English under the title *The Beautiful in Music*, and, more recently, *On the Musically Beautiful*. It seems to me that a better, more idiomatic rendering than either of these is *On Musical Beauty*, and so I shall refer to it on these pages.

In *On Musical Beauty* Hanslick defended two theses: one he called 'negative,' the other 'positive.' The positive thesis will occupy us later on. The negative one is relevant now.

Hanslick's negative thesis was that it is not the sole or primary purpose of music, as an art, either to arouse or to represent what I have been calling the garden-variety emotions. His argument for this thesis was simple and direct. Music, as an art, *cannot* either arouse or represent the garden-variety emotions. *Therefore*, it cannot be the sole or primary purpose of music, as an art, either to arouse or to represent the garden-variety emotions.

Hanslick's negative thesis has been continually misinterpreted by commentators because of the way in which it was stated. Since his thesis is that arousing or representing the garden-variety emotions cannot be the *sole* or *primary* artistic purpose of music, it would seem that Hanslick is allowing the possibility that it is at least a secondary or minor purpose. But, clearly, that cannot have been his intention, because his argument for the negative thesis is that music as an art *cannot* arouse or represent the garden-variety emotions; and if it *cannot* then it follows trivially that it cannot be *any* purpose of music, as an art, to arouse or represent the garden-variety emotions.

Why, then, did Hanslick express the negative thesis in the way that he did, as denying that the *sole* or *primary* artistic purpose of music is to arouse or represent the garden-variety emotions? Simply because these were the theses of his predecessors, and the only *interesting* theses. Someone who maintains that it is a not very important, or even trivial office of music, as an art, to arouse or represent the garden-variety emotions is maintaining something that is really not worth the trouble to refute, because it is not really worth the trouble to entertain. In any case, since Hanslick's strategy, in the negative thesis, was to argue that music *cannot* arouse or represent the garden-variety emotions, in any artistically significant way, there was hardly need for him to point out that it is immaterial whether the theory against which the strategy is deployed is that music's sole artistic function is to arouse or represent these emotions, whether it is music's primary artistic function, or whether it is one of music's minor artistic functions. If the strategy is good, it is good against any degree of involvement of music with the arousal or representation of the garden-variety emotions. What music cannot do *at all*, it cannot do even a little bit.

But there is a second reason why commentators on Hanslick's negative thesis have thought that he was not ruling out, in the negative thesis, at least some intimate involvement of music with the emotions. For having taken as his first task, in *On Musical Beauty*, the proof that music cannot arouse the garden-variety emotions, he seems to turn an about face and claim, later on, that it *can* and often *does*.

However, to the careful reader, Hanslick is reasonably clear about what he is saying in these two distinct places and reasonably clear about why they are consistent with one another. At the outset

Hanslick claims that music cannot, *in any artistically relevant way*, arouse the garden-variety emotions. When he later returns to the question of emotive arousal, he points out the obvious fact that music can, of course, arouse the garden-variety emotions *in artistically irrelevant ways*. It can do this in two ways, both equally irrelevant to artistic function.

If a person is emotionally 'overwrought,' or in some way emotionally 'unstable' or 'abnormal,' a musical work might well send him into paroxysms of rage, or depths of despair, as might a dandelion or a door knob. But this tells us nothing about what any of these things are for or what their nature is. That music, like anything else, can have emotional effects on people with temporary or permanent emotional 'problems' or peculiarities is irrelevant to the artistic nature or purpose of music, and of no concern to the philosopher of art.

More importantly, because easily mistaken for genuine aesthetic effect, music may, according to Hanslick, arouse the garden-variety emotions in listeners who have 'personal associations' with it. Thus, if I first heard Beethoven's Fifth Symphony during a particularly sad period of my life and you first heard it in a particularly happy period of yours, it might, on subsequent hearings, remind you of happy events, me of sad ones, thus, by 'association,' making you happy and me sad. But such accidental personal associations are irrelevant to the content of Beethoven's work, and to our artistic appreciation of it.

The argument for the negative thesis, as we have seen, is that music is incapable of arousing or representing the garden-variety emotions *in any artistically relevant way*. But what is the basis for the claim that music cannot relevantly do this? Hanslick's answer is twofold.

But before we get to that twofold answer, it is important to remark upon another of Hanslick's major points, always to be borne in mind whenever there is a discussion of musical aesthetics, particularly one in which music and the emotions is the subject. It is simply that what we are concerned with here is pure instrumental music without text or dramatic setting: what Hanslick's century began to call 'absolute music,' and what I sometimes call 'music alone.'

Most of the music in the world is now, and always has been, music sung to words. As an art form in its own right, absolute music did not become a subject of philosophical inquiry until late in the eighteenth century. The issue Hanslick is dealing with then, as he makes very clear, is whether *pure instrumental music* can relevantly arouse or represent the garden-variety emotions. Of course, when a text or dramatic setting is given to music for the music to accompany, music's capability in these regards is altered radically. Music with words and musical drama are subjects of great importance, needless to say, to the philosophy of music. They will be discussed at the appropriate time. Until then, what we are considering is absolute music and that alone.

Against the notion that music alone can relevantly arouse the garden-variety emotions, Hanslick presents an argument remarkable both for its cogency and for its foresight. It is an argument that many accept, including myself. Furthermore, it makes use of an analysis of how the garden-variety emotions are aroused in ordinary life that did not gain currency until more than 100 years after Hanslick proposed it in *On Musical Beauty*.

The analysis of which I speak, known today as the 'cognitive theory of the emotions,' is simply that, for a garden-variety emotion, let us say fear, to be aroused, the following must happen. The person feeling fear must, in the standard case, have some belief, or set of beliefs, appropriate to the experiencing of that emotion: must, in other words, have a belief or set of beliefs that can reasonably be thought to cause fear in a person. (She believes, for example, that she is being threatened by a dangerous lunatic.) The fear must have an object: that is to say, the person must be afraid *of* something or other. (In this case, the person is afraid *of* what she takes to be a dangerous lunatic: the dangerous lunatic is the *object* of her fear.) And there usually is, also, although not necessarily, a particular feeling—the feeling of fear in one of its many forms—that the fearful person is experiencing.

Hanslick gives an analysis of emotive arousal very like the one sketched above and then goes on to argue that it is not within the capabilities of music, absolute music, to provide the materials of arousal as so understood. What relevant beliefs could the music impart that would arouse fear or joy or sadness in me? And what would be the objects of these emotions? Seen in this light, Hanslick insisted, the notion that music can relevantly arouse the garden-variety emotions becomes ludicrous: a palpable absurdity. It is hard not to agree. (Whether, of course, music with words or a dramatic setting can relevantly arouse the garden-variety emotions is quite another matter, and will be discussed in the appropriate place.)

Against the notion that music can relevantly represent the garden-variety emotions, Hanslick relies principally on what might be called the 'argument from disagreement'—a familiar skeptical strategy in the history of philosophy. The claim is simply that listeners are in complete disagreement in any given case about what emotive term or description correctly characterizes the music. There is, Hanslick thinks, complete disarray. One listener hears one emotion, another listener another, a third listener no emotion at all, and so on. But, Hanslick asks, can we believe music is able to represent the garden-variety emotions if it elicits no agreement from listeners about what emotion, if any, is represented? The answer he expects and gives is 'No.'

This argument of Hanslick's—the skeptical argument from disagreement—has had a long-lasting and powerful effect on future speculation. It is an argument, if cogent, against the claim not only that music can relevantly represent the garden-variety emotions but that it can arouse them or in any other way systematically embody them. It is somewhat puzzling that Hanslick failed to point this out: failed, that is, to point out that his argument from disagreement, if good, was fatal not only to the representation theory of musical expressiveness but to the arousal theory as well.

In any case, the argument from disagreement seems to have been accepted without question by generations of music theorists and philosophers, pretty much putting an end, for nearly 100 years, to any serious philosophical reflection on the possibilities of understanding music as an expressive medium, at least as straightforwardly expressive of the garden-variety emotions. The lone but important departure from this skeptical orthodoxy—indeed the only philosophically powerful foray into musical aesthetics between Hanslick and almost the middle of the twentieth century—is Edmund Gurney's *The Power of Sound* (1880). Gurney (1847–88) did, indeed, think that music could on occasion be expressive of the garden-variety emotions; and he was also careful to distinguish this phenomenon from that of music's having power to move listeners deeply (which he also affirmed). However, he placed little importance upon the fact that music could sometimes be expressive of the garden-variety emotions, which is why he is usually thought of as being the 'English Hanslick': a musical 'purist' completely in Hanslick's mould. He is far more than that, and we shall return to him later, at a more appropriate time.

A more or less barren sixty years in the philosophy of music, at least in the English-speaking world, separates Gurney's great work and what amounts to the opening, but somewhat premature, event in a veritable Renaissance of the subject, in America and Britain, which continues as I write. It was in 1942 that Susanne K. Langer (1895–1985) published *Philosophy in a New Key*, a work that was to have a profound influence on musical thinking, and that reminded philosophers of art that music was sorely in need of their attention. In particular, Langer revived the question of music's relation to the emotions.

It is not as if *Philosophy in a New Key*, despite its 'musical' title, is a book on the philosophy of music; indeed only one of its chapters, 'On Significance in Music,' is a direct contribution to the subject. But what Langer had to say, there, about where the significance of music lies, which, she thought, is in its potency as an emotive symbol, struck a responsive chord, after nearly 100 years of skepticism, particularly among those music theorists and philosophers who were beginning themselves, perhaps, to grow skeptical of Hanslick's emotive skepticism, and were looking for a way out.

Langer had done her homework. She had read her Schopenhauer and her Hanslick and a good deal more in the history of music aesthetics in the eighteenth century. She accepted as givens something like Schopenhauer's idea that music was a representation or iconic symbol of the emotions, as well as the validity of at least part of Hanlick's skepticism. But how could *both* be true? That was her problem.

The answer that emerged from *Philosophy in a New Key* was that music is not an iconic symbol or representation of the individual garden-variety emotions: it is not, in other words, as if this piece of music were a symbol or representation of sadness, that one of joy, the other of anger or fear. In that respect Hanslick was right. Rather, she thought, music is iconically symbolic of, 'isomorphic' with, as she sometimes put it, the emotive life in general. She adduced, to illustrate her point, the *bon mot* of the American psychologist Carroll C. Pratt, to the effect that *music sounds the way emotions feel*—the emotive thesis of his highly original study in aesthetic psychology, *The Meaning of Music* (1931).

Thus Langer could have it both ways. With Schopenhauer she could hold that emotion (albeit *singular*) was in the music, not the listener, while more or less accepting Hanslick's skeptical conclusion that music cannot represent, and certainly cannot arouse, the individual, garden-variety emotions. What it can do, she claimed, is to represent or symbolize the emotive ebb and flow as a whole, by being 'isomorphic' with it. (Could this have been something similar to what Aristotle meant by that enigmatic proposal in the *Politics* that music 'imitates' the emotions?)

What appealed to many in the musical world about Langer's account of music was, first, that it supported their feeling of aversion to descriptions of music in terms of the ordinary, garden-variety emotions, which they saw as, at best, a sop to children and the laity, and, at worst, simply nonsense, since Hanslick had 'shown' through the argument from disagreement that there was no objective validity in such descriptions. Second, however, it, as well, supported their equally strong feeling that, Hanslick's critique to the contrary notwithstanding, music alone, absolute music, possessed something correctly described as 'meaning' or 'significance,' and that this 'meaning' or 'significance' must have *something* to do with the human emotions. In short, Langer's account allowed them to think that it was silly to call music sad or happy but quite all right to say that there *was* emotion in it for all of that.

But when the philosophical community took the measure of what Langer had said about the emotive significance of music, it was more reluctant than the musicians in its acquiescence. To be sure, she was seen to have pointed philosophy of music in the right direction by putting emotion in the music, as Schopenhauer had done. Philosophers were, however, beginning to be suspicious of Hanslick's unexamined skepticism. There were at least some primitive psychological data to show that, as a matter of fact, there *is* substantial agreement about what garden-variety emotions passages of music are expressive of; and plenty of common-sense considerations that pointed in that direction. People just *do, pace* Hanslick, generally agree about whether a passage of music is sad or happy or angry, and so on. (If you don't believe me, just try out some simple examples on your friends.) And composers agree what kind of music is appropriate for setting sad words, what kind appropriate for happy words, what kind for angry words. As a result, it no longer seemed an advantage of Langer's position that it eschewed descriptions of music in specific emotive terms, in terms, that is, of the garden-variety emotions, and claimed, somewhat mysteriously, so it seemed to some, that music was symbolic of the emotive life 'in general.' (What could that *mean?*)

Furthermore, there had been trouble, right from the start, with the logic of Langer's notion that music might be a 'symbol,' albeit an 'iconic' symbol, a 'picture' symbol, if you will, of the emotive life. For even iconic, 'look-like' symbols must 'mean' by convention. If I hang a plaster fish in front of my shop, it is taken for a fish market, not an aquarium; and the sign by the side of the road with an 'S' on it signifies not 'snakes crossing' but 'curves ahead'—both by 'meaning convention.' But there *is* no meaning convention for music's iconically symbolizing the emotive life, as Langer would have it, rather than any of the other things it might be isomorphic with or 'sound like.' So, as a claim about music's *symbolic* function, Langer's theory won't stand up.

Finally, the placing of the emotion or emotions 'in' the music, as representation or iconic symbol, does not seem to capture how we really experience the emotions in music. Most people would say, I think, that, when they hear, for instance, sadness in a musical theme or passage, they don't hear it the way they see the dog in a dog-picture but, rather, the way they see the redness in an apple: not, in other words, as a representational but as a simple *perceptual* quality.

Langer, following Schopenhauer, prepared the way for contemporary philosophical analysis of the musical emotions by taking the emotion out of the listener and putting it where it belongs, *in* the *music*. But, like Schopenhauer, she saw only one possible way that the emotion *could* be in the music: as representation or iconic symbol. Contemporary analysis, however, now envisions a second way, closer to the way we seem to experience the emotions in music, which is to say, as perceptual properties like colors or tastes. To this, it seems to me, successful new approach to the problem of the musical emotions we must now turn our attention.

CHAPTER 3

Emotions in the Music

There has been a growing consensus among philosophers of music that, contrary to the skeptical claims of Hanslick, it makes perfect sense to describe music in expressive terms, and that, again contrary to Hanslick's skeptical claims, there is more or less general agreement, among qualified listeners, as to what the music is expressive of, in any given instance, if, that is, it is expressive of anything (which need not necessarily be the case). More specifically, there has been a growing consensus that music can be, and often is, expressive of the garden-variety emotions, such as sorrow, joy, fear, hope, and a few other basic emotions like these.

As well, the consensus generally is that, when we say a passage of music is sorrowful, or fearful, or the like, we are not describing a disposition of the music to arouse such an emotion in us, but ascribing such an emotion, as a perceived property, to the music itself. This way in which the musical emotions are perceived, as, rather, in the music, than in us, with the music as their cause, was well captured by the late American philosopher O. K. Bouwsma, when he quipped that the emotion is more like the redness to the apple than like the burp to the cider.

But this view, though initially appealing, is not without its problems, the most discussed of which is *how* the emotion can be *in* the music. We all understand how an emotion can be 'in' something as a 'disposition.' Sad news is news that makes people sad: the sadness is in the news merely in the sense of a tendency of such news to sadden people. There is no 'metaphysical' problem there: that is, no problem about the nature of the property we are ascribing to the news.

Likewise, we all understand quite well what we are saying when we assert that a person is sad: the sadness is a conscious state of that person; that feeling of depression and lassitude one experiences upon losing a loved one or suffering a great disappointment. Again, there is no 'metaphysical' problem about how a person can possess the 'property' of sadness; what its mode of existence is. Sadness is a conscious state and persons are capable of having conscious states.

But music is not capable of being in conscious states (needless to say), so it can't possess sadness in *that* way. And, since it is the consensus that it doesn't possess the thing as a disposition to make us sad, or, as we have seen, as a representational property, that is, as a representation of sadness, how exactly *does* it—the music—possess the sadness? It is all very well to say, with Bouwsma, that it is as the redness to the apple rather than the burp to the cider. However, that does not really answer our question. For, although we have a pretty good idea of how redness 'inheres' in apples and other red things, what we *don't* have is a pretty good idea of how the emotions 'inhere' in the music. Indeed, some people think we don't have any idea at all.

One of the traditional ways philosophers have of dealing with such cases is to try to make an analogy between the problematic case and an unproblematic one that it relevantly resembles. In the present instance, what might make us less uncomfortable with the notion of emotions 'inhering' in music as perceptual properties would be to discover cases in our ordinary experience where we commonly accept as a matter of course the notion of perceptual emotive properties belonging to non-sentient 'objects.'

Such a general argument was advanced by the remarkable American philosopher Charles Hartshorne in his highly original book *The Philosophy and Psychology of Sensation* (1934), many years before the problem emerged decisively for contemporary philosophy of music. Hartshorne adduced the common phenomenon of the emotive tone of colors to illustrate the point that emotions can be part of our perceptual field in perfectly ordinary circumstances well known to us all. Thus, he pointed out, yellow is a 'cheerful' color, not because it makes us cheerful but because its cheerfulness just *is* a part of its perceived quality, inseparable from its yellowness. That's just how we perceive yellow. In the same vein, he instanced other colors, as well as sounds, and other visual aspects of our world. In so doing, Hartshorne drew our attention to the fact that music is not alone in possessing for us emotions as perceived qualities of our sensible experience. The phenomenon is ubiquitous to our perceptual world. It should make us less uncomfortable, then, with the phenomenon in music if we realize that it is not merely a *musical* phenomenon but a phenomenon of human perceptual experience in general.

Nevertheless, the skeptical may reply, the problem of how emotions can be possessed by music, as perceptual qualities, has hardly been solved by discovering that objects other than music possess them. Indeed, it could be argued that the problem has actually been exacerbated. For now we have the problem not only for music, but for the other objects as well. If it is mysterious how music can possess emotive qualities, it is equally mysterious, for example, how colors can possess them. First we had one problem; now we have two.

Hartshorne's answer to how emotive properties constitute part of the perceptual world of insentient matter is unlikely to appeal to the contemporary analytic mind. Indeed, his philosophy is a kind of 'panpsychism': the view that so-called 'insentient' matter has itself at least a degree of sentience. In other words, Hartshorne does *not* explain how insentient matter can come to possess emotive properties, but, rather, blurs the distinction between sentient and insentient; which is to say, to a degree, it's sentience all the way down.

As I say, few will be willing to take such a drastic step with Hartshorne, although, I hasten to add, he is not some wild-eyed fanatic, in touch with astral forces, but a cool-headed philosopher of the first rank whose works abound in useful and penetrating insights. So for those of us who are not attracted to anything as beyond human experience as what Hartshorne offers, a more mundane answer must be sought for the question of how music can possess perceptual emotive properties. It is a comfort, indeed, to know that music shares this expressive aspect with such everyday objects as simple colors, and helps to assure us that there is nothing bizarre or seemingly outside the realm of the human to call a passage of music mournful or jolly or anguished. However, that does not replace the need for an explanation of *how* music can possess such emotions as perceived properties.

One thing to notice, straightaway, about the comparison of the cheerfulness of a musical passage and, say, the cheerfulness of the color yellow is that the cheerfulness of yellow, as yellow itself, is a 'simple' property whereas the cheerfulness of music is a 'complex' one. What this means is that, if I say, 'This kerchief is yellow,' and you say, 'No, it's orange,' there is nothing else I can point to in the kerchief to show or convince you that the kerchief really is yellow and not orange. I cannot respond to your denial by saying something like: 'But don't you see it is such-and-such and so-and-so, so it *must* be yellow.' This, of course, does not mean that there is *no* way I can try to show you that the kerchief is yellow, not orange. The usual procedure would be for us to view it in sunlight rather than artificial light, or make sure one of us is not sight-impaired in some way, and so on. What I *cannot* do, because yellow is a simple property, is to point to something *else* in the kerchief and say: 'It's yellow because of *that*.' Yellow is not a complex property, so there is no 'that' to point to.

The same seems to be true of the cheerfulness of yellow. Like the yellowness itself, it is a simple quality. The cheerfulness just is a quality of the yellowness. Yellowness is not cheerful in virtue of some other perceived quality or qualities that it has beyond the yellowness (which is simply what it *is*).

But when we go from the cheerfulness of the color yellow to the cheerfulness of a musical passage, the situation is radically altered. When I say that a passage of music is cheerful or melancholy, I can *defend* my claim by pointing to *other* features of the music in virtue of which the music is cheerful or melancholy (or whatever). I can say: 'Notice the rapid, skipping tempo, the bright major tonalities, the generally loud level of sound, the leaping, galloping themes. That's what makes it so cheerful.' Or: 'Notice the slow, dragging tempo, the dark minor tonalities, the subdued, quiet dynamics, the faltering, drooping themes. *That's* what makes it so mournful.' In this sense, the cheerfulness, mournfulness, and other emotive qualities of music are 'complex' qualities, not simple ones like the cheerfulness of the color yellow. They are also the kinds of quality that are sometimes called 'emergent,' because they perceptually 'emerge' from the other qualities that make them up. The cheerfulness of the music is a new quality, so to speak, that is produced by the combined force of the bright major tonality, the rapid skipping tempo, the loud dynamics, the leaping, galloping themes.

Calling the emotive qualities of music 'complex' qualities emphasizes the fact that a passage of music is cheerful, or melancholy, or whatever in virtue of *other* musical features that make it so. Calling them 'emergent' qualities emphasizes the fact that they are perceived as distinct qualities in their own right, separate from the qualities that may 'produce' them.

That the emotive qualities of music are *complex* qualities should not be thought to imply that when someone is hearing, say, the melancholy quality of a musical passage, he or she is necessarily aware of the other qualities productive of the melancholy. A person may be hearing the melancholic quality of the music without being aware *that* the music is melancholy in virtue of its slow, halting tempo, subdued dynamics, dark minor tonalities, faltering, drooping themes. He or she may not even know that it is those kinds of musical features that are generally responsible for making music melancholy. But if someone *fails* to hear the melancholy in the music, he or she can, often, be helped to hear it by having attention drawn to those features: 'Listen to its slow, halting tempo, those dark minor tonalities, the subdued dynamics, the faltering, drooping themes. Now don't you hear the melancholy?' Frequently the answer will be 'yes.'

Among those who think that the garden-variety emotions belong to music as perceptual, heard qualities, there is little dissension from the belief that these qualities are complex, emergent qualities in the sense explained just now. Furthermore, there is general agreement about what features of music are associated with what emotive qualities. Indeed, this is not just a 'theoretical' agreement among philosophers but a 'practical' agreement among composers and ordinary listeners as well. We know the latter because for well over 300 years composers have consistently utilized just those musical features to set melancholy and cheerful and fearful texts that we, as listeners, perceive to be the features responsible for the melancholy, cheerful, fearful emotive qualities we hear in textless music, as well as the features that make the music appropriate to the emotive tone of the texts the composers set. This is not a philosopher's pipe dream but a basic fact of musical listening, and of the musical craft in the West for centuries.

However, because there is general agreement that this piece of music is melancholy in virtue of its dark, minor tonalities, subdued dynamics, slow, halting tempo, drooping, halting melody, that piece cheerful in virtue of its light, major harmonies, loud dynamics, fast, skipping tempo, leaping, galloping melodies, does not solve the problem of how or why the music is in the first case melancholy, and in the second cheerful. Why, after all, don't I just hear the dark, minor harmonies, the subdued dynamics, the slow, halting tempo, the drooping, halting melodies? Why do I *also* hear the *melancholy*? This is the problem.

The most tempting approach to the problem of how emotions get 'into' the music is one that I am intimately familiar with, as I have been tempted by it myself. This approach begins with the thought that sad music being in slow, halting tempo, subdued in dynamics, with drooping, faltering melodies, and sad people walking in slow halting gate, with drooping bodies, speaking in subdued halting voice, cannot be altogether coincidental. Nor can it be altogether coincidental that cheerful musical works and cheerful people move rapidly, speak loudly, and even leap about, melodically in the music, bodily in people. In other words, there seems to be a direct analogy between how people look and sound when they *express* the garden-variety emotions (at least *some* of them) and how music sounds or is described when it is perceived as *expressive* of those same emotions. The intuition is that there must be some causal explanation lurking in this analogy: that the way we customarily express the garden-variety emotions must somehow explain why we hear those emotions in the music.

In my 1980 book *The Corded Shell*, later reprinted, with major additions, as *Sound Sentiment*, I attempted to give an account of musical expressiveness based, in large part, on the analogy between musical expressiveness and human *expression*. To facilitate that project I substituted for Hartshorne's example of the cheerfulness of yellow my own example of a St Bernard's sad face.

The St Bernard's face is not *expressing* sadness. The face of the St Bernard is sad even when the creature is happy, it being at the other end that she *expresses* her emotions. The face, rather, is *expressive* of sadness: the sadness is a quality of the face as the cheerfulness is a quality of the yellow color. But, unlike the color yellow, the face of the St Bernard is a *complex* perceptual object and, hence, makes a far better analogue to the expressive musical object, which is also a *complex* one. What does the analogy have to teach us?

It seems fairly clear that the sadness of the St Bernard's face is there in virtue of our seeing it as a kind of caricature—but a recognizable resemblance—of the human visage when expressing sadness. Furthermore, we can point to individual aspects of the canine face—the sad eyes, the wrinkled brow, the drooping mouth and ears, the dewlap—that are exaggerated reflections of just such sadness-expressing features of a human face. The theory of musical expressiveness now under discussion is that expressive music is to human expressive features, overall, as the St Bernard's face is to the 'expressing' human countenance. Can this claim be substantiated?

We might usefully distinguish among the following three kinds of expressive features of music that the theory under discussion must deal with. First, there are the features of music that might be claimed to 'sound like' the sounds human beings make in expressing their emotions: the most obvious being speech. Second, there are the features of music that are said to resemble, in their sound, visible aspects of human expression behavior: for example, human gesture and bodily movement. Third, there are certain musical features, notably the major, minor, and diminished chords (to be explained in a moment), that have, for most people, the emotive tones of cheerfulness, melancholy, and anguish, respectively, but that, because they are, like yellow and its cheerfulness, simple perceptual qualities, do not seem to resemble either the sound of human expression, or its visible aspect. The chords by themselves, in other words, do not have a linear (but only a vertical) structure, and so do not seem to be able to be construed as resembling human expression behavior, which *does* exhibit complex structure: there is no structure in the chords to resemble the structure of human utterance and behavior.

The resemblance of the sounds of music to the sounds of human beings expressing their emotions is something that, as we have seen, has been claimed ever since antiquity, and was the motivating force behind the endeavors of the Florentine *Camerata*, in the sixteenth century, to revive, as they saw it, ancient sung drama. But whereas Plato and the *Camerata* utilized the supposed resemblance to explain how, they thought, music can arouse the emotions, the present project is to utilize it to explain how music can embody them as heard qualities.

The first question for such a theory would appear to be whether there really is a perceived resemblance between the sounds of music and the sounds of human expression. Let us take, for example, music that is heard as melancholy and music that is heard as cheerful.

Certainly this much can be said. Melancholy music and melancholy speech and utterance have some obvious sound qualities in common. Melancholy people tend to express themselves in soft, subdued tones of voice; and melancholy music tends to be soft and subdued. Melancholy people tend to speak slowly and haltingly; and melancholy music tends to be in slow tempi and halting rhythm. Melancholy people's voices tend to 'sink,' and tend to remain in the low vocal register; and melancholy music too exhibits the same characteristics.

In contrast, cheerful people express themselves in bright, loud, sometimes even raucous—certainly not subdued—tones; and cheerful music tends to be bright, loud, and in the high register. Cheerful people are not slow or halting in speech and utterance but bright and sprightly; and cheerful music, likewise, is quick and sprightly. Cheerful people's voices rise energetically into the high register; and so too do the melodies of cheerful music.

In all of this particular attention should be paid to melody. For there is no aspect of Western music that is more amenable to analogy with the rise and fall in pitch of the human speaking voice than the rise and fall in pitch of music's melodic line. Furthermore, melody is that aspect of music that, historically, has been singled out most frequently as the primary *expressive* aspect. This perceived analogy between melody and speech is a leitmotif in writings about music's expressiveness from Plato to the *Camerata* to the eighteenth-century philosophers to the present day. The cheerful melodic line, like the cheerful speaking voice, is high, loud, fast, 'running' and 'leaping.' The anguished melody, like the anguished speaking voice, shrieks and cries, leaps in dissonant intervals, and proceeds in 'jerks,' with irregular pauses.

But beyond the phenomenon of music's 'sounding like' the vocal expressions of melancholy or cheerful people, many listeners perceive an analogy between the heard properties of music and visible human behavior as well. Music is customarily described in terms very similar to those we use to describe the motion of the human body under the influence of such emotions as melancholy and cheerfulness. Thus a musical phrase may leap joyously, or droop, or falter, like a person in motion. To put it more generally, music is customarily described in terms of motion; and so the same descriptions we use to characterize it are frequently the ones we use to describe the visible motions of the human body in the expression of the garden-variety emotions.

I called this theory of musical expressiveness, in *The Corded Shell*, the 'contour theory,' because, to put it somewhat figuratively, the 'contour' of music, its sonic 'shape,' bears a structural analogy to the heard and seen manifestations of human emotive expression. One thing to be noticed straightaway about the contour theory is that it is going to have trouble with our third kind of expressive musical feature, the major, minor, and diminished chords; for *they* do not have any contour at all, so find no analogue, apparently, in the contours of human expression behavior. I shall deal with these seemingly anomalous expressive features in a moment. But before I do I want to complete this account of the contour theory.

The contour theory of musical expressiveness faces immediate problems. To begin with, it must not become a representational theory: it must not, that is to say, be construed as the theory that music 'represents' the voice and gesture of human expression, the way paint on canvas represents the visible features of the world. For representation does not capture the way we experience the emotive qualities of music. We do not, that is to say, hear sounds as representations of melancholy and cheerful behavior, the way we see paint on canvas as a representation of melancholy and cheerful men and women, and *then* hear the music, in virtue of these representations, as melancholy and cheerful. We hear the melancholy and cheerfulness of the music immediately, in the music, and can be quite unaware of the features of the music in virtue of which it is melancholy or cheerful. And even if we are consciously aware of the expressive-making features of the music, which we may frequently be, we do not perceive them as representations of anything.

Furthermore, there must be some explanation produced, in defense of the contour theory, for why it is the similarity in structure between music and *expression behavior* that plays so important a role in the listening experience. After all, the contour of music is probably similar in structure to inanimate sounds and natural objects, as well as to human expression behavior. What's so special about expression behavior that *it* should be singled out for mention above those other things?

Finally, does the contour theory do any better a job of capturing our experience of music's expressive qualities than a representational theory would do? Can it capture the way we experience the emotions in music, namely, as directly perceived perceptual qualities?

In order for the analogy between musical contour and the contour of human expression behavior to work non-representationally, it must work subliminally: that is to say, we must not be fully aware of what is going on; we must not be aware of the analogy. Let us, for the moment, assume that this is what is happening. But why should we hear *emotions* in the music because of this subliminal perception, and not something else?

I believe one possible answer to this question can be found in a well-known perceptual phenomenon. When presented with ambiguous figures, we tend to see them as animate rather than inanimate forms: as living rather than non-living entities. We tend to see living forms in clouds, in stains on walls, in the shadowy things lurking in the woods. We see the stick as a snake. Why? Because, perhaps, we are hard-wired by evolution—by natural selection—to do so. Evolution says: 'Better safe than sorry. Better wrong than eaten.' Living things can be dangers to you. It is better to see the stick, immediately, incorrectly, as a snake, than to be snake bit, in pondering the question, if it turns out to be a snake after all.

Now, if this be true of sights, might it not be true of sounds as well? Might it not be the case that we are hard-wired by natural selection to hear sounds, where possible, as animate: where possible, as in music, as utterance and 'behavior'? I advance that as a possible, perhaps plausible, hypothesis. If it is true, it tells us why we hear the analogue of musical contour to human behavior and not to the other things it might resemble.

But if we hear sound as animate, why do we hear it as *expressively* animate? Well, if you want to carry through the 'survival' idea, it is to our advantage to know what emotive attitude is being evinced towards us by the living creature we may be encountering. If it is anger, we must prepare for fight or flight to be safe. If it is a benign emotion, other behavior is appropriate.

One might also add to these 'evolutionary' considerations the fact that just those 'simple' emotions we tend to hear in music are emotions whose expression behavior in human beings has direct analogues in the expression behavior of the higher primates and other mammals. In other words, their modes of expression seem hard-wired and deep in the inherited nature not only of us, but of other animals as well. This can be seen as corroborating evidence for the evolutionary story already told.

But now a further question presses itself upon us. In the case of ambiguous visual phenomena, we are conscious of what we are seeing (or think we are seeing). I take the stick for a snake and *run*. However, that does not seem to be what is happening in music. We are conscious of the expressive property, the emotion; we are not conscious of taking the musical contour for human utterance or behavior. Is there any plausible reason for this to be the case? We can't just *assume* it to make our theory work.

Well, consider this. The sense of sight is the primary 'survival' sense for human beings (and other of the higher primates). The sense of hearing is *not*, although it may very well have been for our ancestors way down the evolutionary chain. Thus there is no need for us *consciously* to hear things as threatening the way we consciously see things that way. So it is not completely unreasonable to suppose that what may very well have been a propensity consciously to hear ambiguous sounds as animate and (potentially) threatening has atrophied in us, like the appendix, and remains a vestigial relic of a more sound-oriented past. To put it another way, it is not completely unreasonable, on evolutionary grounds, to think that, while the seeing of ambiguous forms as animate remains a conscious phenomenon of human perception, the hearing of sounds that way has sunk back into semi-consciousness as a kind of 'background noise.'

Here, then, is *one* theory of how music comes to embody expressive qualities like melancholy and cheerfulness. It is agreed on all hands that music is melancholy, and cheerful, and so on, in virtue of certain standardly accepted features. It is perennially remarked on that these features bear analogy to the expression behavior, bodily, gestural, vocal, linguistic, of human beings. One can construct an evolutionary story of how and why we might be subconsciously, subliminally aware of this analogy and that this should cause us to perceive the music as melancholy or cheerful or the like as we perceive the sadness of the St Bernard's face. I have named this theory the contour theory of musical expressiveness.

But we have yet to work one further element into the contour theory: that is the expressive chords, major, minor, and diminished. These chords are generally perceived as cheerful, melancholy, and anguished, respectively; and you can hear this for yourself by playing the three notes together on the piano: first, C–E–G (major); then C–E flat–G (minor); finally, C–E flat–G flat (diminished). The problem is that these individual chords, not having a contour, being experienced as simple qualities, do not seem to bear any analogy at all to human behavior—hence must be expressive of cheerfulness, melancholy, and anguish in some *other* way than that allowed for by the contour theory of musical expressiveness. So the contour theory cannot be the whole story.

At least this much can be said for the contour theory straightaway. It is no worse off than any other theory in this regard. There is *no* generally accepted explanation for the difference in emotive quality between the major and minor chords, over which much ink has been spilled in the last 300 years. So, that the contour theory cannot provide one is no great deficit. But there is no harm, anyhow, in trying. Here are two suggestions.

The first suggestion is that we hear the vertical structure of the chords as a kind of contour. Compared to the major triad—that is, the major three-note chord, C–E–G—the minor triad has a lowered third: that is, the E is the third of the C-major chord, the E flat is the third lowered a half step, the smallest interval in the Western harmonic system. (The E is called the 'third' because it is the third note up from the C: that is, C (1), D (2), E (3). The G is called the 'fifth' because it is the fifth note up.) Now think of the lowered third, E flat as kind of sagging, or sinking, depressingly from E to E flat. Might that give a depressing, melancholy cast to the C-minor triad? There is a downward tending contour of the C-minor triad, as compared to the C-major one, like the downcast contour of the melancholy speaking voice or posture. And the diminished triad, C–E flat–G flat, is even more depressed: it has both a sinking third *and* a sinking fifth. Pretty far-fetched? Perhaps so.

Well, then, let's try this. Perhaps the chords should not be considered as isolated elements but in context: that is to say, functioning *in* musical structure. Perhaps it is from their function within musical compositions that they gain their emotive color.

If you go to the piano again, and play the major triad, C–E–G, the minor triad, C–E flat–G, and the diminished triad, C–E flat–G flat, in succession, I think you will perceive a big difference between the first two and the third. The diminished triad is an 'active' chord: that is to say, it sounds as if it must go somewhere; it must, as a musician would say, be 'resolved.' It can't stay at rest where it is. Or, another way of putting it: you couldn't hear it as the final chord of a musical composition. To hear what I mean, now lower the G flat to D flat, and raise the C to D flat. You have, in doing that, 'resolved' the diminished chord, and you can hear for yourself that things are now 'at rest.'

Might one suggest, then, that what gives the diminished chord its dark, anguished quality it its function, in musical structure, as an active, unconsummated, unresolved chord? It is restless, so to say, in its musical function; when it occurs in a compositional structure, at least until fairly recently in the history of the Western harmonic system, it imparts that restlessness to the contour of the melody it accompanies. From its 'syntactic' or 'grammatical' role in music it gains, by association, as it were, even when alone, its restless, 'anxious' emotive tone.

Furthermore, might this not be true, to a lesser degree, of the minor triad as well? It is, indeed, a matter of historical fact that the minor chord, until well into the nineteenth century, was considered more active than the major, which is why compositions in the minor mode for a long time almost invariably ended on a major rather than a minor chord. And, although ending on a minor chord is now no big deal, I think we still feel the minor ending as more restless than the major. You can hear this for yourself by resolving the diminished triad, C–E flat–G flat, two different ways: first, by lowering the G flat one whole step to E (F flat) and rasing the C one half step to D flat; and then doing what you did before, lowering the G flat to F and raising the C to D flat. Do this a few times in succession. Which resolution sounds more 'restful' to you. I would venture to predict that it is going to be the latter: the major resolution. For what you did first was to resolve the diminished chord to D flat minor, and then to resolve it to D flat major. I think you, like your musical ancestors for over three centuries, found the major resolution gramatically and emotionally the more fulfilling one: the one that sounds the most stationary; the one that sounds the most completely *final*.

I don't know if this attempt to accommodate the major, minor, and diminished chords to the contour theory of musical expressiveness is any more plausible than the first. In any event, even where the contour theory does best, with the larger structural elements of music, particularly melody, it is not without serious problems and many detractors.

In the version of the contour theory that I have given, *my own version*, there are numerous difficulties that even I find daunting. Here are some.

To begin with, how convincing *is* the claim that there are recognizable analogies or similarities between music and the 'shape' of human expression? Do melodies *really* much resemble human speech in any significant way? Many people think the similarities adduced pretty far-fetched. And when one goes to supposed analogies between how music sounds and how human expression *looks*, there is bound to be more skepticism still. Does it make any sense at all to say that a passage of music is melancholy in virtue of sounding the way a human being gestures or moves when he or she is melancholy? Can music *sound* like a gesture or bodily posture? Can sense modalities be crossed that way? There is certainly plenty of room for doubt about it.

Furthermore, the whole psychological apparatus that the contour theory requires is highly conjectural, to say the least. What evidence, if any, is there for the claim that listeners subliminally hear the analogy, if indeed it exists, between the contour of music and human expression? And even if they do hear it, does that adequately explain our experience of hearing emotions *in* the music as perceptual qualities. As well, does the phenomenon of seeing things in ambiguous figures—seeing the stick as a snake, or the faces and figures in clouds—transfer to sounds and what we hear (if anything) in them?

Finally, what of the evolutionary explanation offered for, first, the tendency to 'animate' ambiguous figures and, second, the difference between this tendency, as evinced in visual perception, and as evinced in hearing? Are they plausible? Is there evidence for *either*?

The biologist Stephen J. Gould scorns such armchair evolutionary explanations as I have given, labeling them, contemptuously, 'just-so stories,' the point being that a natural selection story, just like Kipling's fanciful 'explanations' for how the leopard got its spots, or the elephant its trunk, can be made up by almost anyone, including an amateur like myself, for any trait you like. So it is probably wise not to place much faith in these exercises. The skeptical, therefore, will be wary of the evolutionary support I have adduced for the claims that, all things being equal, we will see living forms rather than non-living ones in ambiguous perceptual arrays, and, second, that, because of the primacy of sight over hearing as a 'survival sense,' in human beings, our perception of 'animate' forms in sounds, as opposed to sights, will be dim or subliminal, as the contour theory requires.

Add all of these difficulties together and the contour theory begins to look pretty shaky. Indeed, it looks shaky not only to its detractors but to at least one of its supporters as well: *me*. Having vigorously defended the contour theory on two separate occasions, I can no longer say that I am not without serious qualms.

But the funny thing about the contour theory, or, in general, the theory that music is expressive of the garden-variety emotions by virtue of analogy to human expression behavior, both vocal and bodily, is its perennial attraction. It simply refuses to die, in spite of its numerous difficulties. There doesn't seem to be another, more plausible alternative.

That there isn't another game in town, of course, does not constitute much of an argument for the contour theory or its relations. Tomorrow is another day, and may well bring another, more convincing account.

What, then, should we do here and now? When a problem remains unsolved, one obvious strategy is to work at it until it gives up its secret, and only *then* go on to the problem that logically follows next. But that is not the strategy I think will have the best results. I think it a mistake for us to remain bogged down with the question of *how* music comes to embody the garden-variety emotions as perceptual qualities. Rather, since there is a consensus, more or less, that music does exhibit the expressive qualities in this way, let us now go on to examine what role, as so understood, they play in musical structure and the musical experience.

Let us, then, treat music, in this regard, as what the scientists call a 'black box': that is to say, a machine whose inner workings are unknown to us. We know what goes in, and what comes out, but what causes what goes in to produce what comes out—of that we are ignorant. With regard to how music comes to exhibit the garden-variety emotions as perceptual qualities, it is to us a black box. We know what goes in: the musical features that, for three centuries, have been associated with the particular emotions music is expressive of. And we know what goes out: the expressive qualities the music is heard to be expressive of. And rather than becoming obsessed with penetrating this black box, we should, or at least *some* of us should, go on to see what implications this new way of looking at music's expressive qualities (for it *is* a new way) has for our understanding of music as a whole. That is the project I propose to pursue in Chapters 6 and 7. But before I do that I must convey to you some general idea of how music, and our experience of it, are to be construed. Only then will we be able, so to speak, to add the garden-variety emotions, as perceptual qualities, into the mix, and determine the part they play. So we will put aside, temporarily, the question of music and the emotions, in the following two chapters, only to return to it after the necessary groundwork has been laid.

CHAPTER 4

A Little More History

For most people in the world, 'music' means sung music. For most people in human history, 'music' meant sung music.

The modern 'problem of music' is the child of pure instrumental music: absolute music; music alone. What is the problem, and how did it arise?

In the Middle Ages, the Renaissance, and the seventeenth century, the composer's life was devoted mostly to the composition of vocal music: for the Church, for secular occasions, and, later, for the opera house and for occasions of State. This is not to say that music played on instruments alone was unknown in these pre-Modern periods. Some of it was vocal music played on instruments. But some of it, as well, was written especially for the organ, or harpsichord, or lute, or even specified combinations of instruments. There *was*, indeed, instrumental music before the eighteenth century.

But it is generally agreed that something about instrumental music radically changed in the latter half of the eighteenth century. Certainly its 'social status' migrated upwards, and with that the amount of creative time it occupied in a composer's life. This is for historians of music to understand and explain. What it meant for the philosophy of music, however, is altogether clear.

I mentioned, in the first chapter, the formation, during the eighteenth century, of what has been called the 'modern system of the arts.' What this event betokened was the realization that a number of practices once thought of as 'crafts' were better understood as akin to poetry, and henceforth to be classified, along with it, as the 'fine arts': the very practices that we now understand to fall under that rubric.

The last such practice to be gathered in, and the most troublesome, was *music*. It *was* the last, *because* the most troublesome, and the trouble lay in the rise to prominence, in the latter half of the century, of pure instrumental music. Here is why.

As we have already seen, as far back as Plato, there was the belief that music represents or imitates the passionate speaking voice. This belief was given a powerful formulation on the eve of the seventeenth century by the Florentine *Camerata*; and the belief endured through the eighteenth. But always it was *vocal* music that was meant by 'music.' And it was vocal music that the representational theory most plausibly described. Thus, from Plato to the middle of the eighteenth century, the reigning view was that music is a 'representational' practice: it represents the human speaking voice. *Vocal* music, that is.

What of *instrumental* music? Well, it was much more difficult to understand *it* as a representation of the human speaking voice. But, no matter; for while pure instrumental music remained on the periphery, a mere sideshow, there was little need to bother about it. If you had a good theory of *vocal* music, you had a good theory of music, for all intents and purposes.

Why did one need a 'theory' of music? Just because the modern system of the arts demanded it. If the arts of poetry, painting, drama, and the rest were *the* fine arts, there had to be some defining character that they all had in common: something that *made* them *the* fine arts. And that something was agreed on all hands to be 'representation.' To be a fine art required being representational. Vocal music, since antiquity, had been conceived of as representational; and the *Camerata* had reformulated that view in modern terms. Thus it posed no problem for the new project of determining what made the fine arts the fine arts. 'Representation' was the password; and vocal music was in on the secret. For the time being, instrumental music, far harder to see as a representational art, didn't matter.

However, the rise of instrumental music, in the second half of the eighteenth century, changed all that. It became a 'contender'; but its credentials were not at all as clear as those of vocal music. When you hear (and *see*) someone singing, it is not difficult to interpret the singer as representing someone speaking the words she sings, as when you hear the characters in Shakespeare's plays speaking in poetry, you naturally interpret them as representing people speaking in ordinary prose. (The English kings did not speak in verse.) And as we think of Shakespeare's plays as representational works of art—poetic representations of people conversing in ordinary prose—so we do not have much trouble thinking of composers, in their vocal music, as contriving representational works of art—works of art representing speaking or (in opera) even conversation.

However, when confronted with a late-eighteenth-century symphony, by Haydn or Mozart, in which a considerable number of players on various instruments cooperatively produce an intricate sound structure with little apparent resemblance to human vocal expression, it becomes far from easy to conceive of what one is experiencing as artistic representation in any of its familiar forms. But nor, at this point in the history of instrumental music, can such compositions be dismissed as peripheral. In the case of Haydn, they are his central, defining task. Haydn's reputation, by the last quarter of the eighteenth century, was founded, largely, not on his vocal music, but on his compositions for instruments alone. And it was an international reputation. The point is, then, that by this time, if one were going to explain how 'music' was one of the fine arts, one would have to include as 'music' not merely vocal music but instrumental music as well. The problem was that the reliable old formula, 'The fine arts are the arts of representation, music is a representation of the passionate speaking voice, so music is one of the fine arts,' did not work any more, at least not in any obvious way. It did not work any more because it did not *seem*, at least, to work for pure instrumental music; and pure instrumental music was now too important, both as an activity and as a 'social' phenomenon, to be ignored.

One of the central projects of philosophers of art, during the eighteenth century, was to make firm the foundation of the fine arts, which was representation. Absolute music, pure instrumental music, was a stumbling block. It was difficult to place on that foundation. Most philosophers paid scant (if any) attention to the problem of absolute music. The knew little about it (or about music in general) and tended to pass it off as a representational art, with no real discussion of how such a claim might be made out or what substantial difficulties it faced. A prime example is the distinguished Scottish philosopher Thomas Reid (1710–96), who suggested musical harmony be thought of as a representation of pleasant, good-natured conversation, musical dissonance as that of an angry, disputatious one, and let it drop without further attempt at elaboration, commenting only that he knew little about music in the first place.

However, another philosopher, probably no more knowledge-able than Reid, nevertheless went more deeply into whether and how absolute music could be a fine art than any other philosopher of the first rank in the period. That philosopher was Immanuel Kant (1724–1804), who produced, without a doubt, the most profound treatise on the subject of what we now call 'aesthetics' that the eighteenth century was going to see.

Kant's reflections on art and beauty are to be found in his *Critique of Judgment* (1790). This work is divided into two parts, called:

Critique of Aesthetic Judgment, and Critique of Teleological Judgment. The second part, Critique of Teleological Judgment, is concerned with the problem, particularly troublesome in Kant's day, of our judgments concerning the apparent purposes we find in Nature: for example, the 'purpose' of the giraffe's long neck, which is to enable its foraging in the highest branches of trees, or the 'purpose' of the heart, which is to pump blood. ('Teleological' means 'having to do with purpose,' and comes from the Greek word for 'purpose,' *telos*.)

The theory of art and beauty is laid out in Part I of the *Critique of Judgment*. But its title, Critique of Aesthetic Judgment, is liable to be misleading; so it would be a good idea to clear that up right away before we go on. The confusion arises because Kant's use of the word 'aesthetic' differs radically from ours. When we talk about 'aesthetic' judgments, we mean judgments that have to do with matters of art and beauty. Thus, we think the judgment 'The sunset is beautiful' is a typical aesthetic judgment, whereas we don't think that of a judgment like 'This steak tastes good.' But Kant would have thought *both* of these judgments are aesthetic judgments because all *he* meant by an aesthetic judgment was a judgment based on the judger's 'feeling.' The judgment 'The sunset is beautiful,' Kant would have said, is made on the grounds that perceiving it produces in the admirer of sunsets a pleasurable feeling, and the same would be true of the judgment 'This steak tastes good.'

What puzzled Kant was that even though judgments about the beauty of things, just like those about the tastes of food, are 'aesthetic,' that is, based on the subjective feelings of the judgers, they are nevertheless spoken with, as it were, a different 'voice.' When one says, 'This steak tastes good,' one is understood to be saying, 'This steak tastes good *to me*.' The taster is making a singular, personal judgment, and would not be put out if someone else were to say of the same steak, 'This steak does *not* taste good *to me*.' But, Kant thought, not without some justification, I believe, that when one makes a judgment like 'The sunset is beautiful,' one is speaking with a 'universal voice.' One is *not* saying, 'The sunset is beautiful *to me*,' and one *is* put out when someone else says, of the same sunset, 'Not beautiful at all.' The puzzle is *how* there can be judgments that are *both* aesthetic *and* universal, which, Kant thought, judgments of the beautiful are.

The major task Kant undertook in the Critique of Aesthetic Judgment, its defining task, really, was the task of explaining how judgments of the beautiful could be both aesthetic and universal. Like all of Kant's philosophical explanations, it is notoriously difficult to understand, and it would be inappropriate to enter into a technical analysis of Kant's argument in a book such as this one. But I believe one *can*, in an informal way, catch on to what Kant is saying in this regard; and it is important that we do so, because Kant's explanation of how judgments of the beautiful can be both aesthetic and universal has important implications for his account of music, and *his* account of music has important implications for *my* account of music.

Returning, now, to the example of the sunset, suppose we *do* have two opposing judgments. Mr Positive says, 'My, what a beautiful sunset,' and Mrs Negative gives the opposite opinion. Mr Positive then adds, as if to win Mrs Negative over to his view, 'This sunset truly is displaying forth the glory of God,' to which Mrs Negative, not to be beguiled by such maudlin sentimentality, replies, 'This sunset is the result of the appalling air pollution extending over the entire State of New Jersey.'

What is noteworthy about this exchange between Mr Positive and Mrs Negative, from Kant's point of view, is that *neither* has offered what Kant calls a 'pure judgment of taste.' That is because each of their judgments has been tainted, so to speak, by an extraneous belief about the sunset: in Mr Positive's case, a belief favorable to it, in Mrs Negative's case, a belief unfavorable. Seeing the sunset as displaying forth God's glory causes it to please Mr Positive, while seeing it as the result of air pollution causes it to displease Mrs Negative. Each has injected a strain of the personally 'idiosyncratic' into the judgment, making it no more universal than any other judgment based on feeling—for example, judgments about the tastes of foods.

But surely *everyone* has some belief or other, perhaps many more than one, positive or negative, about sunsets. So it looks as if the problem Mr Positive and Mrs Negative are having with their sunset is everyone's problem with every sunset, and, more generally, everyone's problem with *anything* they find beautiful. It is the problem of achieving the pure judgment of taste in the face of all of the prior beliefs, concepts, and other conceptual predispositions that perturb it.

What Kant argues, then, is that if someone can, to stick with our previous example, gaze at a sunset in temporary abstraction from all his beliefs or concepts concerning sunsets, and contemplate merely its visual appearance alone, he will then have achieved the attitude of 'disinterestedness' from which a pure judgment of taste can issue. The idea is that in this attitude of disinterestedness I have removed all of the personal factors that make judgments based on feeling singular rather than universal. So, if you achieve this attitude and, as well, if Mr Positive and Mrs Negative achieve this attitude, then we will all agree, on the basis of feeling alone, that the sunset is beautiful.

What, then, are we agreeing *on*? Well Mr. Positive has, for the moment, ceased to see the sunset as an act of God, Mrs Negative has ceased to see it as an 'act' of pollution, we have all ceased to place it under any of our sunset concepts or beliefs. What's left? The answer is: its *form*. When we agree that the sunset is beautiful, if we have really achieved the attitude of disinterestedness towards it, it is the *form* of the visual appearance that we are talking about. Furthermore, Kant points out over and over again, we do not even make a commitment to the *actual existence* of the thing, whatever it might be, the form of which we judge beautiful. The form of the sunset, after all, is invariant with the mode of the sunset's existence. Whether it is a real sunset, a dream sunset, or a hallucinatory sunset makes no difference. Whatever the existential status of the sunset, the form of its visual appearance remains constant; and it is its *form* that we are reacting to in the pure judgment of taste. This is Kant's 'formalism.'

But why, the skeptical may ask, should we think that, when we remove from our contemplation of the sunset all our personal, acquired beliefs and concepts concerning sunsets, and this one in particular, we will all, as a consequence, necessarily agree in our estimate of its beauty? Perhaps we are *inherently* different in our estimations of the beautiful, not merely different because of our acquired beliefs and concepts. A further argument, then, would seem to be required to show that, when we achieve the state of 'disinterestedness,' our judgments of the beautiful will converge: will agree. And Kant does indeed provide one. In effect, he argues that, as he puts it, we are suitors for agreement because there is a ground common to all of us.

The common ground of humanity that, Kant believed, assures agreement in judgments of the beautiful is the joint operation of two common, basic human faculties: the imagination and the understanding. These are the faculties Kant took to be complicit in our acquiring and making claims to knowledge. But when they are employed in the disinterested contemplation of form, they are then, as Kant put it, in a kind of 'free play' that issues in the pleasure of the beautiful. We all share these faculties in common, as we all share the capacity for knowledge; and when they are in this 'harmonious' free play, not doing any work, as it were, we all share the pleasure thereof—the pleasure that makes judgments of the beautiful, the pure judgments of taste, *both* aesthetic *and*, nevertheless, universal.

So much, then, for the beauty of sunsets and other such natural phenomena, big and small. We are after different game: the understanding of works of art; in particular, the elusive art of absolute music. How does Kant's analysis of the beautiful pay off there?

Contrary to what some people may think, Kant was *not* a formalist in his philosophy of art, if being a formalist means believing that the formal properties of art are its only art-relevant ones (however such properties might be construed). On the contrary, he believed that works of art, being representational, have a 'content' or 'meaning' and that this content or meaning is an essential part of their nature. His teaching here is subtle and (as always) difficult. But the gist of it is this.

Works of fine art are, for Kant, essentially, works of genius. Thus, when Kant talks about the nature of the fine arts, he is speaking, usually, about art at its highest level; and so we shall understand him. (He does have a way of fitting not-so-great art into his scheme, but I cannot go into that here.) Such art, the art of genius, has 'content' at two levels. First of all, it has what might be called 'manifest content.' So, to take one of Kant's own examples, a poem might tell us about the sun going down at the end of a perfect summer day. (Back to sunsets again!) But what its *important* content is, if it is the art of genius, is not *that*. Any mediocrity can write a poem about a sunset at the end of a perfect summer day. What happens in the art of genius is that the manifest content sets in motion, in its audience, a rich chain of ideas, the 'aesthetic ideas,' Kant calls them, which proliferate indefinitely, giving the work its deep, albeit ineffable content: it can be felt, so to say, but never explicitly stated. It is what gives the art of genius its 'spirit.'

The effect of this deep content, the chain of aesthetic ideas, is much the same as the effect of the perceptual presentation when apprehended disinterestedly: it engages the harmonious free play of the imagination and understanding.

Besides their deep content of aesthetic ideas, Kant also believes, quite naturally, that works of art can possess formal beauty as well. But—and this will be very important in his discussion of music—Kant distinguishes sharply, in works of art (and elsewhere), between beauty and what he calls 'charm.' In an oil painting, for example, the visual forms have beauty. The colors, however, even though people may ordinarily call them 'beautiful,' *cannot*, strictly speaking, *be* beautiful; for, as we have already seen, only form can be beautiful:

only form can be the object of the pure judgment of taste. Colors, *per se*, are perceived as simple qualities, without form, hence do not provide the pleasure of the beautiful in the free play of the cognitive faculties. What they can provide is the pleasure of their 'charm': which is to say, pure sensuous pleasure, the pleasure of physical sensation.

To sum up, then, Kant thinks that works of the fine arts, the works of genius, exhibit two definitive characteristics. They possess beauty of form; and they possess representational deep content: the power to excite a chain of ineffable ideas, the aesthetic ideas, which, like the beauty of form, engage the harmonious free play of the imagination and understanding.

The problem of whether music, absolute music, that is, is a fine art, or, as Kant puts it, merely an art of the 'agreeable' (which would be an art of 'charm'), is the problem of whether absolute music possesses beauty of form, and whether it can excite aesthetic ideas capable of engaging the free play of the cognitive faculties. It cannot be *fully* a fine art without both.

Let us take the form question first. Kant's approach to it will seem strange to us; for, rather than talk about the 'forms' of music, as we usually think of them, the large temporal patterns by which musical compositions are organized, and the smaller formal patterns internal to the large ones, Kant concerned himself, rather, with the question of whether individual musical sounds themselves were simple perceptual qualities or whether *they* had form we might perceive. If the latter, then music could fulfill the first criterion of fine art: formal beauty. Kant embraced the latter alternative.

Kant based his claim that musical sounds possess perceptible form on the fact that sounds are *vibrations* of the air, that is to say, are waves, and, hence, have a form (or periodicity). It is this perceptible wave-form that, Kant believed, enables musical sounds to be beautiful. Being beautiful, they give music the first requirement of a fine art: formal beauty. And, on the strength of this, Kant described music as 'the beautiful play of sensations.'

With regard to deep content, music does not fare so well. Music does, according to Kant, have something like manifest content (as I have called it), in the form of its expressive properties. Kant, in other words, thought music could be described in terms of the garden-variety emotions. He even thought this manifest, expressive content could excite aesthetic ideas in the listener. But, for reasons that are not altogether clear (at least to *me*), he did *not* think that the musical chain of aesthetic ideas succeeds in engaging the free play of the imagination and understanding. Rather, he thought it merely effects a purely *bodily* relaxation, so to speak. In a word, then, for Kant, music can interact only with the body, not the mind, through its deep content, and on that account, apparently, fails to achieve the second condition for being a fine art. It is artlike in form, but not in content. (Content, he says elsewhere, is added to music when it is joined with a text.)

The significance of Kant's not granting absolute music full status as a fine art is not something we need go into. What is very important to concentrate on is his positive conclusion: that absolute music is artlike in its possession of formal beauty: that it is a beautiful play of sensations. This conclusion can be considered the seed pearl of musical formalism.

It did not much matter, in the development of musical formalism after Kant, whether or not he thought music one of the fine arts, properly so-called. What mattered was that he ascribed the beauty of absolute music solely to its formal properties. That these properties were the vibrations of sound, not the kinds of formal properties succeeding formalist theorists were at all concerned about, was easily forgotten. What was important was that pregnant phrase, 'the beautiful play of sensations,' and, as well, Kant's comparison of music with the decorative arts. In particular, Kant analogized music without words to wallpaper, designs *à la grecque*, which is to say, free floral designs, and other examples of pure decoration. This was, indeed, formalism. But what Kant's musical formalism totally lacked was any real recognition of the 'logic' behind the form. He gave little evidence, in his reflections on music, of having any knowledge of the principles that lay at the heart of musical structure. His musical formalism was a fruitful idea, but an empty one, really. What it required was fleshing out in real musical terms. That fleshing out was begun by Hanslick. If Kant was the genetic father of musical formalism, Hanslick was its nurturing parent.

It will be recalled that Hanslick presented, in his little book *On Musical Beauty*, a negative thesis and a positive one. The negative thesis, which we have already discussed, was that music's beauty does not at all lie in its expressiveness. The positive thesis, which we are now to look at, holds that it lies in the musical materials themselves, and especially their form.

Although he was not a philosopher by trade, I do not think there can be any doubt that Hanslick was greatly influenced by Kant's philosophy of beauty. He could not bring to his project philosophical genius. But he could bring, as Kant could not, real musical knowledge and true musical sensibility, being a musician and critic.

Hanslick famously described music as 'tonally moving forms.' And it is not, perhaps, too far-fetched to understand the phrase as another way of expressing Kant's thought that music is the beautiful play of sensations. Decoration, for Hanslick, as for Kant, provides the leading analogy. Where Kant speaks of designs *à la grecque*, Hanslick speaks of arabesque. They amount to pretty much the same thing: free decoration.

But it is noteworthy that Hanslick goes quickly from static design to design in motion. Music is, for him, the sonic analogue of the kaleidoscope: a toy that we all have held in our hands at one time or another, and that, clearly, was already familiar in Hanslick's day.

The kaleidoscope provides what analogues such as wallpaper, designs *à la grecque*, and arabesque cannot: decoration in motion, although we must always understand musical motion in metaphorical terms. Of course music does not literally move (unless it is being played by a marching band). It is a pattern of sounds succeeding one another in a temporal order, as the kaleidoscope is a temporal succession of visual patterns.

So far, there is little advancement over Kant. For, even though Hanslick's kaleidoscope may be a more felicitous illustration of tonally moving forms than Kant's wallpaper or designs *à la grecque*, it surely fails to capture an absolutely vital element in music. For, as Hanslick well says, music is not *merely* 'an ear-pleasing play of tones' (surely an echo of Kant's 'beautiful play of sensations'). It is not *merely* a kaleidoscope of euphonious noises.

But what is missing from the characterization of music as, in Kant's words, a beautiful play of sensations, or, in Hanslick's, an ear-pleasing play of tones? Music *is* that, after all, if 'beautiful' and 'ear-pleasing' are given a wide interpretation. Hanslick, in one very dense and suggestive passage in Chapter III of *On Musical Beauty*, tries out a number of images to capture the extra baggage that absolute music carries, over and above the beautiful play of sensations or ear-pleasing play of tones. In contrast to arabesque, Hanslick says, music is a picture, but one whose content we cannot express in words or concepts. Or, unlike arabesque, music has sense and logic—but not in the way that science or history has sense or logic. Its sense and logic are purely musical, which is to say, expressible only in musical terms. Finally, unlike arabesque, music is a sort of language, but—you guessed it!—a language we cannot translate into any other, even though we can 'speak' and 'understand' it. What are we to make of these various images?

It seems apparent that Hanslick is trying, with these images of visual representations, sense, logic, linguistic meaning, to capture *something* about music that separates it from the first images with which Hanslick introduced it as a purely formal art: the arabesque and kaleidoscope. But what is it he is trying to capture?

Let us go back to the kaleidoscope for a moment. When you look through its eye-piece and turn the wheel, you observe a sequence of symmetrical colored patterns succeeding one another. What you do *not* see is any rhyme or reason to the sequence: nothing connects one pattern with the next. They follow randomly as the bits of colored glass configure themselves, tumbling inside the kaleidoscope's tube. But a sense of order, a sense of logic, a sense of 'sense' is exactly what you *do* get in a well-wrought musical composition (or even in a not-so-well-wrought one). And it is that quality of music, as opposed to the random quality of the kaleidoscope, that Hanslick is trying to capture with his images.

The logical and linguistic images are, I think, the most suggestive and appropriate for what Hanslick is getting at. Let us look at the linguistic image for a moment.

Compare the succession of sounds in a paragraph of English prose, read aloud, with the succession of colored patterns in the kaleidoscope. What's the difference? It is that the colored patterns have no logical connection but the English sentences do: they are connected by their *meaning*, and the total meaning of the paragraph that they comprise.

Are the successive tones of music connected in the way the words and sentences are in the English paragraph? Is music a kind of language? Hanslick seems to be suggesting that it is severely constrained, because he insists that music is a language that cannot be translated into any *other* language. If it could, then Hanslick would be turning against his formalism—that music has no extramusical meaning or content, either emotive or any other. However, this is wondrous strange. What kind of language could it be that is impossible to translate into any other language? Indeed, we know that marks on paper or stone, or successions of sounds, are language and not meaningless patterns just because we can translate them into a language that we can understand. (That is how we determined that the Rosetta Stone had linguistic inscriptions on it and not mere decorations.)

What would music *be* if it were a language in principle impossible to translate? It would be a 'language' minus its meaning:

a 'language,' if that is the right word for it, without its *semantic* component.

But what is left of a language if you distill off its semantic component? What is left is its *syntax*: its *grammatical* component. What is left is a collection of inscriptions with rules for their correct combination: rules for the stringing-together of the meaningless inscriptions into grammatical, syntactically correct chains, or, if you will, 'sentences'—except they are 'sentences' without meaning.

It seems, then, that what Hanslick was at least beginning to see is that absolute music is, as it were, a kind of syntax without a semantics: language-like but not a language. It does not convey merely a sense of order. It *does* convey *that*. But it is a very special kind of order: the order of syntactical structure. That, I am certain, is what Hanslick was trying to get at when he said that the progression of musical sounds has a kind of 'sense' or 'logic,' but not semantic sense or logic. This was a tremendous insight, and gave to musical formalism the backbone it needed to do real justice to the deep musical experience—an experience I doubt Kant ever had. What Hanslick realized was that, without having a meaning, absolute music, at its best, has a 'logic'—a quality of inexorable progress and direction. (Listen to Beethoven for your first, overwhelming corroboration of that.)

The direct heir of Hanslick's formalism is frequently said to be Edmund Gurney, whose great 1880 book, *The Power of Sound*, has already been mentioned. Surprisingly, there is no mention of Hanslick in it, although I find it difficult to believe that Gurney was unfamiliar with his predecessor's ideas. Gurney's own characterization of musical structure, 'ideal motion,' is hard not to hear as an echo of Hanslick's 'tonally moving forms.'

Gurney's formalism is almost entirely a formalism of *melody*, which he takes to be the major operator in music—at least any music that Gurney takes seriously. Gurney's basic idea is that, to put it baldly, music is melody, and so the beauty of music is the beauty of melodic form.

But what *is* melodic form? It is, according to Gurney, the flowing *connectedness* of melody; and that certainly sounds right. A melody is individual tones heard as a continuous connected whole. It has, as Hanslick would say, a 'logic,' a 'sense.' It has, as Gurney would say, 'ideal motion.' If you don't hear individual tones as connected, you are not hearing melody. Furthermore, bad melodies frequently sound 'disconnected' to us, in comparison with good melodies. So the sense of connectedness, the sense of 'logic,' helps us to distinguish not only melody from non-melody but good melody from bad. Gurney is onto something here: so far so good.

Two basic problems are generated by formalism, as Gurney understands it. The first is very obvious. Melody simply cannot bear the weight that Gurney places upon it. Even the music Gurney sees as the pinnacle, the music of Beethoven, cannot be comprehended solely, or even largely, in terms of melody. And with music of the Medieval period, and the Renaissance, where melody, in Gurney's sense, is hardly even a major principle, let alone a dominant one, his melodic formalism fails utterly. The failure of his theory to manage the music composed prior to the time of Haydn, Mozart, and Beethoven fazes Gurney not one bit. The music of the Middle Ages and Renaissance Gurney simply puts down as primitive—of historical interest, perhaps, but not of great artistic merit. No one like myself, nurtured in historical musicology, can possibly accept such a historically skewed, historically prejudiced view of the history of music, or such a naive view of musical 'progress,' as if music got better and better as time wore on, like steam engines or printing presses.

Furthermore, there is, in Gurney's attempt to explicate the form of melody, and how we perceive it, something that smacks of mystification, so to speak, and that goes against the grain of the reasonable person. Quite rightly, Gurney is suspicious of trying to identify any obvious formal properties of a beautiful melody that cause it to be beautiful: that are the 'essence' of its beauty. For such formal properties that can be readily identified, he is fond of pointing out, are also present in mediocre, unlovely melodies as well as in beautiful ones.

As a result of this skepticism, Gurney tends to represent ideal motion as if it were some kind of mysterious, non-natural, almost supernatural quality. Consequently, he ascribes the perception of this elusive quality to a special, 'musical faculty' that is as imponderable as the musical quality it is supposed to track. This kind of thing is not helpful, although it is an understandable, and perhaps a healthy, overreaction to the danger of oversimplifying the concept of formal beauty. That a formal property of one melody contributes to its beauty does not imply that it will contribute to the beauty of every melody in which it is present, and certainly does not imply that it will make every melody in which it is present beautiful. But nor does it follow that, because it does not contribute to beauty in one place, it cannot in another. In other words, there is no formal formula for formal beauty in melody, or anywhere else; Gurney is certainly right about that. That does not mean, however, that we cannot, on a case-by-case basis, discern *some* of the reasons why *this* melody is beautiful and *that* one banal. And it certainly does not mean that the formal beauty of melody, or its 'ideal motion,' as Gurney would have it, dwells in some never-never land beyond the ken of our natural faculties. Musical beauty, melodic or otherwise, is a wonder, but not a miracle.

We should not, however, at the end of the day, let these doubts about ideal motion and the special musical faculty obscure or tarnish Gurney's accomplishment. It is agreed on all hands to be a considerable one, all things considered. Given that Gurney greatly overemphasized the importance of melody in Western art music, no one doubts its importance nevertheless. Furthermore, Gurney's formalist analysis, with its emphasis on the sense of connection and logical progression that well-wrought melody conveys, contributed in a significant way to the formalist project. Indeed, it is fair to say that Gurney's *Power of Sound* represents the first complete and persuasive version of musical formalism to come down the pike.

Others, I am sure, will tell a different story of the coming to be and the coming of age of musical formalism in the nineteenth century. But by my lights no such story could plausibly omit the joint efforts, in this endeavor, of Kant, Hanslick, and Gurney. They laid a firm foundation. On it I will build some superstructure in the chapter to come.

CHAPTER 5

Formalism

'Formalism' is an ill-chosen word to describe the account of absolute music that I am about to give. It is, indeed, an ill-chosen word to describe many other versions of musical formalism that resemble mine in general outline but differ from it in major or minor aspects. It is ill-chosen, I think, for two reasons.

To begin with, it suggests that the *only* aspect of music relevant to its appreciation *is* its *form*; and this may be true of the views of Kant, Hanslick, and Gurney, which represent its first flowering. But it is certainly not true of *my* formalism that musical form is the only artistically relevant aspect, and it is certainly not true of other versions of formalism currently in the marketplace.

Formalism is best defined, initially, in negative terms: in terms, that is, of what music *isn't*. According to the formalist creed, absolute music does not possess semantic or representational content. It is not of or about anything; it represents no objects, tells no stories, gives no arguments, espouses no philosophies. According to the formalist, music is 'pure' sound structure; and for that reason the doctrine is sometimes called musical 'purism.'

But once we arrive at the conclusion that, according to formalism, music is pure sound structure, we see immediately that there is more of artistic interest in it than form alone. There are the elements of the construction: the things out of which the construction is made. And, unless you believe that only forms can be beautiful or artistically appreciated, these elements, in themselves, even those that do not have form, will be of artistic interest as well. The sounds of individual notes or chords, the tone colors of the various instruments, all of those things out of which musical form is constructed, will also have their appeal. We want to see the trees as well as the forest.

Formalism, then, is the view that absolute music has neither representational nor semantic content. Absolute music is a structure of sound: but a structure that is of musical interest not only for its form; for that too, of course; but for the elements of that form as well. According to formalism, we are interested, musically, in all of the 'sensuous' properties of the musical work, its form being one of those, albeit perhaps the most important.

The second reason that 'formalism' is not a very good word for the doctrine being put forward here is that the word suggests visual forms ('the human form divine'), static spatial forms; and musical 'form' is temporal, although, of course, it can be, and usually is represented with, spatial diagrams. Musical forms are temporal patterns of sound. But 'formalism' is a term that has been in place for so long that discarding it would cause more confusion than clarity. (I doubt that 'temporal patternism' would catch on if I were to propose it as an alternative.) So 'formalism' let it remain, even though not the perfect name for the thing.

Now, that music possesses formal and sensuous properties we enjoy, in listening to it, no one denies. Even if you believe that absolute music possesses representational or semantic properties beyond its structural and sensual ones, you still must also believe that its structural and sensual properties pleasure us in the hearing, just as the forms and colors of representational paintings do, or the pure linguistic beauty of novels, plays, and poems. Thus, the formalist's question with regard to absolute music, What do we enjoy in our apprehension of musical structure?, is *everyone's* question, formalist or not. It is the question I now want to raise, and, I hope, answer satisfactorily.

Suppose I asked you, What do you enjoy in reading a novel or seeing a movie? Very likely, many people would reply: the fictional events of the novel or movie as they unfold. Needless to say, we enjoy other things as well: the beauty of the language, if it is a literary work, the picture composition if it is a movie, the structure of the plot, and perhaps the profound questions of philosophy and morality the fictional work might pose. But surely what we all principally enjoy about much of the fiction we consume is *the story.* Whatever else the great novelists of the nineteenth century were, they were great storytellers, as were the great Hollywood directors in the golden age of American narrative cinema.

Now let us ask the same question about musical structure that we just asked about fictional narrative. What is it we enjoy in listening to the formal and sensual properties of absolute music unfold in our listening space? If you are a formalist, there is but one reply. As in a work of narrative fiction, what we are enjoying is the unfolding of *events*—but not fictional events, like Hamlet's murder of Polonius or Tarzan's rescue of Jane from a herd of stampeding elephants. The events that we are enjoying, as they unfold, are purely musical events: sound events.

However, even though musical events are not narrated or depicted fictional events, but pure, meaningless sound events, our perception of them, and our enjoying of them, share some common characteristics with our understanding and enjoyment of fictional narratives, whether read, in novels, or witnessed in plays and movies. Roughly speaking, we *think* about the events we are experiencing, in some similar ways, whether they are the fictional events of narrative artworks or the pure sound events of absolute music.

Imagine you are reading a novel for the first time. As you read along, you are introduced to the characters and are made privy to their actions and conversations, even sometimes their thoughts. But you are not a *passive* spectator. You *think* about what is transpiring. You wonder how the hero is going to get out of the fix he is in, and you are surprised at how he manages the business. Or you guess, early on, that he is going to fall in love with his fiancée's cousin, and sure enough, that is what happens. You think that the butler did it; but in the end it turns out to have been the lord of the manor. Or you get the feeling that things are going to turn out happily for the downtrodden peasants—and, lo, their rescuer appears. In other words, when we attend to a fictional narrative, we play a kind of question-and-answer game with it; or *it* plays the game with us. However you want to put it, a fictional narrative plays with our expectations, confounding some, confirming others.

Furthermore, our expectations are conditioned by our previous experiences with the various genres of narrative fiction, and how they work. Thus, for example, my reactions to the twists and turns of a detective story I am presently reading would be quite different if I had never read a detective novel before. And the same for any other genre of fiction. Likewise, the experience I am now having of the detective novel in my hands will alter my future experiences of detective novels, as well as other works of fiction. My expectations are, in other words, in a constant state of flux, as are the other mindsets I bring to my experiences of fiction.

Now absolute music is not fiction, at least for the formalist. Nevertheless, a good deal of the way we react to narrative fiction transfers to our experience of music alone, minus, of course, the fictional content.

What I am getting at is this. Just as, in reading a novel, say, we think about what we are reading, frame hypotheses about what will happen next, have our expectations frustrated or fulfilled, and so on, so we will too in listening seriously, with concentration, to absolute music. Musical works have 'plots': not, to be sure, plots with characters in action; rather, pure musical 'plots'; sound events occurring, as Hanslick urged, with a connecting musical 'logic' or 'sense.' When we follow these plots, we do much the same thing that we do in following fictional narratives. We play question and answer with them.

The way musical 'plots' play with our hypotheses, expectations, surprises, and fulfillments has been brilliantly explicated by the music theorist Leonard B. Meyer in his ground-breaking work in musical aesthetics and psychology *Emotion and Meaning in Music* (1956), as well as in various essays and articles. I don't think a successful musical formalism can be viable without making use of some of Meyer's conclusions. So I want to get the relevant ones, for *my* formalism, on the record now.

Meyer bases his analysis of musical perception and appreciation on what mathematicians call 'information theory.' But don't get scared. You don't have to be mathematical to understand the basic principles; and the basic principles are all we need for our purposes.

To get a basic idea of what 'information theory' is, let us begin with what the word 'information' conveys in ordinary life and ordinary discourse. Suppose I tell you 'The sun will rise tomorrow.' You might well reply: 'That's no news to me; you aren't telling me anything I don't know.' In other words, I have given you no 'information'; for we usually understand that what it means to *inform* somebody of something is to tell her something she doesn't already know.

But now suppose I tell you that the sun will *not* rise tomorrow because of some impending cosmological catastrophe that the astronomers have only just discovered. Surely that would be news to you: startling news indeed.

Furthermore, the events in question, the rising, or the not rising of the sun, would be, respectively, no news and very big news. If you awake to a rising sun, the fact of its rising is no news, because you were as certain, the night before, that the sun would rise on the morrow, as you were of anything else. The sun's rising did not tell you anything you did not already know: it conveyed no information. But, on the other hand, if the sun does *not* rise next morning, that *is* news: you believed with close to certainty that the sun would rise, and it didn't. The failure of the sun to rise was a complete surprise: it told you something you definitely didn't know: it was highly informative.

Information theory is an extension of this common-sense notion of what's news and what isn't. Information theory says that events are on a continuum from the totally expected to the totally unexpected. The more expected an event, the less informative it is if it occurs, and vice versa: an unexpected event is 'highly informed,' an expected event is not.

What Leonard Meyer does is to apply the information theorist's concept of informed and uninformed events to *musical events*. In other words, musical sound events are evaluated in terms of the degree to which they are expected or unexpected. An unexpected musical event is highly informative, like the failure of the sun to rise, or uninformative, if expected, like the sun's rising right on schedule. But what kind of musical 'events' are we talking about? And what causes us to form expectations concerning them?

I will distinguish, for the purposes of this discussion, between two kinds of musical events: what I shall call 'syntactical events' and 'formal events.' By syntactical events I mean those 'small' events that take place within the musical structure. These events are governed by the 'rules' of musical grammar. Some have to do with chord sequences, that is, what chords follow what other chords, and with what frequency. Some have to do with melodic lines: for example, when a melody goes up with a leap, from one note to another five steps above, it 'should,' 'normally,' then descend stepwise. And some have to do with the manner in which melodic lines can be combined in 'counterpoint': for example, when it is permissible for two melodic lines to move in parallel motion, when they must move in opposite directions, what intervals are permissible between them, and so on.

Formal events are the large events of musical structure that are governed by the various musical forms. Thus, for example, it is a formal rule or principle that a symphony is to have four movements, the first one fast, sometimes with a slow introduction, the second slow and contemplative, the third in a lighter vein, either a minuet (in the classical symphony), or a 'scherzo' (since Beethoven), and the final one fast, usually faster than the first movement, and often in rondo form in the classical period.

But the movements within work structures like the symphony, or the sonata, also follow formal rules or patterns of their own (which may vary with historical period). Thus the first movement of a classical symphony by Mozart or Haydn is in what is called 'sonata form.' It goes something like this. There is a first theme or group of themes, a contrasting second theme or group of themes, and a closing theme or group of themes, constituting the first section of the movement: the *exposition* as it is now called. The second section, sometimes called the *free fantasy* section, or *development*, has no fixed form but allows the composer to work with her themes any way her imagination inclines her. The movement closes with a *recapitulation*, which, ordinarily, follows the same pattern as the exposition, first theme, second theme, closing theme, using the same thematic material. This gives sonata movements a three-part symmetrical form: ABA.

So the musical events with which musical information theory deals are, as outlined above, syntactical events and formal events which the listener has expectations about: which, in other words, are expected to occur or not expected to occur, strongly, weakly, or to any degree in between. From whence do these expectations arise?

Expectations of musical events can usefully be divided into 'external' and 'internal' expectations, which is to say, expectations that one brings already formed to a work one is experiencing, and expectations that the work itself generates in one's listening to it. The former are the expectations one acquires quite naturally, without being aware of it, in growing up in a specific musical environment. By listening to Western music, we become enculturated into the musical scale, the harmonic syntax, and the formal structures characterizing our music, whether it be the popular genres, folk idioms, or the classical repertory. We bring this set of expectations, at the ready, to any musical work we encounter; and the composer assumes that they are present in the listener.

The latter expectations, the internal ones, are aroused and frustrated or confirmed by the inner workings of the particular musical work itself that the listener may be attending to. It is part of the composer's craft to play with the formal and syntactical expectations of the listener; and it is part of the listener's pleasure to become involved in this play.

A musical work, then, is, among other things, a structure of sound events, running the gamut from expected to a very high degree to unexpected to a very high degree: in terms of information theory, from a low to a high degree of information. And, according to Meyer, satisfying music, 'good' music, if you like, must cut a path midway between the expected and the unexpected, or at least stay far enough away from the one or the other not to become totally either. If a work's musical events are all completely unsurprising, uninformative in the information theorist's sense, then the music will fulfill all of the listener's expectations, never be surprising—in a word, will be boring. On the other hand, if the musical events are all surprising, all highly informed, the musical work will be, in effect, unintelligible: chaotic. The listener's expectations will *all* be frustrated, or the listener will fail to have any expectations at all, and will not be able to find her way in the work. New works, in novel or unfamiliar styles, will frequently exhibit this character, as will works from musical cultures other than the listener's own, either because historically or geographically remote.

Two questions now pose themselves with regard to this information-theoretical account of musical listening. First, to what extent is this process of expectation, surprise, and fulfillment a conscious process, to what extent operating, as it were, 'behind the scenes'? Second, how can the process work at all when one is listening to a musical composition that has been listened to many times before, and, hence, holds no surprises, because one 'knows the story'?

The answer to the first question is, I think, fairly straightforward. The process of expectation, surprise, and fulfillment, of which the information theorist speaks, operates *both* consciously and unconsciously. I presume that, when I am consciously aware of music, there is, always, an unconscious process going on, in which musical expectations are being aroused, fulfilled, and frustrated. But I am going to leave the unconscious alone. Rather, what I am concerned with is what goes on in the listener's consciousness when he or she is seriously and single-mindedly attending to a musical work, at a concert, or on a recording, for the sole purpose of enjoying the music. In my view, such a person—and I extrapolate here from my own experience—is consciously playing what might be called the 'hypothesis game' with music. He or she is thinking about the musical events taking place, is framing hypotheses about what is going to happen, and is sometimes surprised, sometimes confirmed, in his or her expectations.

Note that the hypothesis game can go on with varying degrees of *self*-consciousness. One may be playing the hypothesis game and also be concentrating on how one is playing it and *that* one is playing it: not merely thinking but thinking about one's thinking. But playing the hypothesis game no more implies that one is thinking about how one is playing it than playing any other game implies such self-awareness. I point this out because people sometimes object to musical enjoyment being necessarily a conscious activity when what they mean is that it is not necessarily a *self*-conscious activity—quite a different thing.

Nevertheless, it may still be objected that I am over-intellectualizing what is going on in the listener's mind in attending to music. Perhaps, it will be said, this is what musicians and the musical experts do, but surely it goes beyond what takes place in the mind of the lay listener.

Well, I don't think so. It certainly is the case that the musical expert has more conceptual apparatus, in the form of what is called 'music theory,' with which to think about the musical experience, as it unfolds (and more of that in a moment). But we all have concepts under which to place the musical events that we attend to; and it is my point that when we are really listening to music as a serious, engrossing activity, not merely as background to some other task, or for 'atmosphere,' we are, in the process, thinking about what we are hearing. Furthermore, part of that thinking is in terms of the information theorist's framework of hypotheses, expectations, surprises, and fulfillments.

But now the second of our questions to the musical information theorists remains. How can we play the hypothesis game with music we have already heard? For the hypothesis game can only work, can only be fun, if we are not certain of the course the musical events will take. If I think, 'Now the melody will come to a conclusion,' and it does, my expectation is fulfilled. If it doesn't, I am agreeably surprised. That is the game. However, if I have already heard the music before, I *know*, am *certain*, what the melody will do. So it makes no sense to say that my expectation has been either fulfilled, or frustrated. There can be no doubt about the outcome, any more than I can be in doubt about the ending of a novel I have read; and if there is no doubt, then the game loses its point, and its pleasure. Obviously the outcome can't surprise me; nor, though, can it confirm my hypothesis either. For there must be at least some doubt about the outcome, some possibility of surprise, for the fulfilled expectation to provide me with aesthetic satisfaction. If I *know* the butler did it, because I have read the book, then the fun of surmising that the butler did it, and turning out to be right, evaporates.

This problem, the so-called problem of rehearing music, has a fairly straightforward solution. To begin with, the rehearing problem exaggerates the degree to which most listeners, even expert ones, can remember, in detail, the course of musical events in any musical composition beyond the most trivial. Repeated hearings of a symphony or string quartet will cause the listener to become acquainted with its general outlines, but hardly give her photographic recall. So most music of substance will bear many rehearings before the danger of total familiarity looms.

Furthermore, there is, in absolute music, as in fiction, what might be called the persistence of illusion. Even though one may know that some formerly surprising event is about to occur in a composition, because one has heard it many times before, one gets 'sucked in,' as it were, once again, by the music, and reacts, essentially, in spite of one's self. It is rather like knowing someone is going to lunge at you but, nevertheless, involuntarily flinching when it happens. To take an example, the ordinary course of events in a symphony, as I noted before, is for the first movement to be fast, the second movement slow, the third movement a minuet or rapid scherzo, the finale fast again. Beethoven adheres to this pattern in all of his symphonies up to the Ninth (except for the Sixth, the 'Pastoral,' which does not follow the usual four-movement form). In the Ninth, he puts the the scherzo second and the slow movement third. And as many times as I have heard the work, I still am, in a funny sense, 'surprised' when the scherzo, a fast movement, occurs when I am 'expecting' the adagio. I, as it were, 'get into the story' all over again, as I do when I see *Hamlet* yet again.

Now it is certainly to be expected that no musical work, no matter how complex, can be listened to *ad infinitum*, without ever losing its effect. Nevertheless, it is the general experience of serious listeners that the great works in the repertory provide a lifetime of normal listening. Thus, the 'problem' of rehearing music does not make implausible, by any means, the information theory of musical appreciation. The hypothesis game does survive the rehearing of music, in usual circumstances, and there is no doubt, I think, that it constitutes a significant part of our listening experience: but *not*, by any means, the *whole* experience. Let me add to it what I shall call the musical game of 'hide and seek.'

So-called classical music, during most of its history, has been a music of more or less complicated structure. And it is in appreciating this complicated, intriguing structure that musical enjoyment has been generated.

Even where melody has been a principal part of the musical experience, as in the period from the beginning of the eighteenth century to the end of the nineteenth, it has been melody embedded, so to speak, in structure of a more or less complicated kind. Thus, a great deal of the interest such music generates is involved in seeking out the melody in the structure. This is what I have referred to as the musical game of hide and seek, or, elsewhere, as *Cherché le thème*.

In the familiar forms that Western art music has taken, in the modern era, the fugue, sonata form, rondo, theme and variation, and so on, the formal principle involved has been one kind or another in which the listener's task is to find, to recognize, the principal melody or melodies out of which the musical structure is constituted. It is the composer's task to vary these melodies, hide them, alter them, dismember them, and generally give the listener puzzles to solve.

Furthermore, the standard musical forms or patterns involve the recurrence of themes at various places. It is the experienced listener's task to recognize when the themes occur, and to orient herself within the musical forms or patterns. Finding one's way in a musical form is part of the hide-and-seek game, and gives part of the satisfaction one derives from such music, and from such musical listening.

We can now put together the two processes of musical listening, the hypothesis game, and the game of hide and seek, into a plausible account of what we enjoy in our encounters with absolute music (and music with texts as well). What both of these games suggest is a kind of puzzle play, much like, as I suggested earlier, the kind of thing that goes on when we take in a fictional narrative, whether read (as in a novel) or seen (as in plays and movies). In a story we are held captive because we want to know what is going to happen: how things will turn out. But we are not completely passive observers of the fictional proceedings: not intellectually passive, that is. A great deal of our pleasure in the experience of fictional narrative is the pleasure we take in wondering what is going to happen, making conjectures about what is going to happen, and, of course, finding out what is going to happen: finding out if our conjectures are on the money or not. Narratives pose riddles we try to solve.

The forms of absolute music are plots without content. Or, if you like, they are purely musical stories. But, just as fictional narratives pose us questions and then answer them, so too do musical plots. Just as fictional narratives may hold surprises in store for us, so too may musical plots. Musical plots, like fictional ones, display 'events' for our enjoyment: in the latter, fictional events; in the former, sound events.

But it cannot be emphasized too strongly, in this place, before I go on, that, although absolute music may bear an analogy to fictional narrative in the ways I have just described, it is emphatically *not* literally fictional narrative. For, both internally and externally, as we shall see in Chapter 8, music is *repetitive* to a very high degree. Musical 'plots'—and they are 'plots' in an attenuated sense only—repeat themselves in a way, and to an extent, that would be intolerable in narrative structure (as will become apparent). The reason we enjoy this repetition, at least to a point, is not altogether clear. What is clear is that, because music is pattern without content, the repetition plays the same role in music as it does in abstract visual patterns. Indeed, as should be plain, you couldn't *have* pattern without repetition. *That* is what pattern *is*.

I have spoken, above, of the hypothesis game and the hide-and-seek game in musical 'plots.' However, if the hypothesis game is endemic both to fictional narrative and to musical 'plots,' the hide-and-seek game seems more musical than literary, just because it is so much a function of design repetition. The seeking and finding of themes, which plays such an important part in the musical experience, does indeed play a part in the literary experience as well. The recurrence of words, or phrases, or fictional events of certain kinds, or philosophical points, or metaphors, certainly occurs in fictional narratives; and the seeking-out of such literary 'themes' is certainly part of our enjoyment of at least the higher forms of fiction. But I think such thematic structure plays a far greater role in absolute music than in literature just because there is no fictional 'content' in absolute music to organize its 'plots.' And, indeed, when theme recurrence *does* occur in a literary work to an unusual degree, the work is frequently said to have a 'musical' character on that account, so closely are music and theme recurrence associated with one another.

In any event, whether with regard to fictional content or theme recurrence, to understand a fictional narrative is to understand what took place. To show you understand what took place you describe what took place. Is that also true with musical plots? I think so; but that requires some explanation.

A person who understands a fictional narrative understands it because he can put what he reads under the appropriate concepts. If a child should read *Pride and Prejudice*, he would understand some of it, perhaps; but he would miss out on a great deal because, to put it bluntly, he wouldn't know what Jane Austen was talking about. For large portions of the story, he literally wouldn't know what really is happening because he does not possess the concepts necessary for story comprehension.

But what, exactly, does a musical listener understand? There is no fictional plot—just musical events. Well, it is the musical events that are understood, in the sense that the listener attends to those events; and, if he attends to those events, then he perceives them as happening in certain ways.

Now many readers may think that, again, I am over-intellectualizing the listening experience, which is often thought of as more like a semi-conscious, dreamy reverie in which one is bathed, as it were, in sound. That, of course, is a way of listening to music (or, rather, a way of *not* listening to it). But it is simply not the way of listening to music that we are trying to understand. We are trying to understand what goes on when someone, whether or not a musically trained someone, listens to music seriously, attentively, the way a serious composer intends and hopes. *That* person is attending to musical sound events not with a mind completely blank and bereft of thought, nor a mind occupied with thoughts and problems for which the music may serve as a soothing background, but a mind occupied *with the music*. A person with his or her mind so occupied is a person who, I think, can fairly be described as thinking about the musical events to which he or she is attending.

The music, when seriously listened to, is what philosophers would call an 'intentional object': that is to say, an object perceived under certain descriptions. For example, you and I might both be looking at a man. I believe the man to be a well-known actor. You don't know him at all: he is just a tall, good-looking man to you. The 'intentional object' of my gaze is 'a tall, good-looking man who is a well-known actor, famous for his Hamlet.' Your 'intentional object' is merely 'a tall, good-looking man.' We both see the 'same man'; but, depending upon what we know, or believe about the man, we see 'different men'; we see different 'intentional objects.' I see an actor famous for his Hamlet; you just see a man.

Music, when listened to seriously, as I have described above, is an intentional object of the listener's attention. And what intentional object it is will depend upon what beliefs the listener has about the music. In particular, it will depend to a large degree on what musical knowledge, and what listening experience, the listener brings to the music. The more knowledge and experience one brings, the 'larger' the intentional object will be: the more there will be to it; for the more we know about the music, the more elaborate our description of it will be, and the more elaborate our description, the more features, literally, the intentional object, the music, will possess for us to appreciate.

It begins to look, then—and I welcome the conclusion—that increase in musical knowledge will tend towards increase in musical appreciation or enjoyment. The reason for this is that, since increase in musical knowledge enlarges the intentional object of musical appreciation, it, quite simply, gives us more to appreciate or enjoy. Furthermore, this view of the matter helps us to understand another aspect of the musical experience that some people find puzzling: the role, in musical appreciation or enjoyment, of what is called 'music theory.'

'Music theory' is not 'theory' in the sense in which Darwin's theory of evolution, or Einstein's theory of relativity, are 'theories.' It is not, in other words, a 'theory' in the sense of some deep explanation of how things in nature work. It is, rather, an elaborate technical description of musical events that does not seem to have an analogue in any of the other arts. And it has been a matter of contention, among music theorists and philosophers, as to how, or whether, music theory can play any part in musical appreciation or enjoyment. I think that it does play a part, and that the way of looking at musical listening I have outlined above tells us how and why.

Now one conclusion we certainly want to avoid is that knowledge of music theory is a *requirement* for a rich appreciation of music. Vast numbers of people, who comprise the audience for classical music, have no such technical knowledge; and it is hard to believe that such people would devote the time and treasure they do to an art form that afforded them little satisfaction.

But, on the other hand, I think we want to avoid, too, the (to me) equally unwelcome conclusion that acquiring the technical knowledge of music constituted by music theory should not contribute to an increase in musical enjoyment. That has not been my experience, nor that of others I know. There is a tendency in our democratic-minded society to be wary of an 'elite' cadre of aesthetes who possess secrets that open to them and close to us the higher forms of art and culture. We should not allow this inbred distaste for an inherited aristocracy to cause us to bring musical appreciation down to the level of the uninformed.

We already have in our possession the argument to suggest that technical knowledge of musical syntax and structure will tend to increase our musical enjoyment. For what it gives us is an increased capacity for describing the intentional object of musical appreciation; and what *that* gives us is an enlarged intentional object of musical appreciation. The ability to describe music in music-theoretical terms provides us with tools for distinguishing, in the musical object, events that are closed to the listener without such tools.

Again, this is not to say that a rich appreciation of music cannot be achieved by those lacking knowledge of music theory. But nor should we shy away, out of some kind of 'democratic' scruples, from acknowledging that not all music is equally accessible to the naive and the learned. Large portions of the classical repertory are greatly enhanced by music-theoretic knowledge, even while accessible, to some degree, to all. If that is the bad news, the good news is that music theory can be learned by *anyone* with an ear for music (and don't let the experts tell you anything different). *Anyone* who enjoys, who appreciates, classical music, or *any* music, for that matter, can acquire music-theoretical knowledge, if he or she is of a mind to do it. In that sense there is nothing 'elitist' about knowing the basics of musical grammar. Anyone who wants to can be in on the secret. If you don't want to, well, of course, that is your own business. If *that* is aesthetic 'elitism,' then I am all for it.

I have, then, to recapitulate, presented absolute music in the form of two 'games': the hypothesis game, which is essentially the information theorist's formalism, and the hide-and-seek game, which, I presume, is part of everyone's formalism. At this point, though, the reader may be beginning to wonder about how far this really goes in explaining *what we enjoy in music*. How, why, are these games enjoyable?

I confess that I cannot answer this question. But maybe it is not really a philosopher's task to answer it. After all, he can only go so far; he must, eventually, reach something that he can but ask the reader to take for granted or accept 'on faith.' Here is what I mean.

I have posed the question: What do we enjoy or appreciate in absolute music. And I have answered: We enjoy musical 'plots,' in something like the way we enjoy fictional stories, except, of course, that the musical 'plots' are 'merely' sequences of musical sound events, not stories about fictional events. Furthermore, I have tried to spell out two ways—not necessarily the only ways—in which we interact with musical 'plots,' as we do with fictions: they are 'games'; the game of hypothesis and the game of hide and seek (although the latter is more a musical game than a literary one).

But, if you accept this argument, then, really, you already have a kind of answer to your question. You have brought with you to these proceedings the belief that games are inherently enjoyable to human beings: they are paradigm instances of what humans enjoy. So, if you accept that the games of hypothesis and hide and seek are an important part of what goes on in our appreciation of absolute music, you have learned why, to that extent, listening to absolute music is enjoyable: it consists in part in these games, and games, generally, are enjoyable to us. One way to satisfy someone's curiosity about why S is p is to show that person that S is q, and that, *as you have always known*, all p's are q's.

Now, of course, this does not mean you are unjustified in wanting to know *why* p's are q's. You are not unjustified in wondering *why* games of the kind we are talking about are enjoyable to human beings. It is a legitimate question. But it goes beyond what the philosopher of music can, or is obliged to, explain. Perhaps it goes beyond even what the philosopher of *anything* can or is obliged to explain. Perhaps we now require the psychologist or biologist or both. The philosopher of music, however, has taken you as far as he can.

At this point we have a pretty good idea about what shape my musical formalism takes. But so far two rather important topics have been avoided. First of all, it will be recalled that I thought 'formalism' an ill-chosen term for my (and others') view, because it apparently singled out music's formal elements as the only ones relevant to its appreciation; whereas there are, as well, in our appreciation of music, elements of pure sensual beauty—tone colors, individual chord qualities, chord progressions and modulations, and so on—that appeal to us as well. Second, I have said nothing at all about the concept of beauty itself. Surely it matters to us whether the music we hear is beautiful or not: we take pleasure in, appreciate, music to the extent that it is beautiful or, more generally, musically 'successful' to a high degree. How does the concept of the beautiful fit into the formalist creed?

As for the sensual elements of music, there is little one can say that is not just plainly obvious. Musical form is realized in heard sounds. These sounds are produced by instruments constructed to produce as beautiful a tone as possible, in their characteristic timbres, and are played by performers who are (one hopes) trained to elicit from their instruments as beautiful a tone as possible. Music that is written for groups of instruments is constructed in ways that make use of the distinctive timbres of the different instruments in sensually beautiful ways. Music written for a single instrument exploits, as beautifully as possible, the distinctive sounds it makes in its various registers.

The beauty of chords, chord progressions, modulations, and other such 'individual' elements of the musical fabric of course begin to have 'form': they certainly have 'parts.' Nevertheless, they remain, in the big picture, elements out of which musical form is constructed. Of course their beauty is not a 'natural beauty,' a natural property, like the beauty of a sparkling gem, or a shiny gold nugget, any more than the beauty of a whole symphony is. Some large part of their beauty is a cultural artifact: the famous chord in Wagner's *Tristan und Isolde*, which succeeding generations have found so fascinatingly beautiful, would have been an ugly dissonance to the eighteenth-century ear.

Furthermore, the beauty of individual chords, chord progressions, or modulations is frequently owed to how they are situated in larger musical areas: how they 'emerge' from the forms of which they are the elements. Nevertheless, the beauty of these elements is, more or less, like the 'natural beauty' of gems and precious metals in that they are experienced, within musical structure, as its sensually beautiful elements, simply qualities like the beauties of colors.

Well, there it is. Beauty. Beauty. Beauty. Music has sensual beauty; and its forms are realized in that beauty. But what makes the sounds of the various instruments of music beautiful? What makes the sounds of individual chords, chord progressions, and modulations beautiful? And what makes musical compositions realized in those beautiful sounds beautiful? Surely the philosopher of music has not completed his task until he has answered those questions.

Here, I think, the philosopher of music cannot beg off and say: The question of musical beauty is someone else's question, not mine. Who else's question could it be? It is a *philosophical* question if ever there was one; and it is clearly the philosopher of music who should answer it.

Nevertheless, I shall not try to answer the question of what constitutes musical beauty or 'success.' It just *may* be an unanswerable question. In any event, *I* cannot answer it, nor do I know anyone else who has, or can. For, if you mean by answering it, giving some set of properties that, together, are necessary for any music's being beautiful, and being sufficient for its being beautiful, I think Gurney was quite right in being skeptical about there being such (as I think he was).

The fact that we despair of an answer, in terms of necessary and sufficient conditions, to the question, What is musical beauty?, should not, however, paralyze us into dumbness about saying what, *in particular cases*, contributes to the beauty of a musical composition, or a part thereof, as I think it did Gurney. Indeed, everything we have so far seen, about what is enjoyable in musical form and material, is an answer to what, in particular cases, may contribute to musical beauty. And everything that is to come will contribute as well. What we must *avoid* concluding is that no music can be beautiful without such features as I have discussed, or that having such features will assure its beauty. That no one can say with good reason.

What more *is* there to say about the outlines of musical formalism? The attentive reader will, no doubt, have noticed that, so far, nothing has been said about the emotive properties of music in this regard. Yet, as we have seen, there is general consensus, and I share in it, that there *are* emotive properties in music, which we perceive there when we listen to it. Are these emotive properties to play no part at all in the musical formalist's account of the musical listening experience? Some have thought so. I do not. I promised at the end of Chapter 3 to return to the question of how the garden-variety emotions, *in* the music, function there, after I had laid the necessary foundations of musical formalism. I have now laid these foundations. So I can delay no longer in keeping my promise. To the musical emotions, in the following chapter, we again direct our attention, and to some other relevant things as well.

CHAPTER 6

Enhanced Formalism

Traditional formalism—the formalism of Hanslick, Gurney, and their followers—has always been associated with the denial that music can be described in emotive terms. Hanslick, as we have seen, denied flat out that music could embody the garden-variety emotions, in the only two possible ways he could envision: as dispositional properties of the music to arouse the emotions, or as representations of the emotions.

Gurney may have been somewhat more liberal; but his formalism, in the end, amounted to the same thing as Hanslick's as regards any possible role for the garden-variety emotions in musical aesthetics. For, although he did allow that music could be sad, happy, and so forth, he thought this was completely irrelevant to the aesthetic structure. In other words, the fact that a passage of music might be sad had no more to do with its beauty, or other relevant aesthetic features, than the fact that a peach is fuzzy has anything to do with its taste.

The explanation for the total exclusion of emotive properties from music in the early formalist creeds of Hanslick and Gurney is fairly clear. Both of them saw the battle lines cleanly drawn between the traditional theory, which they opposed, that the whole of music's beauty, or artistic significance, lies in its emotive properties, however they might be conceived, and their own theory, which denied this. It must have seemed to them, then, that it was all or nothing: either emotive properties did play a role in the musical work of art, or they did not. If their view, formalism, was right—if the beauty or artistic significance of music lay in its forms alone— then there was no room, in formalism, for the emotions. So 'formalism' became synonymous with the exclusion of emotions from the musical experience. If you were a friend of formalism, you were an enemy to the emotions.

The early formalistic creed, of Hanslick and Gurney, was, furthermore, reinforced in its rejection of the emotions in music by, as we have seen, a very limited choice of options for *how* music might *be* describable in emotive terms. The possibilities on offer were that music was sad, say, in a dispositional sense: it had the property of making listeners sad; or that music was sad in a representational way: it represented sadness the way a painting represents flowers or fruits. What was not contemplated was the possibility that music is sad in virtue of possessing sadness as a heard property, the way a billiard ball possesses roundness and redness as seen properties. But, once the possibility of emotive properties as heard properties of the music is conceived of, then it immediately becomes apparent that emotive descriptions of music are compatible with 'formalism,' broadly conceived as the doctrine, outlined in the previous chapter, that music is a structure of sound events without semantic or representational content. For, if emotive properties like sadness are heard properties of the music, they are just properties of the musical structure, and to say that a passage of music is sad, or cheerful, is no more to describe it in semantic or representational terms than to describe it as turbulent or tranquil. A tranquil passage of music does not represent tranquility or mean 'tranquil.' It simply *is* tranquil. And the same is true of a passage of music that is melancholy. It does not mean 'melancholy' or represent melancholy. It just *is* melancholy, and that ends the matter.

Now there are those who argue that, if a musical passage is describable in emotive terms, that, *ipso facto*, implies that the music has at least minimal 'content.' I shall deal with this claim later in the chapter. But for now I will take it that formalism broadly conceived is perfectly consistent with music's possessing heard emotive properties. This view has been aptly characterized by the philosopher Philip Alperson as 'enhanced formalism.' And that is how I shall refer to it on these pages.

The task at hand now is to explain what role or roles emotive properties might play in musical structure. They cannot, at least in many important cases, just *be* there, for no reason at all.

When emotive properties of music were thought of as either dispositional or representational, their reason for being present was fairly straightforward. If sad music aroused sadness, that was the way music moved us emotionally; and being emotionally moved by works of art is an inherently good thing. Or, if sad music represented sadness, then there was no problem either, because representation in art is an inherently good thing: naturally pleasing to human beings, according to Aristotle. But, if emotive properties of music are neither dispositional nor representational, just heard properties, what are they *doing*? There has to be an aesthetic or artistic reason why there is a major chord of a certain kind in this measure of a symphony, and a diminished chord of a certain kind in the next. And appeal to musical 'syntax' and the overall structure of musical works is the approved method for explicating it. What, though, do we appeal to in trying to explicate why there is a cheerful passage of music followed by a melancholy one, if not to representation or arousal?

Why not say that the emotive properties of music play the same kind of role as the chords and motives and melodies? Why not say that what we should do is appeal to musical 'syntax' and the overall structure of the piece, in trying to explain why the music is cheerful in one place and melancholy in the next? I think that *is* the right thing to say. However, to be convincing, that answer needs some spelling out.

Before one even gets to talking about the more elaborate functions in syntax and structure the emotive qualities of music might perform, it would be helpful to point out that there are perfectly simple and obvious functions that can be ascribed to them as well—functions they share with many other heard properties of music, or seen properties of the visual arts. I take it as a truism that emotive properties of music, like other of its artistically relevant properties, are inherently *interesting* properties. That is to say, they are properties of music that add to its aesthetic character, and are inherently pleasurable to experience. But, furthermore, like other heard, aesthetic properties of music, they help constitute the sonic pattern. Patterns, whether sonic or visual, are a matter of repetition and contrast. Thus, if, in observing a visual pattern, a fine Persian rug, for example, you ask, Why is this square figure just *here*?, I might reply, Because this rug is a pattern of squares and ovals, and a square is what is required here if the pattern is to be consistent. But why, you then ask, is it a *red* square?, and my reply then might be, Well, it is for contrast, since the oval next to it in the pattern is black.

In other words, the emotive properties of music, like such other properties as turbulence, or tranquility, or its being major at one point, minor at another, or simply that it has one kind of melody here, and another kind next, can be explained, initially, in terms of the simplest facts of musical structure: that is, sonic patterns, and that patterns consist in repetition and contrast. And the appeal to repetition and contrast as explanations for why a musical work is of a certain character here, another there, is an appeal valid for *any* musical qualities, including, of course, emotive ones.

Furthermore, it bears mentioning that part of the human appeal of absolute music, as a pure abstract art of pattern, is its emotive properties. I do not suggest, by any means, that abstract visual patterns cannot possess emotive properties as well, abstract expressionism being a recent and impressive case in point. But it may in fact be, for reasons I do not fully understand, that sonic patterns, when they are *music*, are richer in emotive properties than abstract visual patterns as a rule are. If that is so, it may make them particularly appealing to the human animal, which is, for better or worse, an *emotional* animal. Absolute music , even though it is a pure, abstract, 'formal' art form, is not a 'cold' formalism. It has human 'warmth,' because it has human emotions as a perceptual part of its structure.

It needs remarking as well that the presence of emotive qualities in music sometimes requires no explanation at all, because the composition in which they occur is working out musical structure that simply has nothing to do with the emotive properties it possesses. For example, a composer may write a musical composition predominantly in major keys, and with bright, brisk melodies, that will be, of necessity, because of that, cheerful and exuberant. Yet the composer may have had entirely other things on her mind than these expressive properties. She is interested in writing a piece that exhibits certain structures and patterns involving just these keys and melodies. These structures and patterns have nothing to do with the emotive tone of the piece, which simply occurs because the piece is written in major keys and with bright brisk melodies. The emotive tone, so to speak, comes with the territory; comes along for the ride. But it plays no particular part in the proceedings, and hence need not be noted or explained in an analysis of the piece, and what is musically going on in it.

But, needless to say, in an abundance of music in which expressive properties occur, they do play an important structural role. And, although the simple function of making patterns and providing contrasts goes some way towards explaining, in such cases, why emotive properties are where they are, there is frequently more to be said for their presence and particular place in a musical composition.

As I suggested just now, it is tempting to try to understand the role of emotive properties of absolute music in terms not only of patterns and contrast, and other 'surface' features, but in terms of musical syntax and deeper structure as well. How this might be done, I hasten to add, is not by any means clear, at present. Indeed, as a research project, in my own work, it has only just begun. Nevertheless, I think I can give the reader at least a vague idea of what a 'syntactical' explanation for the musical function of emotive properties might look like.

One of the most prominent and most often written about 'syntactic' features of the kind of music we are concerned with is what is usually described as 'resolution.' In very general terms, the music of which we speak moves from moments of rest, to moments of tension, or instability, and then resolves tension or instability into stability or rest.

More specifically, certain chords are active chords, and must be 'resolved' into stable chords that provide resting points, either temporary or permanent. Such resolutions from tension to rest are called 'cadences.' They are either the temporary resting places of musical movements, sometimes called 'half-cadences,' if they occur during the course of the movements, or they are permanent resting places, when they occur at the ends. Frequently, what makes a chord 'active' is that it contains a dissonance; and the process of its 'resolution' involves resolving the dissonance into a consonnance. But this needn't always be the case. Thus, a G-major chord, the triad G–B–D, has no dissonance in it, nor does the C-major chord, the triad C–E–G. In the key of C major, however, the G-major chord performs an active syntactical function: the G-major chord resolves to the C-major chord; and when it does, it goes from tension to rest, even though it does not go from dissonance to consonance but from consonance to consonance.

If you add F to the G-major chord, you *do* get a dissonance: the F with the G. (Play those two notes alone on the piano and you will hear it.) This is known as a 'seventh' chord, because the added F is the seventh note up from G. This chord, as well, by virtue of the dissonant F–G is even a more active chord, in C major, than the plain

G-major triad, and the resolution to the C-major chord that much more a 'resolution': a greater release of tension.

You can hear how the resolution from dissonance to consonance works, syntactically, with even greater clarity, in the following musical commonplace that has been employed over the centuries in the combining of two or more melodies together. I will write it out in musical notation for those who can read and play it.

Notice that the passage begins at rest, with the consonance C–E. The top melody then moves down to D, while the lower melody remains on C, thus producing a dissonance. (This is called a 'suspension' because the C is held over the bar line to the following measure.) The dissonance is resolved in the second measure, but only comes to a partial close (with another suspension) onto the G-major chord. There is no dissonance now, but, as we saw, the G-major chord is an active chord in C major, and naturally calls for a final resolution to the C-major chord in the fourth measure. Thus these four measures give us a progress from rest to tension to partial resolution to full resolution. It is a very common musical technique: indeed a musical cliché But within its tiny dimensions it provides an example of the most pervasive structural-syntactic feature of Western art music since, I would guess, the very beginnings of musical notation in the Middle Ages. Western art music, in its small, medium, and large-scale aspects, is a process of movement from rest, to tension of varying degrees, to rest of varying degrees, to a final stability or closure. And, if a composition *departs* from this model—if a composer writes tensionless music, or music that avoids closure, 'restless' music—part of its effect lies, of course, in its being projected against a background of the enduring tradition of music in the rest–tension–release mode.

As well, it must be cautioned that what constitutes a 'restful' chord, a chord on which it is permissible to close, is not written in stone, but is historically relative. Thus, there was a time when a musical composition could not come to rest on a chord with a third in it: the third was considered a dissonance. There was a time when a musical composition could not come to rest on a minor third: the *minor* third was a dissonance. And the kinds of chords that are chords of rest, of complete closure, in our own times would have been considered inappropriate as closing chords in the nineteenth century. Musical closure is a syntactic concept, and syntax in music, as in natural languages, changes with time.

If one takes, for example, the most popular large musical form, the symphony, one can, in the paradigm cases, the great symphonic works of the eighteenth and nineteenth centuries, see clearly (and hear clearly), from the smallest musical units, to the large thematic groups of the individual movements, to the overall direction of the individual movements, to the whole four-movement work, a process that goes from rest to tension to rest. It is, if you will, the overarching syntactical figure that all other syntactical figures serve.

Now a brief comment must be made at this point about what exactly we are experiencing when we experience the tension and resolution in music of which I have just now been speaking. Some people would want to say that what is happening is that we describe moments of music as moments of tension when the music makes us feel tense, and we describe moments in music as moments of resolution or release when our tensions, which the music has excited, the music now dissipates, or, as the musical term would suggest, 'resolves.'

I myself don't like this way of describing things at all. It seems to me far more congruent with my own musical experience to say that the tension and resolution about which I have been speaking are not tension and resolution experienced in me as emotional episodes in my own psychological 'biography,' but, rather, things that are happening in the music, and that I hear happening there. In other words, like the garden-variety emotions, they are in the music, not in the listener. Not only does this way of speaking seem better to represent what I perceive I am experiencing. As well, the other way of speaking seems to me implausible. Here is why.

The feeling of tension is very pronounced and usually distressing. One feels tense when one is expecting something unpleasant to happen: the dentist is preparing to extract a tooth. Or one feels tense when one is about to do something fraught with difficulty and the threat of failure: before making a speech or playing a concerto. It seems doubtful that hearing tension in music is anything like *that*.

But, it may be replied to this, you have maintained in the previous chapter that one of the principal ways of attending to absolute music, the hypothesis game, is a process of arousing expectations and having them fulfilled or frustrated. If one feels tension in expectation of the dentist's forceps, or the giving of a speech, then doesn't one also feel tension in expectation of the melody going this way, or the dissonance resolving that way? They are *all* cases of expectation, after all. And, if tension is aroused by the non-musical expectations, why not by the musical ones as well? What's the difference?

I think the answer is, quite simply, that not all expectations arouse tension: only those where the outcome might be such where tension would be the normal, appropriate response. I feel tense in the dentist's chair, or waiting to go on stage at my Carnegie Hall debut, but not when expecting a visit from my best friend or a delivery of groceries. And there doesn't seem to be anything about *musical* expectations that would cause tension in the listener, at least the normal listener under normal circumstances. (Someone who was made tense by *every* expectation would surely require the care of a therapist or a heavy dose of valium.)

Of course, a particularly persistent customer might go right on to insist that it is in the very nature of every expectation to be productive of at least some degree of tension, no matter how minimal. He might argue: to be in a state of expectation is *ipso facto* to be in a state of tension. I have no particular objection to someone speaking in this way, just so long as it is recognized that it is a strange way of speaking that squeezes every bit of juice out of the concept of 'feeling tense' and leaves only the empty husk behind. Everyone knows the difference between expecting the dentist's forceps, or that cadenza, bristling with difficulties, that you must play before a hostile audience of New York critics, and expecting your best friend or the delivery boy with the groceries. In the former case you are in a tense state, a state of anxiety, in the latter a state of calm anticipation. If the tough customer insists that all are tension states just by virtue of all being expectation states, he has simply legislated a change in language, but has changed our concept of tension not one bit. We will just have to find a new word for our old concept: philosophy will not be advanced; rather, communication will be impeded.

So I will rest content with my way of speaking about tension and resolution, in which not all expectations are productive of tension in the one expecting, musical expectations being a case in point. And I will rest content too with my belief that the best way to view musical tension and release, or resolution, is, like the garden-variety emotions, as being heard events *in the music*. That being said, it now is time to see just how the garden-variety emotions in the music might play a part in the tension-resolution syntax. As we shall see, the syntax of tension and resolution provides rich possibilities for the emotions in music to play a structural role. I do not believe it is the *only* role they play. But it will be something of an accomplishment, and as much as I can hope to do here, at least to show how they function in the syntax of tension and release. As I said earlier, this is not a complete theory but an ongoing project in progress.

The first thing to notice is that the terms 'tension,' 'release,' and 'resolution' themselves refer to psychological states that could at least broadly speaking be described as garden-variety emotions, along with ones like happiness, melancholy, love, anger, and the like. They are, after all, common enough, and, most would agree, fall within the general category of the emotional. Thus it would be no surprise that, when tension, release, resolution occur in musical works, the other garden-variety emotions are involved as well. After all, when tension, release, and resolution occur as mental states in human beings, the garden-variety emotions occur along with them. I am angry, and my anger 'resolves' into forgiveness. Or I have an enormous reservoir of pent-up anger and it is 'released' in an outburst of abusive language. And so on.

A second very important point to notice, or, rather, to remember, is the connection of the garden-variety emotions in music to the distinction between major and minor tonalities: in particular, the major mode with cheerful, light emotions, the minor with the darker, melancholy ones. For the remainder of this discussion I will concentrate on the major–minor contrast as it plays out in the cheerful–somber one.

Recall that when I talked about the melancholy quality of the minor triad, I observed that, for a long period of its history, it was considered a dissonant chord. Thus the ending of a composition in the minor key was frequently on a major chord. For example, a piece in the key of C minor would end on a C major chord rather than a C minor one. This was felt to be a more complete, more final resolution; and I think the feeling still persists, at least to some degree.

But note, too, that, since the association between major and cheerful, minor and somber, there is another big difference between resolution to the major and resolution to the minor. A resolution to the major is an emotive resolution from dark to light: from a somber emotive tone to a cheerful one. But, from the emotive point of view, the resolution, in a minor key, to the minor close, would be no resolution at all. Nor would there be any emotive resolution, in a major key, to a major resolution.

It is, I think, reasonable to suppose that the resolution in music from the darker to the lighter emotions would be a *stronger* resolution, a more restful, decisive close, than *merely* a resolution from dissonance to consonance or from an active chord to a stable one. In other words, the resolution of minor to major, which is a firmer resolution than minor to minor, is even *more* decisive because it is *also* a resolution from dark emotive tone to light. Furthermore, by consequence, the movement from dark to bright emotive tone will tend to be a movement, in and of itself, from tension to rest.

What begins to become apparent, then, is that, in the larger elements of tonal structure, the alternation of somber and bright emotive tone colors is an alternation between tension and rest, just as is the alternations of dissonance with consonance, or active chords with stable ones. In other words, the emotions in the music are, in this respect, performing a syntactical function: the most central one in Western art music, which is to say, the syntax of tension and resolution.

What I have been trying to show, in these reflections, is that the emotive properties of music, which is to say, absolute music—music with words and dramatic setting is quite another matter—have a purely structural role to play in the musical works in which they occur. But, it is sometimes objected, as soon as one has allowed music to be described in emotive terms, one has, *ipso facto*, gone beyond musical formalism, because, if music is somber, say, or melancholy, or cheerful, then it has at least minimal semantic content; and musical formalism denies semantic content absolutely. What are the grounds for this claim? And are they justified?

It appears that the reasoning goes something like this. The most basic condition for semantic content is 'reference': that is to say, the function of pointing, so to speak, to something that the referring term or expression is supposed to denote. Nouns like 'dog' or 'house' are said to denote, or refer to, those things: dogs and houses. Thereby they have a semantic dimension: they have content; they are 'about'; they mean. But, so the reasoning goes, if music is melancholy, or cheerful, it must, *ipso facto*, have reference to, denote, melancholy and cheerfulness. So formalism 'enhanced' with emotive properties is formalism no longer, properly so-called. Music that is melancholy must refer to melancholy; cheerful music must denote cheerfulness. And so semantic content, at least of a minimal kind, has insidiously infiltrated the musical structure through emotive reference.

I do not find this argument at all persuasive. Even if it *is* good, it yields, it seems to me, a trivial conclusion.

First of all, there are all sorts of other properties besides the emotive ones that we ascribe to music, with terms drawn from everyday life. We say that music, like rivers, can be turbulent or tranquil. We say that music, like food, can be sweet or, like children, can be raucous. Does this mean that turbulent music must, *ipso facto*, be referring to turbulence, tranquil music to tranquility, and so on? That seems to me to be absurd. Why should it be the case that, if something can be described in these terms, it must denote the properties named? Some things do indeed refer to some of the properties they possess. A boot, for example, hung outside a shop to indicate boots are sold inside has properties that might be thought to denote those properties. And 'short' is a short word denoting shortness. But there seems no good reason to think that properties of music serve such a function. The turbulence of passages in Beethoven's symphonies no more denotes turbulence than does the turbulence of the Colorado River. But suppose, anyway, that we accept the claim that music refers to its phenomenal properties: if it is melancholy, it denotes that property, likewise for its turbulence or tranquility or sweetness or raucousness. What has been accomplished?

Some may answer: If it refers to these properties, then music is 'about' them; and if it is about them, it has semantic content. So enhanced formalism is no longer formalism properly so-called.

Whatever victory this conclusion might be for the opponents of formalism, it seems to me a hollow one. For the absolutely minimal sense of 'aboutness' that mere reference accomplishes will hardly work anyone's passage from enhanced formalism to a musical semantics: it will get you only from enhanced formalism in letter and spirit to a musical semantics in letter, not spirit, and an enhanced formalism, still, in spirit. That is because, in order for music to be semantically interesting, semantically significant as an art form, it must not only refer but say something interesting and significant *about* what it denotes. If it cannot do *that*—which indeed it *cannot*—

then its *only* significant interest remains in just those non-semantic features that enhanced formalism recognizes: those of formal structure, syntax, and sensuous appeal.

I have presented, in the preceding pages, a version of what I have been calling 'enhanced formalism': the doctrine that absolute music is a sound structure without semantic or representational content, but, nevertheless, a sound structure that sometimes importantly possesses the garden-variety emotions as heard qualities of that structure—an enhancement, in effect, of formalism as it has traditionally been understood. I have, furthermore, tried to defend enhanced formalism against the charge that, in allowing absolute music to be describable in emotive terms, I have gone beyond the bounds of formalism properly so-called, because, if music *is* describable in emotive terms, then it must, *ipso facto*, denote emotions, be 'about' them, and, by consequence, have semantic content.

There are, however, other objections to the doctrine of formalism that adduce characteristics of so-called absolute music supposed to prove either that it isn't 'absolute,' or that, in any event, it cannot be understood on purely formalist assumptions, even when 'enhanced' with emotive properties. I want to conclude this chapter by considering three such objections. I shall refer to them, respectively, as 'historicist factors,' 'functional factors,' and factors of 'social setting.'

It is sometimes said that formalism is an 'ahistorical' doctrine and, therefore, cannot be true. For absolute music, so the argument continues, like all other arts, is embedded in its history, and its history imparts important properties to it. Whereas, so it is claimed, formalism is 'timeless.' The formal properties of music, so it is said, at least as the formalist construes them, are independent of historical incursions. A triangle, after all, is a triangle, then, now, and forever. Its concept is eternal and unchanging. So, if the formal properties of music, *its* forms, are like geometrical forms such as the triangle or circle, then they too are 'timeless' entities. They exist 'outside history,' recognized by you, me, and an ancient Greek alike for what they are. And, if that is so, like geometry, music can be appreciated in a completely ahistorical way. You needn't, for example, have any notion at all of the historical relationship of Haydn's, Mozart's, and Beethoven's symphonies fully to appreciate them. You needn't even know that Haydn came before Brahms. But that surely is absurd, so the critic of formalism concludes. It is *obvious* that you can't fully appreciate music, or any other art, without knowledge of its historical background and place. If formalism implies that you can, which it does seem to do, then formalism must be false.

The problem with this argument is that musical formalism is in no way committed to construing musical form (or any of the other artistically significant features of musical structure, for that matter) ahistorically. On the contrary, any sensible formalist will say that one big difference between music and geometry is that geometrical forms are ahistorical and musical forms are not. What the form of a musical work *is* is in part a function of its place in the history of music. There must be many aspects of musical form that are historically determined. I will mention two.

To begin with the obvious, a formal structure may exhibit art-historical features. Thus, many of Beethoven's piano sonatas have their first movements in clearly recognizable 'sonata form': the same form exploited to such perfection previously by Haydn and Mozart. But in numerous ways, especially in key structure, they are *innovative*. And you cannot perceive this innovative quality without perceiving them in their historical context, as both emulations of and artistic responses to the sonata movements of his great predecessors.

Now philosophers of art have argued over the years about whether these art-historical features of which I have just now been speaking are truly features of works of art, and appreciated as such, or whether they are, rather, features of art history and, therefore, to be appreciated and understood as historical events rather than aesthetic properties. I myself gravitate towards the former view of the matter, and, for what it is worth, the people who write about music, and the other arts, in a more or less popular vein, seem implicitly to agree. It is the stock in trade, for example, of those who write program notes for classical music concerts, to try to get listeners to hear the innovative and 'original' features of the works that are to be played as part of their listening experience. Be that as it may, however, there is no need for us to put all of our historical eggs in that one basket. There are ways in which musical form is historically contingent in the perfectly straightforward sense that the form of the composition is 'formally' different when listened to historically as opposed to 'ahistorically,' or, to put it more precisely, when listened to in the manner of its contemporaries, as opposed to the way our listening habits of the past 300 years would dictate. Here is one such example.

The British musicologist Margaret Bent, among others, has pointed out that it is very easy to 'mishear' certain tonal events in Medieval music as instances of the most common and basic musical event in our modern harmonic system. This is the progression, in the key of C major, for example, from the active chord, G–B–D, to the chord of rest, C–E–G. The chord, G–B–D is called the 'dominant' chord of C major, the chord C–E–G the 'tonic' chord. And the progression from dominant to tonic is the very foundation of all our listening habits in the modern tonal system. In particular, the progression from dominant to tonic is the closure event in the major–minor harmonic system. It is always the progression from tension to resolution, from active to restful. It is the most common musical 'ending.' To remind yourself how it sounds, play the following two chords at the piano.

Now in music of the Middle Ages and Early Renaissance, there are musical events that sound *to us*, because we live in the historical period of the major–minor tonal system, exactly like the dominant tonic cadential figure: the moving from tension to rest. But in the syntax of that historical period, they perform an entirely different function: in particular, they perform a *continuing* function rather than a cadential one from tension to rest. So, if a musical composition is continuing rather than coming to rest at a certain point, then it possesses, quite literally, a different form, a different formal structure from a piece, *making exactly the same sounds*, that is coming to rest there.

Consider, now, a piece of Medieval music, call it *C*, that we hear performed. At a particular place we hear a dominant–tonic cadence, but a Medieval audience would have heard a continuing passage. They were hearing a piece with a different formal structure from the piece we are hearing. Furthermore, it is arguable that *they* were hearing correctly, we not. However that may be, it is clear that the formal structure of *C* is different in the two cases. Musical form, it would seem, is as much a hostage to history as any other artistic feature the historicist might pick. There is nothing about enhanced formalism implying that musical form is a timeless or ahistorical thing. The historicist's argument against formalism, enhanced or otherwise, comes to nothing.

The two remaining objections to enhanced formalism stem from what I called functionalist considerations and considerations of social setting. And, since these two objections are closely related, and sometimes even mixed up with one another, I think it best to treat them together.

To begin the discussion, it would be useful to make a few brief historical remarks. These concern a radical change that seems to have taken place towards the end of the eighteenth century, in how we listen to music; and I will confine my remarks to pure instrumental music, which is the crucial case. Before the change of which I am speaking, instrumental music was listened to in a variety of social and institutional settings: in the home, in the manor house or the palace, in the church, in ceremonies of state, in social functions, and so on. In these various settings, the music had various distinct functions in addition to the common one of providing objects for aesthetic contemplation (which it certainly must have had as well). It provided background for social events, it was danced to, it formed part of religious or ceremonial rituals, it was a teaching method for students, and many other things.

But in the last half of the eighteenth century these various settings and functions of instrumental music were more or less put into the shade, though not, of course, completely replaced by one single venue: the public performance space, which is to say, the concert hall. The eighteenth century invented the public concert.

The concert hall, the aural version of the art museum (also an eighteenth-century invention), is a place for doing one thing: listening with rapt, aesthetic attention to (for the most part) absolute music. Music in *this* social setting is meant to perform but one function: to be the most interesting possible object *for* that rapt attention. In *this* setting, all its other past social settings and functions have been obliterated.

With this historical fact in hand, one can understand why some might claim that at least a great deal of so-called pure instrumental music is not pure at all: is not absolute music properly so-called. It was never meant to be solely an 'aesthetic' object of pure contemplation. It had various social settings and various functions within those various settings. These settings and functions, so the argument might continue, are a part of its artistic, musical fabric. And, if they are, then even enhanced formalism can't be a true account, at least of *these* works, which, after all, represent a substantial segment of the instrumental repertory. Instrumental music has a long history *before* the initiation of the public concert space, after all.

Now there is a good deal of truth in this combined social-functional critique of formalism. For both the social settings of music before what might be called the 'great divide' between it and them, as well as music's diverse functions in these pre-concert hall settings, might be thought to impart to music before the great divide artistic properties that cannot be reasonably thought of as formalist ones.

The social setting itself might be thought of as, in many cases, part of the musical work of art: for example, the spectacle of a state ceremony in which the music is embedded, or the church service of which it is a part.

Furthermore, functions themselves provide aesthetic satisfaction in functional works of art. So dance music, for instance, might be enjoyed and appreciated not merely in terms of its formal properties but for how well adapted it is for the dances it is meant to accompany. Thus in both of these respects—social setting and social function—music before the great divide has aesthetic, artistic properties imparted to it that are not part of its formal structure as normally construed.

These points are well taken, but should not be taken to prove too much. First of all, if musical formalism is understood in its negative sense, as denying that pure instrumental music possesses semantic or representational content, then it is perfectly consistent with what we have been saying about instrumental music before the great divide. For neither its diverse social settings nor its diverse social functions impart to it *either*. Instrumental music before the great divide neither *means* nor *represents* its social settings or its functions. Indeed, it sounds like utter nonsense to assert that it does.

But what of the features that its settings and functions *do* impart to instrumental music before the great divide? If they are not formalist features, even for enhanced formalism, and they do not seem to be, what does that say about formalism and about this music? Well there is no need for the formalist to start wringing his hands over the question. Nor, however, should it be brushed aside. The formalist must take it seriously.

Music after the great divide was designed with the concert hall in mind. It was meant for a setting where its sole purpose is to be an object of rapt aesthetic attention. Music before the great divide was, of course, also meant to be contemplated aesthetically for the purpose of musical appreciation and enjoyment, but, one presumes, in varying degrees, depending upon its particular social setting and function. However composers may have felt about this, it was a fact of their creative lives.

When, however, we take music composed before the great divide out of its original settings and put it into the concert hall, we are, essentially, setting it up to be heard just as the music written especially for this venue: that is to say, with rapt aesthetic concentration to the exclusion of all else. When it is thus attended to, some works will have a higher aesthetic payoff than others. But, regardless of its original place and purpose, that payoff, in the modern setting, will, the formalist will claim, correctly, I think, have to be measured in purely formalist terms: enhanced formalist terms, that is. That is precisely the point of the transfer from the original place to the other.

The question may well be raised with regard to the music composed before the great divide as to whether it might have a higher overall aesthetic payoff if restored to its original settings. It is an altogether fair and sensible question, and has been raised with increasing frequency by proponents of 'historically authentic' performance (of which I will have something to say in a later chapter). But there is no universal, theoretically mandated answer to this question. Music that has much in its structure to be taken in and appreciated may prosper more in the concert hall than it ever did in its original setting, where its function and setting would have interfered with the attitude of rapt aesthetic attention necessary for appreciating its complexities. On the other hand, a composition that does not possess the wherewithal to sustain extended or deep aesthetic scrutiny might well take on, in its original setting, serving its originally intended function, an aesthetic interest far exceeding what it would excite in the concert hall. Such a composition would, clearly, be a prime candidate for restoration to its native, pre-concert hall habitat. (Although if it were true that Handel's coronation anthems come off better at a coronation than in a concert performance, it would still hardly make sense to wait for a coronation to perform them, since kings and queens frequently live a long time nowadays, and, anyway, invitations to coronations are not easy for the average guy to come by.)

Thus, the upshot of these considerations is that instrumental music composed before the great divide may well have aesthetic, or, if you will, musically significant properties that go beyond even what enhanced formalism allows. But there is, on the other hand, no reason to think that recognizing formalism's limits deals it a mortal blow. It is a doctrine that came into being after the great divide, to provide an account of just that kind of music that began to flourish in the new musical environment of the public concert and concert space. That it can deal only partially with music composed before the great divide is to be expected. But, we should remember, it *can* deal with pre-concert hall music to just the extent that that music is well suited to being resituated in the public concert space. The partial failure of formalism, even enhanced formalism, in accounting for *everything* of aesthetic interest in 'early' instrumental music, should not be allowed to obscure the fact of its great success in accounting for much of what continues to make that music interesting and valuable *to us*. And, if the core of formalist doctrine is that 'pure' instrumental music is music without semantic or representational content, that core is left completely intact. Neither its diverse social settings before the great divide, nor its diverse functions, gives any aid and comfort to the idea that this music either 'means' or 'depicts': it has its functions, and it has its settings. It neither 'means' nor 'depicts' either.

I have tried, in this chapter, to present an enlarged version of formalism, enhanced formalism, that countenances emotive properties as a part of its structure and syntax. And I have tried to defend it against some frequently stated objections. But one very serious objections remains. It is as follows.

It will be recalled that one of the chief motivations of the arousal theory of musical expressiveness was that it made of the musical experience a deeply moving one. And that seems right. That is to say, it seems to be true that we are, at least at some of the supreme musical moments, deeply moved, emotionally aroused, to a significant degree by the music we hear. Furthermore, the arousal theory had a ready explanation for this. Music moves us by arousing in us the emotions it is expressive of: anger, fear, melancholy, joy, and so on—the garden-variety emotions. Thus, the arousal theory has the same explanation for what makes music expressive of the garden-variety emotions and deeply moving. It is a neat package.

Enhanced formalism has, however, moved the garden-variety emotions *from* the listener *into the music*. The emotions are not, on this view, felt, but 'cognized.' For this reason the view is sometimes called 'emotive cognitivism.' Further, it is sometimes argued that this view cannot be right. The argument simply is this. If emotive cognitivism is true, we are not emotionally moved by music. But we are emotionally moved by music. So cognitivism cannot be true; and, since emotive cognitivism is a necessary part of enhanced formalism, enhanced formalism can't be true either.

This is indeed a serious objection and it will require a separate chapter to reply to it. In particular, it needs to be shown that the truth of emotive cognitivism is consistent with the palpable fact that listening to music frequently turns out to be deeply moving, and rightly so. I undertake this task in the next chapter.

CHAPTER 7

The Emotions in you

Recall that from the onset of the modern discussion of music and the emotions there were two issues at stake: the expressiveness of music, and its power to move us emotionally. The issue of expressiveness is the issue of what it is in virtue of which we describe music in terms of the garden-variety emotions: happy, melancholy, angry, and the like. The issue of music's emotive power over us, its power to move us emotionally, is the issue, of course, of how, why, we are so moved.

The simple arousal theory of musical expressiveness had, as we have seen, the same answer to both questions. Music, according to that theory, is described as 'melancholy,' 'cheerful,' and so forth, because it makes normal listeners, under normal conditions, melancholy and cheerful: it is melancholy and cheerful in the dispositional sense: it has the disposition to make listeners melancholy or cheerful or whatever. But it is emotionally moving for the very same reason: that it arouses melancholy, and cheerfulness, and so on. It moves us to those emotions. Music that is *not* expressive of the garden-variety emotions, then, music that is *not* describable in emotive terms, cannot, on this theory, be emotionally moving at all. (I shall return to this implication of such theories later on.)

The general consensus nowadays, as I have remarked before, is that we do *not* call music melancholy or cheerful (or whatever) in virtue of its causing us to be melancholy or cheerful. Rather, we hear the melancholy and cheerfulness *in* the music as heard properties of it. But, if we recognize the emotions *in* the *music*, don't feel them in *us*, how can we make out a case for the music's being emotionally moving?

Now, of course, there is one *obvious* way in which music can arouse the garden-variety emotions that no one can deny. Even Hanslick, that arch-enemy of the musical emotions acknowledged it. Hanslick called it music's 'pathological' effect. But he did not mean by 'pathological' anything like 'diseased' or 'abnormal.' Rather, what he meant was that, depending upon the special circumstances of an individual listener's experiences, or, perhaps, that listener's particular emotional state at the time of her hearing a piece of music, the music might, because of those special circumstances, or that particular emotional state, arouse a very real emotion like melancholy or cheerfulness in the listener. I prefer to call this the 'our-song' phenomenon. ('They're playing *our* song, Cynthia, the one that was playing the first time we met, in that little bar on the corner.') Here are two examples, one of music's emotional effect on a person because of his particular emotional state, the other of music's emotional effect on a person because of his special circumstances. (The two kinds of case are not, as a matter of fact, all that different.)

In the first case, a homesick soldier returns to the United States, after three years of fierce combat, during the Second World War. You can well imagine the tumultuous emotional state he is in when he steps off the gangplank of the troopship that has brought him home. As he places his foot on American soil, after three years of danger, hardship, and loneliness, the Marine Band strikes up

'The Star-Spangled Banner.' He bursts into tears and experiences a tremendous emotional upheaval: a strange mixture of joy of home-coming, grief over lost comrades, and so forth. There is no denying that the music has had a real, palpable, indeed overwhelming emotional effect on him, because of his heightened emotional state at the time of its being played.

The second case I adduce is probably the most famous of all, at least among movie-goers, of the 'our-song' phenomenon. In the movie *Casablanca*, Rick, the American saloon-keeper, has forbidden Sam, his friend, and the joint's piano-player, *ever* to play 'As Time Goes By.' That is because it was the favorite song of Rick, and his lost love, Ilsa, and whenever he hears it, it reminds him of her, and arouses in him a mixture of deep melancholy and passionate anger. (*She* left *him*—but, as it later turns out, for very noble reasons.)

No one should doubt that these are real cases of real music arousing real garden-variety emotions in listeners. (I put aside the added complication that both cases involve songs, with words as well as music.) The problem, as Hanslick long ago correctly concluded, is that they have absolutely no aesthetic or artistic relevance at all. The account we need is one that connects the emotionally moving character of music with its aesthetically or artistically significant features. 'The Star-Spangled Banner' has a kind of strident, heroic quality to it, as befits a national anthem. And 'As Time Goes By' is a sentimental love song. But the emotions they arouse, respectively, in the homecoming soldier, and in the unfortunate Rick, have nothing to do with the aesthetically significant emotive qualities of these two songs. Rather, what arouses the emotions has to do with the particular lives of these two listeners. And for entirely different reasons, 'The Star-Spangled Banner' might arouse anger in someone, an anti-American, for example, whereas 'As Time Goes By' fills *me* with nostalgia for my childhood. The solution to our problem cannot lie with the 'our-song' phenomenon or with listener 'pathology.'

Why, however, can't we say that, although music is expressive of the garden-variety emotions in virtue of our recognizing them in the music, as heard properties of it, there is not a second step to the process, in which recognizing the emotions in the music somehow serves to arouse them in us. In other words, we can have our cake and eat it too. We can avail ourselves of the contemporary insight that we call music melancholy or cheerful because we hear those qualities *in* the music, while still maintaining that music also arouses those emotions in us, and so can be deeply moving emotionally after all. So the proposal is: music makes us melancholy *because* it *is* melancholy, and we recognize it as such; music makes us cheerful *because* it *is* cheerful, and we recognize it as such; and so on. The music is deeply moving because it does this.

This approach has the obvious advantage, as the previous one did not, of connecting the emotions aroused with the right thing: not the individual pathology and circumstances of individual listeners but recognized aesthetic properties of the music, namely, the garden-variety emotions it is expressive of. However, the crucial question is, as the reader may already have surmised, *how* the melancholy music makes us melancholy, *how* the cheerful music makes us cheerful. *Why* should it do that? After all, my dog may have a 'sad' countenance; but looking at her scarcely makes me sad, because I know that she is happy—she is wagging her tail madly and leaping around like a mad thing.

There are two at least seemingly plausible theories abroad (among a host of obviously implausible ones) that purport to explain how it is that melancholy music makes us melancholy, cheerful music cheerful, and so on. The first I will call the 'persona theory,' the second the 'tendency theory.' The rationale for these names will soon be apparent.

The persona theory has it that we hear a piece of music as a human utterance. A symphony, for example, if it has abundant expressive properties, can be imagined as embodying an agent, a musical 'persona' as some people call it, that is making these expressive utterances. The persona successively expresses melancholy, joy, anger, and so on as the symphony progresses.

The music theorist Edward Cone called this persona, at one time, 'the composer's voice.' But, as Jerrold Levinson, the chief proponent of this view, has insisted, there is no need to imagine that the persona, say, of Mozart's great G Minor Symphony, is the musical representation of Mozart; no need, in other words, to think that this persona, when expressing the grief or sorrow of the opening measures of the work, must be expressing Mozart's grief or sorrow. All we need do is imagine the persona as a fictional character expressing these emotions. The persona need no more be thought to be expressing Mozart's grief and sorrow than Hamlet's 'To be, or not to be' is expressing Shakespeare's indecision as to whether he should commit suicide or not (if that, indeed, is what Hamlet is really expressing in the speech).

The persona theory then goes on to suggest that, as we hear the expressive utterances of the musical persona in the symphony, we come, quite naturally, to feel the emotions that we imagine the musical persona to be expressing, just as we 'empathize' with a real person when she expresses her emotions. Thus, just as I 'feel with' Jane, feel her sadness when she cries, her joy when she laughs, so, in the Minuet and Trio of Mozart's G-Minor Symphony, I feel with the persona as that being expresses somber but vigorous emotions in the Minuet, lighter, more cheerful ones in the Trio, and then, again, the vigorous, somber ones when the Minuet returns. I imagine the Minuet and Trio as the expressive utterance of the persona, and feel just those emotions that I hear the imagined persona to be expressing.

It may be objected, at this point in the argument, that we feel with Jane, feel the emotions she is feeling and expressing, because Jane is a real person with real emotions: real pains and real pleasures. Whereas the musical persona is a mere imaginary entity, with no real emotions, pleasures or pains at all. What is the musical persona to us that we should share this imagined being's imaginary emotions, pains, and pleasures?

The defender of the persona theory will reply, quite correctly, I think, that we regularly say that we feel real emotions in response to fictional characters in our encounters with novels, plays, and movies; and since there is nothing surprising in that, there should be nothing surprising or implausible about our emotional reactions to the imaginary emotive expressions of the fictive musical persona. The musical persona is to symphonies what heroes and heroines are to movies, plays, and novels: a fictional character that, in the same way as in the other cases, elicits our emotional reactions.

As I say, at *this* point in the argument, this is a perfectly adequate response (although we shall have occasion to re-evaluate its adequacy later on). *Just* because the musical persona is fictional should not of itself rule out the possibility of empathy or sympathy, and emotive arousal, since most people think that fictional characters in novels, movies, and plays have this power quite as a matter of course. This is not to say that whether and how fictional characters in literary and other narrative works of art raise real emotions in readers and spectators is unproblematic. On the contrary, since the characters *are* fictional and, therefore, we don't really believe there is *anyone* experiencing the emotions we are supposed to be responding to, it becomes difficult to explain how or why we should react to them emotionally at all. Indeed, because of this problem, some people even deny that we *do*. (The full details of this difficulty will become more apparent later on in this chapter.)

But for present purposes I am going to assume that fictional characters in novels, plays, and movies *do* in fact arouse the real, garden-variety emotions. Indeed, I am *not* one of those who denies it. Nevertheless, even giving this to the proponents of the persona theory, it seems to me to have serious problems that make it, I believe, an unsatisfactory account of how music can move us emotionally. I will adduce three.

First of all, I myself was deeply moved by music long before I was ever introduced to the idea that one can imagine musical works as having personae. I am not aware that, in those days, I ever imagined any such character expressing emotions in the musical works I listened to. Nor do I do it now. As far as I can tell, music moves me deeply without my being aware at all of musical personae expressing their emotive states.

Nor will it do for the proponent of the persona theory to reply that I do not need to be consciously aware of the emotion-expressing persona for the persona to have the appropriate emotional effect on me. That would be like claiming I do not need to be consciously aware of Anna Karenina's unhappiness for me to be made unhappy through sympathy with her. It is just that awareness of her misery that causes me to share it, just as, in real life, I cannot 'feel with' Jane her emotional ups and downs, unless I am aware of them.

But I do not wish to rest the argument against the persona theory solely on 'anecdotal' evidence. My claim that I do not perceive emotive-expressing personae in musical works can perfectly well be countered by Jerrold Levinson's claim that he does. And, if we simply leave it at that, it is an intractable stand-off. There is, however, more to be said that does not rely on first-person reports.

The second and, I think, more serious objection to the persona theory is that it relies on an analogy between the musical persona and the characters in narrative fiction; and that analogy simply won't stand up. Upon closer scrutiny, it completely breaks down and, along with it, the arousal machinery of the persona theory.

Maybe the reader noticed that I never used the pronouns 'he' or 'she' in reference to the musical persona. That was on purpose, because the musical persona is such a vague, abstract, shadowy being that even 'its' sex cannot be determined. It is just that complete lack of specific personal qualities that distinguishes the musical persona from the 'real flesh-and-blood' characters of the great movie-makers, novelists, and playwrights. And it is the latter that have the power to arouse real emotions in us, if any fictional characters do. We say of a bad novel, or play, or movie, 'The characters were so shallow, so wooden, so lacking in credible, "real-life" qualities that I simply couldn't identify with them. They left me emotionally cold.' But even the most shallow of fictional works have characters with more flesh and blood on them than the musical persona. If *they* fail to arouse emotions in the sophisticated reader or viewer, how can the musical persona, whose sex, even, cannot be ascertained, be expected to do so. Compared to the musical persona in the greatest of Beethoven's symphonies, the characters in the most tawdry soap opera are living, breathing beings.

There is no real mystery in all of this. Language and pictorial representation have the power to put flesh and bones on characters, to limn in the details of their personalities, that music alone does not possess. Anna Karenina does not express her emotions in grunts and groans. She *speaks*. But the musical persona can say nothing of his, or her, or its emotions. All the persona can do is 'say' 'melancholy,' 'cheerful,' 'fearful.' So, even if you do succeed in imagining the emotion-expressing persona in Beethoven's Fifth Symphony, he, she, or it will be a character without qualities that you might be able to empathize with or, therefore, be aroused by to the garden-variety emotions. There is more 'personality' in Peter Rabbit.

Finally, even if the musical persona *did* have the depth of character of Anna Karenina or Hamlet, the machinery *still* wouldn't work in the way required, because the theory, not infrequently, tracks the wrong emotion. This is, indeed, a defect not merely in the persona theory but in theories of narrative fiction as well that rely on 'identification,' and 'empathy' or 'sympathy' to explain emotive arousal. Here is what I mean.

In 'real life,' my emotional reactions to other people's emotive expressions is not simply: You express grief, I feel grief; you express anger, I feel anger. What emotion I feel depends not only on what emotion you express, but who you are, who I am to you, and under what circumstances the emotion is expressed. If you express anger, I may get angry, to be sure; but I may, rather, become afraid. If you express grief, I may experience grief with you, to be sure; but I may, on the other hand, rejoice in your grief, if you are my enemy.

Sometimes I may 'identify' with you, and feel your emotions. But not always, or even as a rule.

By the same token, I do not always, by any means, 'sympathize' with fictional characters. Anna Karenina's sorrow may make me sorrow with or for her. But Iago's final discomfiture makes me glad, not sorry; and Othello's jealousy hardly makes me jealous; rather, furious at or fearful of his obtuseness.

As bad a theory as the theory of identification with characters, and feeling their emotions, is for narrative fiction, it is worse for absolute music. Suppose we agree with the persona theory that our music listening involves hearing an emotion-expressing persona in music. The defender of the theory then has two options. He can claim that, unlike *both* 'real life' and fictional narrative, we *always* feel the same emotion as that being expressed. That has the happy result of the listener's always feeling the emotion that the music is expressive of, which is exactly what the defender of the persona theory wants. But it has the unwanted consequence of forcing the persona theorist to explain why this should be true *only* of music. Why should I *always* feel the musical persona's emotion, when I don't always feel Iago's emotion, or Desdemona's emotion, or my best friend's emotion?

The defender of the persona theory may answer: perhaps it is because it is always, in the music, the appropriate emotive response to feel the musical persona's emotions, because the circumstances in which the musical persona is are always those where that emotive response is appropriate. But what *are* the circumstances that the musical persona is in? That is just what absolute music does not have the resources to tell us. So we will have to accept it on faith. Why should we?

The second alternative open to the defender of the persona theory is no more inviting than the first. She may say that, just as in real life and in narrative fiction, the listener to the musical persona sometimes feels the persona's emotion in response, and sometimes feels another. But *that* yields the absurd conclusion that sometimes the listener is deeply moved to sadness by happy music, and sometimes deeply moved to happiness by sad music, just as I am deeply moved to sadness by the happiness of the villain, deeply moved to happiness by the sadness of the villain, whereas the whole point of the theory is to get the result that sad music is deeply moving (when it is) by making us sad, and happy music deeply moving (when it is) by making us happy. The persona theory cannot get that result, and should be rejected on those grounds alone by anyone who thinks that music is moving in virtue of the emotions it is expressive of being aroused in the listener.

The second theory of how music moves by arousing the garden-variety emotions it is expressive of, the tendency theory, is leaner, more economical, than the persona theory. It relies solely on the expressiveness of the music to account for the arousal: no musical persona need apply. Here is how it goes.

It is commonly acknowledged that yellow is a cheerful color, black a somber one. We perceive these qualities of cheerfulness and somberness in the colors themselves: they are part of the color's perceived quality. Nonetheless, it surely is 'common sense,' in no need of argument or experiment, so the theory goes, that the cheerfulness of yellow has a *tendency* to make people cheerful, and the somberness of black has a *tendency* to make people somber. That, presumably, is why a hotel would prefer yellow to black for the walls of its breakfast room. (Management wants you to be cheerful before you get the bill.)

But surely the same 'common sense,' the theory continues, would apply to the expressive properties of music as well. At least so argue the philosophers Colin Radford and Stephen Davies. If the cheerfulness of yellow has a tendency to cheer us, so too, it stands to reason, should the cheerfulness of a symphony by Haydn. And if the somberness of black has a tendency to make us somber, so too, it stands to reason, does the somberness of Brahms, when he is in his somber vein. Furthermore, if the expressive properties of music have a *tendency* to arouse those emotions in us, they would, it seems reasonable to assume, sometimes do that. The *tendency* of aspirin to cure headaches may not always be effective: often enough, however, it is.

Davies illustrates his tendency theory with the following telling example. We are all familiar with the classical comic and tragic masks, the one expressive of gaiety, the other of melancholy. Suppose you worked in a factory that manufactured tragic masks: the kind people hang on their walls. Day in and day out, eight hours a day, five days a week, you are surrounded by tragic masks: everywhere you look there is that tragic frown. Surely, Davies argues, that would be pretty depressing. The melancholy of the masks must inevitably affect your mood. The tendency of the mask to produce melancholy would eventually have its way with you. So too, it seems apparent, would melancholy music.

Now I am not, I confess, all that convinced that 'common sense' is right about the expressive qualities we are talking about. 'Common sense' has a distressing propensity for turning out to be common *nonsense*; and I am reluctant to accept, without evidence, that all expressive properties have the tendency to arouse their respective emotions. But never mind. Let's grant the defender of the tendency theory his premise: that all expressive properties, and, in particular, the expressive properties of music, have a *tendency* to produce in the perceiver the emotions they are expressive of. On closer examination, I think the reader will agree with me that not very much has been granted, not enough, certainly, to establish the tendency theory of how music moves us emotionally.

What should be noted straightaway is that something can truthfully be said to have a tendency, without that tendency ever being effective. An automobile, for example, may have a tendency to swerve to the left when driven over 90 miles per hour. But if, in its whole career, it has never been driven over 90 miles per hour, that tendency will never have an effect: the car with the *tendency* to swerve to the left will, nonetheless, never swerve to the left.

So now let us ask ourselves, given the assumption that melancholy music has a *tendency* to make us melancholy, cheerful music a *tendency* to make us cheerful, what have we really committed ourselves to? Does this tendency ever get cashed out? Or, like the car's tendency to swerve left, does it remain unfulfilled? A brief return to Davies's telling example of the tragic mask factory will, I think, show us that it is telling *against*, rather than for, the theory that the tendency of expressive music to arouse the emotions it is expressive of arouses such emotions in the listener, even if such a tendency does in fact exist, given the circumstances under which normal human beings customarily experience musical works. The tendency, if it is there, is completely ineffectual.

Millions of us have tragic masks hanging on our walls, live with them, and suffer no observable depression at all from their presence, in spite of their purported tendency to that effect. In order for Davies to make out his case, he must adduce a far from normal example: working an eight-hour shift in a tragic mask factory. The analogous musical example would have to be of someone exposed, eight hours a day, five days a week, to music of unremitting melancholy. But who listens to music *that* way? Thus, even if melancholy music *did* have a *tendency* to make us melancholy, even if cheerful music *did* have a *tendency* to make us cheerful, these tendencies seem no more likely to make us melancholy or cheerful than decorating our offices and studies with tragic and comic masks. *Nor is there any evidence that these tendencies, if they exist, have any such effects.* People who go to concerts of melancholy music, at least in my experience, show no signs, either in the concert hall, or outside it, immediately thereafter, of having been depressed by the experience. More often than not, if they are music lovers, and the performance has been good, they are exhilarated.

Thus, it appears to me that the tendency theory is doomed to the fate of winning a trivial battle but losing the war. To win the point that melancholy music has a *tendency* to make us melancholy, cheerful music a *tendency* to make us cheerful, sounds at first like a real triumph for the arousal theory of how music moves us emotionally. Dig a little deeper, however, and you perceive how trivial the point really is. For, unless the circumstances are such as to allow the tendency to have its effect, its presence is irrelevant. The circumstances under which the *tendency* of melancholy music to make us melancholy could really make us melancholy, if they are anything like the circumstances Davies proposes under which a tragic mask might depress us, would simply never occur in the normal listener's experience of music. They would have to be of a kind that would completely saturate the listener's environment in a way that just never happens in our musical world. For this reason, I think the tendency theory, like the persona theory, fails of its purpose.

The theory that music moves us emotionally by arousing in us the emotions it is expressive of has, doubtless, more versions than the two I have canvassed. But these two, the persona theory and the tendency theory, seem to be good exemplars of the genre. Neither of them works, for reasons specific to each. It would, I think, be tiresome, both for the reader and for me, to examine any further examples. In lieu of that, though, let me make one further criticism, which applies, I think, to *any* theory holding that music moves by arousing the emotions it is expressive of, if they are construed as being the garden-variety emotions. Not everyone finds this criticism altogether convincing; and there have been many attempts to answer it. However, I find it a telling point, and making it will serve as a good transition to my own account of how music moves us, which has, in my view, among its other virtues, that it is immune to this oft-stated criticism.

The point is simply this. If music were moving in virtue of arousing the garden-variety emotions, then a good deal of music would result in very unpleasant experiences. Cheerful music would make us cheerful, to be sure. And who would shun that? But melancholy music would make us melancholy, angry music angry, fearful music fearful. And who would *seek* that? Who would gratuitously, as a matter of choice, undergo the experience of melancholy, anger, fear? Yet there is no evidence that people shun music expressive of the inherently unpleasant emotions. So it seems implausible to think that it is moving in virtue of arousing them. Indeed, when, because of personal experiences, a piece of music acquires the power to arouse unpleasant emotions, as in the case of the unfortunate Rick and 'As Time Goes By,' the listener *does* shun the music. 'Sam! *Didn't I tell you never to play that song!*'

Various answers have been proffered to this objection. It has been pointed out, quite rightly, that works of narrative fiction are agreed, by most, to arouse unpleasant emotions; and we don't shun them for it. (*King Lear* scarcely leaves us untouched by emotions of the most deeply unpleasant sort.)

But the problem with this response, the analogy to works that employ the resources of language and pictorial representation, is, as previously, how *different* absolute music is from these kinds of works of art: novels, movies, plays. It is, indeed, a philosophical problem of long standing why people should seek out such works as *King Lear* and *Oedipus*, whose emotional effects on audiences seem to be so palpably unpleasant at the well-known tragic moments. Do the works somehow make the inherently unpleasant emotions pleasurable through some kind of artistic 'transfiguration'? Or is there a beneficial effect, as Aristotle thought, of experiencing these emotions, making the experience of them worthwhile, painful though the experience may be?

Most people find the notion that an emotion inherently unpleasant can be 'made' pleasant and still remain the emotion that it was unacceptable, indeed, bordering on the absurd. 'Pleasing melancholy,' although perhaps a nice literary conceit, is, when taken literally, pretty hard to credit. This being the case, most philosophers of literature try to show how the unpleasant emotions, particularly the tragic ones, that have been an object of study and dispute since Aristotle, when aroused by narrative fiction, serve some deep purpose of moral or psychological education.

Such appeals to the psychological or moral benefits or 'pleasures' of experiencing the tragic emotions have abundant conceptual materials to work with in novels, plays, and moving pictures, provided by the linguistic and representational elements of such works. But when philosophers try out such strategies on absolute music, the pickings are pretty slim and the results predictably unpromising. What claims for the imparting of moral or psychological education can be made that do not sound trivial, or silly? If one 'over-interprets' a musical work, making it 'say' things we know musical works cannot 'say,' it sounds silly. (More of that in a later chapter.) And if we try to stay within the bounds of what it might sound reasonable to claim music 'says,' it sounds trivial. One person claims that the transition from being expressive of joy to being expressive of gloom, in a passage of music, 'says,' can 'teach' us that joy can follow sorrow in a human life. Another tells us that Beethoven's Fifth Symphony's message to the world is that we should defy obstacles and adversities. Do we need great symphonies to tell us that? If they did, would *that* make experiencing the sorrow worth the pain and trouble? If someone were to come to a teacher or guru he respected, and ask to be directed to those works of art that could educate his moral sensibilities, would she really, if she were worthy of his confidence, direct him to the symphonies of Beethoven instead of the plays of Shakespeare or the novels of Jane Austen? This is not to say something *bad* about Beethoven's symphonies. It is to say that they are with us for other purposes than those of moral and psychological education. They do not have the resources for that job, and were not put on earth to do it. (What they *were* put on earth to do I will say something about in the last chapter of this book.)

There is raging dispute among philosophers about why we enjoy, if indeed we do, the tragic and other dark emotions in our encounters with narrative fiction, and those who deny outright that such works are a source of moral, psychological, or any other kind of knowledge. And if these claims are so contentious in the literary arts, and the cinema, where the prospects seem so much more favorable to them than in absolute music, would there not be a distinct advantage, on these grounds alone, for having a theory of how music moves us emotionally that does not have to explain why we enjoy having unpleasant emotions like melancholy and fear aroused in us? In the remainder of this chapter I shall develop such a theory. Its basic, underlying premise is simple. We do not have to explain why we enjoy those of the garden-variety emotions that music moves us to, that are unpleasant, because it does not move us to the garden-variety emotions at all, either the pleasant or the unpleasant ones. Or, perhaps, more accurately, it moves us to another familiar emotion, call it 'garden variety' if you like, that raises no such problems, as we shall see in a moment.

In order to develop the theory I have in mind, of how music moves us emotionally, we must return to basics. The basics we have to return to are the basic ways in which ordinary emotions are ordinarily aroused in our ordinary lives.

Recall that Hanslick had already at least vaguely sketched out what has come to be accepted by many contemporary philosophers as a reasonable analysis of what is happening, in many of the normal, ordinary cases in which a human being experiences an emotion. According to this analysis, when I am angry, for example, there is, in the ordinary, normal cases, an *object* of my emotion. I am angry *at* someone. Let's say I am angry at my friend. *He* is the object of my emotion.

Furthermore, *ordinarily*, I am in an emotional state I am experiencing for a reason, which can be cashed out in terms of a *belief* or set of *beliefs*. I am, normally, not angry for no reason at all. So let's say that I am angry at my friend because I believe he cheated me in a poker game. So my emotion has an *object*, my friend; and a reason (or cause), my *belief* that my friend has cheated me. And, if my belief should change, if I should cease to believe that my friend has done this bad thing to me, then it is logical to suppose that my anger will dissipate, since the reason for my anger, its cause, will have ceased to be operative. Emotion, in this regard, is not detached from reason, as has been frequently claimed, from Plato onwards.

It is, by the way, because of the *belief* condition that there is paradox and dispute connected with the arousal of emotion by fictional narrative. Because fictional characters *are* fictional, we do not believe such characters exist, do not believe *anyone* has done and undergone whatever it is they, fictionally, have done and undergone. Therefore, there is no reason for us to have our emotions aroused by them and their doings. The *belief* condition is absent. If you don't believe anyone has done anything to justify an emotion, you don't, ordinarily, have the emotion. And in fiction, one doesn't believe *anything*.

Finally, in ordinary cases of emotive arousal, an emotion frequently has a *feeling* component. Emotions are usually said to be *felt*. This is not to say that every time I feel angry, for example, I feel the same way. There is explosive anger, the so-called slow burn, as well as anger of great duration that may, in the long term, not be associated with any particular feeling at all, but, rather, expressed in beliefs and dispositions to behave in certain ways, in various circumstances. But, in any case, there is, ordinarily, a feeling component to the garden-variety emotions.

So, to sum up, in many of the ordinary cases of having an emotion, there is an *object* of the emotion, a *belief* or set of *beliefs* that causes the emotion, and causes it to have the object it does, and a certain *feeling* aroused in the one experiencing the emotion. This is not to say that there cannot be cases where an emotion has no apparent object, or no apparent belief associated causally with it. The word 'emotion' covers a lot of ground. And human beings experience emotions in all sorts of ways, some of them odd, some of them inexplicable, some of them downright abnormal. None of this is being denied. There may well be emotions that fall outside the net of the *object–belief–feeling* analysis. All that is being maintained is that this analysis of emotions does seem to fit a lot of the central cases. So what I want to try to show now is that it fits the case of music. Applied to music, it can show us how music moves us emotionally.

I begin with an observation about the persona theory and the tendency theory. Both of them have what seems to me to be the highly objectionable result that the perceived beauty or general excellence of the music has nothing to do with whether or not it moves us. If a piece of music is expressive, say, of melancholy, it must move me to melancholy, if, that is, I recognize the melancholy in it, whether or not I am dazzled by its beauty, and think it is a masterpiece, or am utterly bored by it and think it is schlock. But being aroused to melancholy by the music is synonymous, on both of these accounts, with being moved by it. And it seems absurd to me to be told that I am customarily moved emotionally be music that I take to be bad music. In my experience, I am moved only by music that overwhelms me with its beauty, magnificence, or other of its positive aesthetic qualities possessed to a high degree.

Closely related to this point is one, mentioned early on. It is a consequence of arousal theories of how music moves us emotionally —the persona theory and the tendency theory being paradigm instances—that music not expressive of the garden-variety emotions cannot be deeply moving: cannot move us emotionally. For the expressive properties are an essential part of the musical machinery that moves us.

Some people may not be uncomfortable with this conclusion, since so much of the music talked about in the philosophical literature is rife with expressive qualities, and the musical works probably most listened to by the average classical music lover are from the Romantic era, where 'expression' is, of course, the central concern. But there *is* music that is not expressive, and *not* being expressive is *not* a condemnation. There is wonderful, beautiful, magnificent music that either is not expressive of the garden-variety emotions by design, or not expressive of them by accident. And such music *can* be deeply moving, at least in my experience.

Perhaps an example here might be helpful. If you listen to some of the works of the Renaissance composers writing in the late fourteenth, fifteenth, and early sixteenth centuries—and such music is easily accessible on recordings, these days—you will frequently hear works that have a kind of serene, untroubled quality about them. They flow in an effortless way, with the strands of melody of the various voices interweaving in the most intricate patterns imaginable, but giving no impression of rising to big, attention-getting climaxes, as in so much music we are used to listening to, from later historical periods. I am not, by the way, saying that *all* of the music of this period is as I have been describing it so far. I am only saying that *some* of it is, and that that is a kind of music frequently encountered in the composers of these times.

This serene quality of the music which I am speaking about is further facilitated by the way the music is usually performed, which is to say, by voices alone, without accompanying instruments: *a capella*, as it is called; literally, 'by the choir.' There are no independent instrumental parts composed for this music, although some scholars think that instruments may have sometimes accompanied the singers, playing the same notes that the singers sang: 'doubling' them, as musicians call the procedure. But whether or not this is true, many of the recordings you are likely to hear will be *a capella*. And because there are no instruments playing along, there is a more subdued sound produced.

Furthermore, women were not permitted to sing in churches in these times (and it is liturgical music that I am discussing here). The high parts were sung not by female singers but by choir boys. And some conductors these days prefer to perform this music as it was performed in its own time: with all male choruses. Now boys have crystal-clear, almost passionless, ethereal voices. And if you get a recording of the music about which I am speaking, sung *a capella* by a choir of men and boys, you will get the most vivid example of that serene, almost passionless quality one can frequently hear in such music: some of the music, for example, of Josquin des Prez (*c*.1440–1521) or Orlandus Lassus (1532–94), arguably the greatest composers of the high Renaissance, and two of the most frequently performed today of that period.

The point I want to make about this music is that it is wonderful, beautiful, magnificent music. But a lot of it is not *expressive* music in the sense we have been talking about. It is not, by turns, expressive of sadness, happiness, anguish, and fear, and the limited other garden-variety emotions music may be expressive of: it is not that kind of music at all. It is, overall, serene, tranquil music. But it is, nonetheless, deeply moving music: music that deeply moves and excites us by its serene, tranquil beauty, not by its being expressive of the garden-variety emotions, which it is *not*.

What, then, can we make of all this? Well, it seems to me that the most obvious thing to make of it is that what deeply moves me emotionally by music is just that very beauty, or magnificence, or other positive aesthetic properties it may possess to a very high degree. The *object* of the 'musical emotion,' if I may so call it, for want of a better term, is *music*. (What else?) Or, more exactly, the object of the musical emotion is the set of features in the music that the listener believes are beautiful, magnificent, or in some other ways aesthetically admirable to a high degree. Thus the first requirement of the *object–belief–feeling* analysis of how music moves us emotionally, an *object* for the emotion, is now in hand.

What of the *belief* requirement? That, clearly, is fulfilled by the listener's belief that the music she is listening to, or an aspect of it, is beautiful, magnificent, or in some other ways possessing positive aesthetic properties to a very high degree. This means that, if she ceases to have this belief or set of beliefs, the music will cease to have any (or much) emotional effect on her, just as when I cease to believe that my friend has cheated me at cards I cease to be angry with him. And this sounds right, doesn't it? For music that once deeply moved me has now ceased to have an emotional effect. Why? Because, so to speak, I have 'seen through it.' What I once thought was a stirring example of musical magnificence I now see as a cheap trick: shallow and showy. Whereas music that once seemed turgid and dense, lacking in melodic spontaneity, now 'knocks my socks off.' In short, my musical allegiances have switched from Liszt to Bach.

Fortunately, there is no need to raise and answer the question of whether, in some 'objective' sense, Bach's music is better than Liszt's, although, as a matter of fact, I think it is. All that is necessary for the *object–belief–feeling* analysis to go through is that there is *belief*. If you *believe* that what you are hearing is musically magnificent or beautiful, or splendid, if it 'knocks your socks off,' then it will move you emotionally, even if it is *my* trash and leaves me untouched. (There needn't *be* ghosts for little boys to be afraid of them. 'You gotta *believe*,' that's all.)

So we now have in place the second component of our analysis: the *belief* component; the belief that the music we are listening to is beautiful, wonderful, magnificent music. What of the third component? What of the *feeling* we are moved to by music? What kind of a thing is *that*?

Here there might seem to be some trouble lurking. For I promised an account of how music moves us emotionally that would be quite 'ordinary': that would, in other words, make the phenomenon of being emotionally moved by music explainable in just the ordinary, everyday way we explain how our friend makes us angry, how our lover makes us jealous, or how our foes make us fearful. But that's just it. These ordinary, garden-variety emotions, these feelings of anger, jealousy, and fear, all have specific names by which we know them. What is this 'musical emotion,' though? It sounds like something special and mysterious. To readers of the past philosophical literature on aesthetics, it will recall, unpleasantly, various failed theories of arcane 'aesthetic emotions' that were supposed to be aroused by works of art and other aesthetic objects. That is the last thing in the world I want to suggest.

But not to worry. There really is no mystery here. The emotion that music arouses does have a name. It's just that the name is not specific to music. The name is 'excitement,' or 'exhilaration,' or 'wonder,' or 'awe,' or 'enthusiasm.' It is the name for that emotional 'high' one gets when experiencing things that one thinks are wonderful or beautiful or sublime or . . . . Though if someone asks you what that feeling *feels* like, I think the best, the only, way you can respond is to say: 'Well, it's the feeling of excitement or exhilaration or enthusiasm . . . that one gets when listening to great, to wonderful, to magnificent music.' In part, in other words, it is the object of the emotion that helps define or determine not just what the emotion *is*, but how it *feels*, which, after all, is to say no more for this emotion than for any of the garden-variety ones with names like 'fear' or 'anger' or 'melancholy,' or 'love.' For how fear or love 'feels,' when you really think about it, is best described with reference to *what* it is that is feared or loved. You say: 'Well, it's the feeling you get when you love your son, or your dog, or your violin.' But those feelings 'feel' different, even though they are all 'love'; and how else can you describe the difference of the 'feels' than to say what the particular objects of these 'loves' are?

In summary, then, I have tried to give here an *object–belief–feeling* analysis of how music moves us emotionally. The *object* of the emotion is, in a word, the beauty of the music; the *belief* is that the music is beautiful; the *feeling* is the kind of excitement or exhilaration or awe or wonder . . . that such beauty customarily arouses. But I promised, when I began this analysis, that the result would be free of the problem theories such as the persona theory, or the tendency theory, face, of why one would want to listen to music that aroused the unpleasant emotions—fear, anger, melancholy, and the like. Now we are in a position to see why this indeed is so: why my analysis does not have that problem.

Let's take, for example, the experience of a piece of deeply melancholy music, even funereally melancholy music: say, the slow movement of Beethoven's Seventh Symphony. I find this movement deeply moving, as do all lovers of classical music. But what am I moved by? Well, certainly, the movement contains many musical features to be wondered at and enjoyed: features that are awesomely beautiful, magnificent, and so on. *One* of those musical features is its deep, funereal melancholy. Recall: the expressive properties of music are, I have argued before, *musical* properties. So, among the many musical properties of this movement that deeply move me in this movement is its profound, stately, funereal melancholy.

Now to be moved *to* funereal melancholy is to be moved to a very unpleasant state indeed. But to be moved *by* funereal melancholy to excitement and enthusiasm and joy over its musical beauty is, on the contrary, to be moved to an emotion devoutly to be wished. Thus the presence of the dark, unpleasant emotions in deeply moving music presents no problem for the view being outlined here. For on this view, when we are moved by these emotions in the music, which certainly I do not deny we are, we are not moved *to* them but *by* them. We are moved by their musical beauty. If it is melancholy, we are moved by how beautifully melancholy the music is. If it is fear or anger, we are moved by how magnificently fearful or angry the music is: *musically* magnificent, of course. The emotions in music, when it is beautiful or magnificent music, and when expressively beautiful or magnificent music, are, without a doubt, implicated in the phenomenon of our being emotionally moved. *They* move us; but only in the way that any other musical qualities in the music move us. They move us by their beauty, or other positive aesthetic qualities, to an emotional high over the music. And there is no reason at all to think that, because experiencing them would be unpleasant, the experience of their beauty would be. Why would the experience of artistic beauty be anything but the opposite?

There are two further points I would like to make before I close this discussion. And to do it I must return very briefly, once again, to the persona and tendency theories.

In my previous discussion of these theories I omitted a point that now requires raising. Both Levinson and Davies, in presenting their theories of how the expressive properties of music arouse those respective emotions, make a very important qualification. Both of them deny that the emotions aroused are *literally* those emotions:

they are not quite full-blooded. They are 'quasi-emotions,' or 'emotion-like': quasi-melancholy or melancholy-like.

The reason for this qualification is that both of them, as we all, recognize that real, full-blooded emotions have what might be called a 'motivating component,' whereas their musical counterparts do not seem to. In life, when I am afraid, I am motivated to flight, when I am angry, I am motivated to fight, and so on. But I am motivated neither to flight nor fight when I am in the presence of 'fearful' or 'angry' music. So the 'fear' or 'anger' that music arouses lacks that motivating component and is, in that respect, on the views of Davies, Levinson, and others, therefore, only quasi-fear and anger, or fearlike or anger-like: quasi-emotions or emotion-like. (I should add that Davies thinks music arouses but two emotions: happiness and sadness.)

But, now, *in a certain sense*, the emotion that, on my view, is aroused, say, by the melancholy quality of a musical passage might also be described as quasi-melancholy or melancholy-like. When, on my view, the melancholy quality of a piece of music moves us, it is the melancholy of the music that is the object of the emotion, even though the emotion is not melancholy. Thus, the musical emotion that beautifully melancholy music arouses in me, though not melancholy, has melancholy as its object. And in that respect it is like melancholy in life, or in fiction, when I feel melancholy over someone else's melancholy. In that sense it is melancholy-like or quasi-melancholy. So perhaps the persona theory, the tendency theory, and my own theory are not so far apart as they might seem. At least there might be some room for accommodation.

Furthermore, if my view of how music moves us emotionally is correct, it might offer some explanation of why many people, mistakenly, I think, are convinced that they are made melancholy by melancholy music, fearful by fearful music, cheerful by cheerful music. What is happening to them, I conjecture, is that, if the music is beautifully melancholy, or beautifully fearful, or beautifully cheerful, then this music moves them to a high state of emotional excitement with melancholy or fearfulness or cheerfulness as its object; and when this happens, they mistake this emotive excitement for melancholy in the first instance, fear in the second instance, cheerfulness in the third, since these are its objects. I have no proof or evidence that that is what is happening. But it is not, so far as I can see, an unreasonable suggestion; and I will leave it at that. (Perhaps the psychologists can do something with it.)

What I have been trying to do in this chapter, and the preceding two, is to outline a view of absolute music that I have been calling, for reasons you now know, 'enhanced formalism.' And I have, as well, been trying to defend it against various objections that have or might be raised against it. In the chapter following I must confront not exactly an objection to formalism, although you might see it as that, but, rather, a whole school, or set of schools, of musical interpretation that, apparently, by their very practice, assume, at least implicitly, that formalism is false. I suppose it might be said that the mere existence of such a school, or set of schools, of musical interpretation is an argument against formalism, even in its 'enhanced' version.

However you may want to look at it, these non-formalistic practices of musical interpretation flourish, and are on the increase. It is, therefore, necessary for anyone defending formalism to confront them. I do not think at this stage of the debate that it is really possible to present some sort of philosophical argument to demolish all non-formalist interpretations of the absolute music canon. But certainly it is possible to examine this set of practices critically, and lay bare some of its problems and assumptions. Furthermore, it is incumbent on anyone who writes an introduction of the kind I am presenting at least to acquaint the reader with the opposition. For to leave him or her with the impression that, at this point in time, musical formalism, even enhanced musical formalism, is the dominant force or in the ascendancy would certainly be to create a false impression. So let us now at least reconnoitre the enemy camp, and test its fortifications.

CHAPTER 8

Foes of Formalism

Absolute music presents an apparently stark contrast with the two most powerful and pervasive traditions in Western art: visual representation and narrative fiction.

The distinction between visual representation and narrative fiction is not, I must add by way of clarification, a clear one. Both movies and plays, as opposed to novels, short stories, and narrative poems, employ visual representation as well as language to tell their stories. And the visual arts of painting and sculpture can, in a limited way, be narrative, as well as, of course, represent fictional characters. That being said, I shall, nevertheless, throughout this chapter, treat the arts of visual representation and narrative fiction as separate and distinct. It will be easier, that way, for present purposes.

Throughout its recent history, from the end of the eighteenth century to the present time, the absolute music canon has been subject to interpretations that analogize it both to the visual arts of representation and to the arts of narrative fiction. But by far the most predominant non-formalist interpretational approaches to music alone are of the latter kind. This is not surprising. For both absolute music and narrative fiction are *temporal* arts. Their 'objects' are not present at once but 'unfold' before us. Or, to put it another way, both musical works and works of narrative fiction are processes in progress. You cannot perceive the end until you have perceived the beginning and the middle.

This is not to say that the visual arts of painting and statuary do not take time to perceive. You must 'take in' a statue or a painting, take in its parts and aspects; and that, of course, takes time, just as listening to a symphony or reading a novel. But a painting or statue is there for you all at once. And, although looking at it is a temporal process, it is a temporal process directed by *you*, whereas the sequence of events constituting a novel or movie or symphony is under the direction of the artist: if you are going to experience *that* work of art, you must experience events in *that* order. The experience of paintings and statuary takes time. The experience of novels, plays, movies, and symphonies takes strictly ordered time.

Because musical works are temporal works, in the same way that narrative fictions are, it seems natural that narrative fictions, rather than pictorial or sculptural representations, should provide a nonformalist model for the interpretation of absolute music. And in recent years that has indeed happened more and more. But it is fair to ask, before we begin to examine these narrative interpretations of the absolute-music canon, *why* they have been resorted to in the first place. Or, to put it another way, why do many people find the formalist interpretation of this canon, even in its 'enhanced' version, wanting?

To begin to answer this question, let me allude to an experience that many of us have had, in the profession of philosophy, but that is by no means unique to that academic discipline. (I am sure many of you have it in other contexts.) Philosophy has a reputation for being 'profound,' 'difficult,' and of great 'complexity.' This reputation can be exploited to the advantage of those who really have nothing much to say that is profound, or even interesting, but who have mastered the art, if that is the right word for it, of putting their non-thoughts in the complex and difficult way many people associate with the expression of great ideas. When we read such utterances we are inclined to say that they are 'meaningless marks on the page': 'nonsense on stilts,' as it was once happily put. And when we hear such utterances in lectures and conversation, we will say, analogously: 'meaningless noise.' That is the supreme insult to the speaker of words.

But isn't that just what the formalist is saying absolute music is? Isn't she saying that the symphonies of Beethoven, the string quartets of Haydn, the organ fugues of Bach are 'meaningless noise'? And what greater condemnation could there be of a human enterprise? 'You spent your life making meaningless noises.'

Furthermore, music is not only a human artifact. It is an aural artifact. It is a human construction made up of sounds. These sounds are highly organized, and the whole enterprise is embedded in an elaborate system of rules and practices. In this it most closely resembles spoken language. It is, I suppose, no big deal to declare that a human artifact such as a bicycle, or a hat, is 'meaningless.' Indeed, it sounds a bit silly. 'Meaning' is not something bicycles and hats were brought into being to serve in the first place. But absolute music is humanly constructed sound; and the only other such major sound construction is speech, which exists, obviously, for the sole purpose of conveying the speaker's meaning to others. Music, then, as the formalist sees it, looks to the non-formalist as meaningless babble.

All of this, I think, weighs heavily on people's minds, who find themselves unable to accept the formalist creed that absolute music is 'merely' an appealing structure of sound. It is a human utterance. If it is meaningless, it is worthless, or, at most, 'mere decoration': 'sonic wallpaper.'

As well, the formalist account of absolute music, even where, as in enhanced formalism, human emotions, in some form or other, are allowed in, seems to make such music 'remote,' so to speak, from the world of the 'humanities,' of 'arts and letters', to which, since the end of the eighteenth century, it has been seen to belong. It seems to be made an occult science, practiced by a secret society, with no attachment at all to the needs and concerns of normal human beings. Yet normal human beings *do* love and cultivate absolute music, and at least a small but significant number think that the appreciation of such music is part of a full education and a well-rounded life. The 'remoteness' and 'emptiness' of musical formalism make these attitudes and practices seem incomprehensible. If formalism is true, what is absolute music to *us*?

Such, I believe, are some of the considerations that drive some people away from the formalist understanding of absolute music. But, one may well ask, why are such people driven into the arms of fictional narrative as an alternative? The obvious answer is: Because it is there. In the temporal arts, narrative fiction is its most popular and populous manifestation. It seems natural enough that the 'emptiness' of musical formalism should seek sustenance in the 'content' of the 'storyline.' Absolute music, like the other temporal arts, has form, to be sure. But if, like them, it tells a tale, it has content as well.

There must, however, be more to the matter than this. For the question of why 'telling a story' and listening to one should be important to us is as vexed a question as why purely formal patterns of sound should be.

Narrative fiction, in its 'important' instances, as high art, is frequently said to be 'meaningful' not only in the obvious sense of having stories as its content: being about Odysseus and his adventures, or Don Quixote and his. But it is frequently said to express, through these stories and characters, important philosophical, moral, political, or social truths, hypotheses, ways of life, that make such narrative fiction an important source of knowledge, particularly (but by no means entirely) self-knowledge or knowledge about 'how to live.'

There have been and are, however, those who have vigorously denied that narrative fiction has any such powers to impart knowledge of any importance to us. Some of these, indeed, have been formalists with regard to literary fictions as well as the visual arts and music. And, if formalism were true with regard to narrative fiction, it would hardly be an escape from musical formalism to show that absolute music is a kind of narrative fiction.

Formalism in narrative fiction and the visual arts of representation is not currently a very popular doctrine, however. I certainly do not subscribe to it; and if it were the only threat to the fictional interpretation of absolute music, I would not think that the purveyors of such interpretations need be running scared. But the demise of formalism in the representational and narrative arts does not in itself mean that, if one could reveal absolute music to be one of the narrative art forms, one could, *ipso facto*, have shown that it should be any more 'important' to human beings than the ordinary narrative forms such as novel, play, and movie. Here is why.

There is considerable dispute among philosophers of art, and has been since antiquity, as to why the experiencing of narrative fictions itself, in its familiar forms, should be important to us. Certainly there is no doubt whatever that all human beings, everywhere, enjoy fictional tales, from storytelling around the campfire to the most sophisticated forms of narrative art. But, after all, there is certainly no doubt whatever that all human beings, everywhere, enjoy the beauty of pure formal design, whether it be visual or sonic. If all that can be said for narrative fiction's importance to human beings is that they have an innate propensity for taking pleasure in it (which isn't such a bad defense, when you really think about it), then the foe of formalism has gained no advantage, in explaining the importance of absolute music by showing that it really is a narrative art form. For in that regard—in regard to importance for human beings— narrative art and the arts of pure design may well be on all fours with one another. The 'justification' (if that is the right word) for all of them is the same: we just take pleasure in them, enjoy them; they entertain and divert us; they are recreation. (And whether this is innate or acquired makes no difference in the argument.)

Now it would be disingenuous of me to leave the impression that I agree with the argument I have just outlined above. What I wanted to show was that whether narrative fiction *does* have the knowledge-providing function that some ascribe to it is highly contentious. And if you are a skeptic in this regard, then you will not find the project of interpreting absolute music as narrative fiction promising as an explanation of its importance: *if*, that is, you think that lacking the knowledge-providing factor, the only other importance of narrative fiction is enjoyment, pleasure, or however you want to put it.

As a matter of fact, I hold the view that *one* of the important features of *some* narrative fiction is the expression of important knowledge claims. And I presume, as well, that no one who believes in the knowledge-providing function of narrative fiction believes that *all* such works have that as even part of their function. I imagine we all, no matter what our stripe, believe that *some* narrative fiction exists for the sole purpose of entertainment. (We don't turn to detective novels or soap operas for philosophical or moral illumination.) From this it follows that, even if there is a knowledge-providing aspect to fictional narrative, which accounts, in part, for its importance to us, showing that absolute music can be interpreted as fictional narrative will not, *ipso facto*, make this knowledge-providing factor available to absolute music as an explanation of its importance to human beings. What has to be shown is that absolute music is not only fictional narrative but *the right kind of fictional narrative*—the kind that has the knowledge-providing aspect, not merely the kind that is 'pure entertainment.' And, whatever the prospects are for interpreting absolute music as fictional narrative— and I shall get to these prospects in a moment—the prospects for showing that it is the *kind* of fictional narrative that can impart knowledge or moral illumination are dim indeed, as I have already suggested in a previous chapter.

All this being said, it is, indeed, an important question whether absolute music is subject to narrative interpretations, whether or not it is the kind of interpretation that would yield knowledge or moral insight.

But before I get to the strategies for the narrative interpretation of absolute music, it must be added that narrative interpretation is not the only game in town that the foes of formalism play. There is, as well, in the literature, the strategy of interpreting works of absolute music not as fictional narrative but, rather, as, so to speak, 'philosophical discourse.' Instead of treating symphonies and string quartets as stories, such practitioners treat them as, essentially, direct expressions, by means of music, of philosophical or moral or religious precepts. And, although the problems surrounding the narrative interpretation of the absolute music canon are problems for 'philosophical' interpretations as well, the latter do deserve a separate hearing after the narrative strategies are discussed.

It seems, then, at present, there are the following non-formalist options for the interpretation of the absolute music canon. Works of absolute music can be treated as narrative fictions that, through their narrations, 'express' significant knowledge claims or hypotheses. They can be treated as, so to speak, 'discourses' that express such knowledge claims or hypotheses directly, without the use of fictional narrative. Or they can be treated as fictional narratives that have no further significance beyond their 'entertainment' value as fictional narratives. (Of course, the non-formalist might avail herself of all three strategies, depending upon the particular work she is interpreting.)

There are, these days, as I see it, two basic strategies for the interpretation of absolute music as fictional narrative. I shall call them 'weak' and 'strong' narrative interpretation. And which of these practices one indulges in depends upon how detailed one is willing to get about the stories absolute music is supposed to tell. The basic problem is to steer a course between making the stories so vague or contentless—remember the musical 'persona'!—that they cannot possibly have any aesthetic interest whatever, and making them, instead, so detailed and specific that the interpreter will be charged with reading things into the work that couldn't possibly be there, in other words, using the work simply as a stimulus to her own imagination. Let's look at 'weak' interpretation first.

A very fashionable way, right now, to interpret musical works is to claim that they don't have plots but, rather, that they have what are called 'plot archetypes.' This, I gather, is a strategy that is supposed to avoid the extreme of overly detailed interpretations. To see what the strategy amounts to we must first get a handle on the concept of the plot archetype.

Consider the plots of those two masterpieces of the Western literary canon, *The Odyssey* and *The Wizard of Oz*. (Come on: don't get snooty; *The Wizard of Oz is* a masterpiece—of a kind.) In the *Odyssey*, as we all know, Odysseus leaves his happy home, goes off to war, and then, through many and great trials and tribulations, finally returns home to live (we hope) happily ever after with his faithful wife Penelope. In *The Wizard of Oz*, Dorothy (involuntarily) goes off to Oz (or is it really a dream?) and then, through many and great trials and tribulations, finally returns home to Kansas to live (we hope) happily ever after with her aunt Em and uncle Henry.

In both works, the *Odyssey* and *The Wizard of Oz*, the storyline consists almost entirely of the events involved in the journey home: the story is really the journey. Now, of course, the characters, events, settings, and other details of the plots are vastly different. But the general plot structure is the same. We might call it 'the long voyage home.' That is the plot archetype that the *Odyssey* and *The Wizard of Oz* have in common. Their plots are very different; but when you strip away the differences, there is revealed, in them both, the same plot archetype.

Again, in the Hollywood comedies *Holiday* and *Bringing Up Baby*, the plots are very different. In *Holiday*, Cary Grant meets a beautiful, rich young woman on a skiing vacation, they quickly become engaged, and, when they return to New York, she brings him home to meet her (very rich) family. Among them is her far less glamorous, but far more interesting sister, played by Katherine Hepburn.

Katherine Hepburn falls in love with Cary, and eventually, he with her. He goes from the 'wrong' girl to the 'right' one.

In the far more well-known *Bringing Up Baby*, again the Grant–Hepburn pair play out the same plot archetype. In this one, many of you will remember, Cary plays a paleontologist, engaged to his assistant, another paleontologist, who is 'dry as bones.' He meets, on the golf course, Katherine Hepburn, gay, full of fun, utterly zany, and, of course, quite irresistible. He resists her (or seems to) for the whole movie and, of course, falls in love with her in the end.

So, *Holiday* and *Bringing Up Baby*: two very different plots, but the same plot archetype: call it the wrong-girl–right-girl archetype.

The idea for musical interpretation is that works of absolute music do not have plots, but plot archetypes. For example, many works of literary fiction have the plot archetype: struggle through adversity to ultimate triumph. The *Odyssey* might be said to exhibit that plot archetype in addition to the long voyage home one because Odysseus' 'odyssey' is a struggle through adversity to ultimate triumph (the slaying of his wife Penelope's suitors and the regaining of his family and home). And one of the most oft-repeated claims of the plot-archetype people is that Beethoven's Fifth Symphony is the quintessential exemplar, in music, of that very struggle-through-adversity-to-ultimate-triumph plot archetype of which I have just now been speaking. It begins in the key of C minor and displays throughout a musical fabric that certainly can be characterized with such expressive descriptions as dark, passionate, turbulent, stormy, embattled. Then, in the triumphant coda, it breaks into victorious C major fanfares. It ends in triumphant joy.

So powerful was the effect of the 'Mighty Fifth' on composers following Beethoven that, so the practitioners of plot-archetype interpretation tell us, its plot archetype was used by them over and over again. The prime example, perhaps, is the First Symphony of Johannes Brahms, also in C minor, also ending with a broad, joyful theme (although it is a tranquil and serene joy, rather than a strident joy that that well-known theme seems to express). Another instance is Mendelssohn's Scotch Symphony, in A minor, ending with a triumphal, hymnlike theme in the tonic major key, that is, A major.

Now it is fairly clear what benefits are supposed to be reaped from ascribing a plot archetype rather than a *plot* to Beethoven's Fifth Symphony. If you say that the symphony has a plot that goes from struggle to triumph, you are obliged to tell us what the details of the plot are. Is it Odysseus' struggle to return home to slay the suitors and reclaim his home? Is it Wellington's struggle to rid Europe of the Napoleonic yoke, ending triumphantly at Waterloo? Or . . . ? Who can tell? The symphony does not have the resources to paint such pictures, to tell such stories, the formalist will insist.

Not to worry, the defender of the plot-archetype approach will respond. We do not say that Beethoven's Fifth Symphony has a plot, so we are not obliged to tell you whether it is about Odysseus or the Duke of Wellington or anyone else. What we say is that it has a plot archetype: struggle through to triumph. And any sensible person can hear it. Isn't it obvious that the symphony is expressive first of struggle and adversity, then of triumph?

The problem with the plot-archetype approach, however, is quite simple. It is logically absurd. A symphony can no more have a plot archetype without having a plot than a man who is not married can get a divorce. It is, plainly, a logical or conceptual truth that only married people can get divorces. Likewise, it is plainly a logical or conceptual truth that only works of art with plots can possess or exhibit plot archetypes. The former, in each case, in other words, is a logical condition of the latter.

Think, for a moment, about how you figure out what plot archetype a literary work exhibits. First, you have to know the details of the story. *Then* you figure out from them what the plot archetype is. In other words, you 'abstract' from plot to plot archetype: you, so to speak, strip away the individual details of the plot to 'get to' the plot archetype. It is absurd to be asked to tell someone what the plot archetype of a work is, unless that person *first* tells you what the *plot* is. But that is exactly what the defender of the plot-archetype approach sanctions, and claims to do: to tell you what the plot archetype of a work is *without* having to tell you or even knowing what the plot is. Indeed, he insists, there is no plot to tell.

If you think, as I do, that logic doesn't end where music begins, then you will wish, as I do, that people would stop talking about musical works having plot archetypes without having plots, since that is logic gone on holiday.

Of course, the defender of the plot-archetype approach does have one thing right. Symphonies can be *expressive of* struggle and triumph and other such things, as Beethoven's Fifth is. But that is no more than enhanced formalism allows. And, because music can be expressive of these emotions and actions, and possess other structural and sensual properties, it can be *used* to underlie plots and plot archetypes when it is set to texts or dramatic situations. That, however, is another thing entirely, and will be dealt with in the following chapter.

Where, then, does that leave the foe of formalism? She can't, somehow, do an 'end run' around the details of real literary plots, which many people find it difficult to credit absolute music with having, by resorting to the notion that it has, instead, plot archetypes, which aren't encumbered with those details. That's just a logical absurdity: the smile without the cat. The obvious alternative is just to bite the bullet and claim, outright, that works of absolute music *do* have plots, details and all. That alternative approach we must now consider.

Perhaps the most ardent proponent of 'strong' narrative interpretations is the American musicologist Susan McClary. She has been particularly disturbing to some because her interpretations have frequently involved sexual and 'gender' content. But that particular aspect of her interpretations is not at issue here. What is at issue is whether the kind of narrative interpretation she practices, 'strong' interpretation, regardless of its specific content, is justifiable. Let us approach this issue by first having a specific example before us.

Her target, in the example I wish to discuss, is Tchaikovsky's Fourth Symphony. McClary begins with the claim that, prior to Tchaikovsky's Fourth, symphonic form was dominated by what she calls the paradigm of adventure and conquest. But the Fourth Symphony of Tchaikovsky departs from that paradigm, so she claims. It is, rather, a narrative about a man who is the victim of his father's expectations for him, and his 'entrapment' by a woman. This combination of unfortunate circumstances impedes the development of his true self. The father's expectations involve, as the interpretation makes clear, a heterosexual relationship for the son. The relationship turns out to be an 'entrapment' and keeps the son's true nature, which is homosexual, from reaching fulfillment. (It certainly is a narrative 'for our times.')

A number of difficult questions are raised by McClary's interpretation of Tchaikovsky's Fourth Symphony. Can a work of absolute music really tell such a story? If it can, what criteria are there for determining whether it tells *this* story or some *other* story? Could Tchaikovsky really have intended his symphony to tell this story? If he didn't—couldn't—intend it to tell this story, could it tell this story anyway? And, if the symphony does tell this story, can it really much matter to our appreciation of it?

These questions are difficult because they go to the very heart of the philosophy of criticism and interpretation for all of the arts. They are questions that, in other words, cannot be answered for music without one's taking a stand on basic questions in the philosophy of art that are quite beyond the confines of an introduction to the philosophy of music such as this one.

Nevertheless, we can certainly explore some possibilities here and, I think, reach some tentative conclusions, even though these conclusions will fall short of the kind of closure that a broader study might achieve. But, before I begin to explore these possibilities, and probe the questions just posed, I want to place before us one other interpretation of a work of absolute music, this time of a philosophical kind. For, remember, there are being touted, among the foes of formalism, interpretations of absolute music that treat it not just as narrative fiction, but as philosophical discourse as well. Here is one such example.

Another American musical scholar, David P. Schroeder, hears, in many of the great symphonies of Joseph Haydn, an expression of the eighteenth-century Enlightenment ideal of what he calls 'tolerance' (and what the eighteenth century would call 'toleration'). According to him, the conclusion of the first movement of Haydn's Symphony No. 83, one of the so-called Paris Symphonies, expresses a deep philosophical thesis. The thesis is that in human life there will inevitably be conflict of opinion. Furthermore, the best way to deal with such conflict of opinion is not through suppression, and the establishing of dogmatic systems of belief from which no dissent is permitted, but to 'resolve' it through toleration. That is to say, the way to resolve conflicts is not forcefully to put down dissent; it is to leave the marketplace of ideas open to all offers. Such is the Enligtenment thesis Schroeder hears in the first movement of Haydn's Symphony No. 83.

As in the case of McClary's sexually charged interpretation of Tchaikovsky's Fourth Symphony, difficult questions are raised by Schroeder's 'philosophical' interpretation of Haydn's No. 83. Can a work of absolute music really express such philosophical theses? If it can, what criteria are there for determining whether it expresses *this* thesis or some *other* thesis? Could Haydn really have intended his symphony to express this thesis? If he didn't—couldn't—intend it to express this thesis, could it express this thesis anyway? And if the symphony does express this thesis, can it really much matter to our appreciation of it?

The question of what control the author's intention (or lack thereof) exerts on her works' meaning is perhaps the most argued about question in the philosophy of criticism, and has been for more than half a century. In a nutshell, the anti-intentionalists claim that once, the work of art leaves the workshop, it is a 'public object' of scrutiny that the critic can make of what he will (as can the rest of us), regardless of the intended meaning. The intentionalist, on the other hand, claims that, as the philosopher Noel Carroll puts it, the interaction of the audience with the work of art constitutes a 'conversation' with the artist, and conversation depends upon each of the participants knowing what the other intends to convey by his or her words. If one mistakes the intentions of the other, communication has broken down: and communication is the whole point.

The intentionalists do not maintain, it must be cautioned, that the intention to embody meaning in a work of art will, alone, assure that the meaning is there. One can *fail*, for various reasons, to embody in a work, or in speech, for that matter, the meaning one intends to express (slips of the tongue being an obvious, if trivial, example). And later on I will suggest that that is precisely why, with regard to absolute music, establishing the composer's intention to embody meaning is not much of an argument for its being there.

In any case, this cannot be the place to establish or argue for either the intentionalist or the anti-intentionalist position. All I can do is put my own cards on the table: they are intentionalist cards. I am on the side of the intentionalists and believe, with Noel Carroll and others, that the meaning of works of art is directly attached to the intentions of their makers, certainly in the negative sense that what the maker did not, or could not, intend a work of art to mean, it cannot mean. But, fortunately, whether or not that is so will not be necessary for us to decide in the present context.

For what it is worth, most of the foes of formalism with whom I am acquainted are also, at least judging from their practice, in the intentionalist camp. For, in their narrative and philosophical interpretations of absolute music, they frequently spend a good deal of time trying to convince the reader that the composers in question really could have intended to mean by their works what these interpreters hear in them. McClary and Schroeder are both cases in point.

McClary makes use, in the defense of her narrative interpretation of Tchaikovsky's Fourth Symphony, with its clearly homosexual overtones, of the now generally accepted biographical fact that Tchaikovsky himself was homosexual. Given that, and other known facts of the composer's life, it is supposed to be seen as at least possible that Tchaikovsky could have intended to tell a story of patriarchal expectations and feminine entrapment in his symphony. Far from being something that could not possibly have occurred to him, it might well have been 'the story of my life.'

Similarly, Schroeder tries to defend his philosophical reading of Haydn by, in part, trying to make it plausible to think that Haydn could have intended to express this philosophy by, first, trying to show that Haydn was acquainted with the philosophical literature of his times. For if he were not, then it would seem quite implausible that he could have intended the ideas this literature contains to be in his symphonies, it being quite implausible that he could have thought them up himself, as he was a musical genius, not a philosophical one.

Now I myself find neither McClary's nor Schroeder's attempt to show the possibility of intention at all plausible. I remain unconvinced that Tchaikovsky could really have intended to tell McClary's 'homosexual story' in his Fourth Symphony or Haydn to expound Schroeder's philosophical thesis in Symphony No. 83. But my readers will have to decide that question for themselves by reading for themselves what McClary and Schroeder have written. Whether or not Tchaikovsky or Haydn could have intended their symphonies to 'mean' what McClary and Schroeder think they did will not be an issue in these proceedings. What will be an issue is whether *if* they had these intentions to 'mean,' they could have *succeeded* in making their symphonies mean what they intended them to mean. It does not appear to me that they could have.

McClary's narrative interpretation of Tchaikovsky's Fourth Symphony is, from the literary point of view, remarkably vague: indeed, not much more detail is present than in the plot archetypes just now discussed, and probably with good reason. For to get much beyond even the low level of plot detail that McClary provides would begin to case doubt on the credibility of the interpretation. But, after all, even McClary's plot requires resources of conceptual expression absolute music may not possess.

According to McClary, Tchaikovsky's Fourth Symphony tells a story of patriarchal expectations and feminine entrapment. There is nothing new in the description of musical themes as 'feminine' and 'masculine,' and nothing outrageous in claiming that one theme might be expressive of femininity, another of masculinity. One problem with that, however, is that it is difficult to know whether a given theme is expressive of femininity or, perhaps, gentleness, or lassitude, whether a given theme is expressive of masculinity or strength or aggressiveness. And being 'patriarchal' begins to stretch the potential of textless music. Grandfather's theme in Prokofiev's *Peter and the Wolf* certainly might seem 'patriarchal'—but that is because there is an accompanying text to help. Without it, 'pompous' or 'grumpy' or 'ponderous' might serve equally well. (How text and music combine to be expressive will be a topic of the next chapter.)

Furthermore, when we go from here to the concepts of 'patriarchal expectations' we are beyond what music can be expressive of and into the area of what language alone can express. To tell even the minimal story of a 'hero' without a name, a father who has expectations for him, for a heterosexual relationship, in response to which expectations the hero without a name becomes entrapped by a wife without a name, requires nouns, verbs, adjectives—in other words, the full resources of a language with a syntax and semantics; with, that is to say, grammar and meaning. Absolute music possesses neither.

But is it really true that one could not tell McClary's story without grammar and meaning? Could one, perhaps, tell it in pictures, like a comic book? And might not music, as well as the visual arts, tell a story in pictures? A sound cartoon, if you will?

Well, it is doubtless true that a minimal story can be told in pictures, although one should not forget how much comic books and cartoon stories, and even silent cinema, rely on written text as well. But that aside, it is important to bear in mind that visual representations are universally recognizable. Recognizing them is, indeed, part of our 'built-in' perceptual apparatus, as has been abundantly demonstrated by experiment. (Even animals can recognize representations.) Such is clearly not the case with musical sound, where representation, even within a single culture, is severely limited, and certainly not recognizable cross-culturally. Show a picture of a man, a woman, a dog, a tree, to *anyone*, *anywhere*, and it will be immediately identified for what it is. Play Tchaikovsky's Fourth Symphony and see how many listeners come up with patriarchal expectations and female entrapment.

But surely, the reader must be thinking, a composer *can* make her music say what she wants it to, just as I can make numbers mean words and sentences in order to communicate with my friends without outsiders knowing what we say. This is true. It should not, however, be confused with 'meaning' in the sense of a negotiable, public commodity. Meaning, as philosophers have been arguing for many years now, is a public, not a private, matter. And that, in general, is true of the meaning of art as well as the meaning of conversation or the daily newspaper. The normal speaker and reader of English can read (or be read to) *David Copperfield* and understand the story reasonably well. That is what, I think, we take narrative meaning to be: understandable by a wide audience of ordinary speakers and readers.

To make more plain what I am saying, let us distinguish among three different phenomena that I think the foes of formalism may tend to confuse: meaning plain and simple, private meaning or code, and suppressed meaning or program.

It has become clear, in the light of historical research, that some composers, and their inner circles of friends, have had private meaning or significance attached to certain passages in their instrumental works. But since these associations were not made public, and not made part of the works in question by accompanying titles or written texts, they are best thought of as private meanings or codes, and, consequently, *not part of the work as the composer intended it and as we possess it*. The work, therefore, does not mean, in the ordinary, public sense, these private, personal things.

Closely related to private meaning, or code, is what I have called the 'suppressed' meaning or program. Program music, the nature of which we shall examine in Chapter 10, is music the composer issues to the public with an accompanying text, saying in words the story the music is supposed to represent or tell. Now a composer might intend his symphony to be programmatic, to have a text, but, for a variety of reasons, suppress the program. This may be the best way to understand, for example, some of the symphonies of the great twentieth-century Russian composer, Dmitri Shostakovich (1906–75), whose private papers have revealed that he attached various political meanings to those works, highly critical of the Marxist-Leninist regime under which he lived, and, therefore, highly dangerous to express publicly.

If we treat these political critiques as suppressed programs rather than codes or private meanings, then what we are saying is that they are to be considered legitimate parts of Shostakovich's symphonies, of which we were previously ignorant but which we should now add to them in accordance with the composer's real intentions. It is rather like discovering that a work had an additional movement or movements (say) that accidently became detached through some accident of history: like discovering, for example, the rest of Schubert's 'Unfinished' Symphony.

Perhaps McClary's narrative is Tchaikovsky's private meaning for his Fourth Symphony. Or perhaps it is a suppressed program. What it cannot be, in my view, is the symphony's meaning, in the ordinary public sense in which the well-known story of *David Copperfield* is *its*. Absolute music can't *do* that; only language can.

With these distinctions in hand, we can now, I think, turn to Schroeder's interpretation of Haydn's Symphony No. 83 and make fairly quick work of it. To start with, if I am right that music cannot, but only a language with a syntax and semantics *can*, express the narrative McClary ascribes to Tchaikovsky's Fourth Symphony, then it seems clear that the philosophical thesis Schroeder ascribes to the Haydn symphony cannot, for the same reasons, be expressed by *it*. To expound philosophy, you need the resources of a language.

Perhaps, then, the lesson of tolerance that Schroeder thinks Haydn's symphony is teaching is a private message between Haydn and his cronies, or a suppressed program. That can be determined only by historical research and decisions about how, in the light of that research, one wants to constitute Haydn's work—whether, in other words, one might want to 'restore' the repressed program, and perform it with that written text distributed to the audience. But what the formalist, the enhanced formalist, urges is that we do not confuse a private code, or a suppressed program, with meaning properly so-called: public, negotiable meaning. *That* absolute music cannot possess.

I might, at this point, consider the matter settled, and the proponents of strong interpretation defeated. But there is yet another very persuasive general argument that seems to me to encourage deep suspicion at least of all narrative interpretations of absolute music: it is that absolute music, to put it bluntly, is very repetitious. *Repetition* is an integral part of musical form, both *internally* and *externally*.

By *internal repetition* I mean repetition within any given form. Thus, within the movements of a symphony, passages and melodies occur and reoccur periodically, making patterns in sound. Just as your wallpaper or your rug repeats small designs to make the larger ones, so too, in the movements of a symphony, the internal structure is a structure of repeated musical entities: melodies, melody fragments, or smaller musical 'motives'.

But the movements themselves are also built upon large-scale, literal repetitions, indicated by the musical sign: ⊞ When that sign appears at the end of a large musical section, it indicates that the performer is to go back to the beginning of the section and play it over again. Such repeats are not rare occurrences in classical music but very common. Indeed, they are the essential building blocks of most musical forms, during the past 300 years. Musical form, as we now know it, would be impossible without them.

Consider, now, what a typical narrative form, say the stage play, would be like if *it* were constructed with internal and external repeats of the kind about which I have just been speaking. Suppose *Hamlet* were constructed that way. Then, instead of saying 'To be, or not to be . . .' once, and then getting on with his life, Hamlet would repeat, every few minutes, 'To be, or not to be . . .'. Not only that, but each act of *Hamlet*—it has five!—would be performed twice, the first act being repeated before the second act could be presented, and so on. The absurdity of this procedure hardly needs further comment.

But if a symphony were a fictional narrative, like *Hamlet*, it would be a fictional narrative with just the kinds of internal and external repeats we have seen would be so absurd in Shakespeare's play. It would be a fictional narrative in which the speeches or events— whatever of these the melodies and melodic passages are supposed to represent—would be repeated over and over again. And it would be a fictional narrative in which large segments, comparable to the acts of a play, or chapters of a novel, would be repeated before getting on with the story. This would be as absurd in a musical narrative as in a literary one.

What should we conclude from this? I think the most obvious conclusion to draw is that absolute music is *not* a narrative art form. Narratives just don't *do* that. Absolute music is the fine art of repetition: it thrives on repetition. Were narrative fiction as repetitive as absolute music, it would not be the art of narrative fiction as we now have and understand it. And were absolute music as *un*repetitive as narrative fiction is, *it* would not be the art of absolute music as we now have and understand it. No more, I think, need be said. But there *is*, however, more that I *can* say, in conclusion, by following a well-known philosophical strategy, and granting my opponents, for the sake of the argument, the truth of their thesis. For, if the thesis is granted, enhanced formalism, surprisingly enough, remains pretty much intact. Or, to put it in a slightly different way, even if the thesis is true, it can be seen that absolute music remains, in two very important respects, so different from the linguistic and pictorial arts, that enhanced formalism remains in place as the most cogent account of its 'important' properties.

The first respect in which absolute music stands apart markedly from the pictorial and linguistic arts can best be explained through the following 'thought experiment,' involving three characters whom I shall call Moe, Larry, and Curly.

Moe presents himself as a lover of Renaissance painting above all other kinds. He frequents museums with well-stocked collections of it, and buys countless reproductions. But he suffers from an odd perceptual deficit. *He can't see representations.* The only thing he sees, and enjoys, in Renaissance painting, is the beautiful patterns and colors.

Larry, for his part, professes a love of German poetry. Oddly enough, he has a very large collection of German poetry recitations, on records and discs, but not a single *book* of German poetry. And that is because *he does not understand a word of German!* He just says that he loves the sound of it being spoken, and has no notion of what it means.

Finally there is Curly. He is an avid listener to classical music, and particularly favors instrumental works. He loves the sound structure, the harmonies, and the tone colors of the various instruments. *But he perceives absolutely no narrative, philosophical, or other 'content' in it*, just as Moe perceives no representational content in paintings, Larry no content whatever in German poetry. The odd thing is that, unlike Moe and Larry, Curly isn't 'odd.'

No one would say that Moe appreciates Renaissance painting, or that Larry appreciates German poetry. You can't even *begin* to appreciate the former if you are blind to representation, or *begin* to appreciate the latter if you don't understand any German. Moe and Larry are very odd cases indeed (and, so far as I know, do not occur 'in life'). But Curly is far from odd. Indeed, he represents a very large group of listeners to absolute music, some of whom are among the most sophisticated around: conductors, performers, music theorists. And no one would deny that these sophisticated listeners are appreciating absolute music richly, even fully, in complete ignorance of, or complete scorn for, such narrative and philosophical interpretations as we have just now been considering. Unlike the content of representational painting and the narrative arts, the content of absolute music can be, and apparently is, ignored, if it is there at all, by a significant number of its devotees. This difference between it and the arts of representation and narrative fiction is hardly trivial: it is, indeed, absolutely stupefying, if absolute music were really an art of narration, or of philosophical significance, in any important way. And this brings us to the second aspect in which music is markedly different from at least the linguistic arts and meaningful discourse, either philosophical or what you will.

Recall that we began this chapter by posing a question that the foes of formalism are supposed to be addressing, namely: Why should anyone be interested in it—why should it merit anyone's interest—if absolute music is merely 'meaningless noise'? And isn't that just what the formalist, even the enhanced formalist, says that absolute music is: sound without significance?

The answer to this question, which we can perhaps extract from the writings of Mclary, Schroeder, and others of their stripe, is that absolute music is *not* sound without significance. The Fourth Symphony of Tchaikovsky's means: 'A male person tries to fulfill patriarchal expectations of a heterosexual relationship and ends up being entrapped by a female person, and rendered unable to realize his true (homosexual) identity.' Haydn's Symphony No. 83 means: 'Conflict is inevitable in human life; but the best way to deal with it is not through dogmatism and repression; it is through tolerance.'

Now if that is the best the foes of formalism can do to answer the question of why we listen to or care about senseless noise, sound without significance, I guess my feeling is that they needn't have bothered. Who could possibly be satisfied with McClary's narrative or Schroeder's philosophical content as an 'explanation' for the deep satisfaction absolute music gives, or for the love and devotion it inspires?

Think, for a moment, of the satisfaction you might get from a novel with the same 'story' as the one McClary ascribes to Tchaikovsky's Fourth Symphony. It clearly is not produced merely by *that* narrative content. It is produced by the numerous incidents, happenings, conversations, description, character delineations, reversals of fortune, and the rest, that fill a well-written work of fiction. It is absurd to think that any satisfaction at all could derive merely from the plot line outlined by McClary for Tchaikovsky's Fourth. Say that it is there, if you like; but it cannot much matter for the slight (if any) satisfaction it might impart, over and above a pure formalist reading of the work. It leaves unanswered the question of why we enjoy meaningless noise, because it does not impart enough 'meaning' to make a difference.

Furthermore, if one thinks the value and satisfaction we find in fictional works sometimes accrues, at least in part, in virtue of its expressing, through its narrative, moral or philosophical hypotheses and arguments, then one can hardly hold out very much hope for musical narrative along these lines. For the poverty of narrative that music is capable of, if it is capable of any at all, is such that there seems no possibility at all of its conveying anything of real moral or philosophical import. To do that one requires a complexity and detail of plot structure music cannot be capable of. And that is plainly apparent in the emptiness of content that characterizes the musical narratives most foes of formalism produce. If even the devotees of narrative interpretation, such as McClary, can give us no more than what she gives in the way of a 'storyline,' then the notion that music can, through narrative, present anything of intellectual interest in the way of philosophy or morals is simply a non-starter.

Consider again, now, the 'philosophical' thesis Schroeder ascribes to Haydn's Symphony No. 83: 'Conflict is inevitable in human life; but the best way to deal with it is not through dogmatism and repression; it is through tolerance.' A philosophy book might well begin by stating it. But it would *then* be followed by 300 pages of close analysis, argument, and examples. It is the *rest* of the book, not the mere statement of its thesis, that provides philosophical satisfaction and value. But analysis and argument even the great Haydn's music is unable to provide. So it is folly to think that, even if it could state the thesis, it would matter very much. You cannot add the thesis to 'meaningless noise' and get anything *more* to enjoy than the 'meaningless noise' itself. And the only game in town to offer hope of understanding why we listen to and enjoy meaningless noise, even if it is 'meaningless' noise enhanced with the kind of meaning that Schroeder (and McClary) impart to it, is enhanced formalism.

Thus, to sum up this last part of the argument against the foes of formalism, even *if* the kinds of narrative the foes of formalism ascribe to absolute music were there, it still is the case that, unlike the visual arts of representation, and the narrative fictional arts, the art of music can be, and *is*, appreciated by large numbers of people who place no narrative or representational content at all on it. Furthermore, the stories and philosophical content ascribed to absolute music by the devotees of such musical interpretation, the sane ones, at least, seem to have little if anything of value or enjoyment beyond what is already there in the sensuous qualities and formal structure. In short, absolute music, unlike the representational and narrative arts, can be fully appreciated, and has been since the beginning, by those who hear no content in it. And the content that responsible interpreters ascribe to it, in the form of story or philosophical significance, is of such paucity that it seems to add little or nothing in the way of value or appreciation to what is already there: that is, expressive musical form and structure.

Of course there are, and always have been, the *irresponsible* interpreters. But of these we need say nothing.

Here my defense of formalism must end, and I must move on to other matters. The first is the matter of music with words, and dramatic setting. And it is really most appropriate that a consideration of this topic should follow the examination of the kind of narrative and philosophical interpretation that writers like McClary and Schroeder ascribe to absolute music. For many of the musical characteristics and techniques that they allude to in absolute music, as possible bearers of meaning, although they cannot, on my view, do the job the foes of formalism ask of them, *can*, when combined with words and (in opera) dramatic setting, do the job of enhancing and highlighting what meaning words and dramatic setting *can* impart. These, and other matters relating to them, we must now take up.

CHAPTER 9

First the Words; Then the Music

I have had occasion to remark previously that music without words —music for instruments alone—forms but a very small part of the music people ordinarily listen to now, as well as what they listened to in past times. Yet it has, so far, occupied us exclusively in this book. That is because it raises the most distinctively philosophical problems; and this book, after all, is an introduction to a *philosophy* of music and not anything else.

Nevertheless, the combination of words with music cannot be totally ignored by the philosopher of music attempting to introduce his subject. It does raise philosophical issues, and now, in this chapter and the next, is the time to consider them, as well as some related issues.

But, because words and music have been together for such a long time, and the singing of words has existed, and continues to exist, in every culture and civilization we know, it is necessary to limit the range of our discussion. In effect, though, the *modern* philosophical debates and questions surrounding the combination of words with music are easy to locate and circumscribe historically. They begin with two events of great importance to the history of music in the West: the invention of musical drama, or opera, as we usually call it; and the religious movement that historians call the Counter-Reformation. Both occurred during the last half of the sixteenth century: in other words, during the waning days of the Renaissance and the beginning of what historians think of as the 'modern era'—*our* era. The reader is already familiar with my penchant for introducing philosophical issues regarding music with a little history. So it will not be surprising that I do so again in this place.

The Counter-Reformation, in which the Catholic Church, in the second half of the sixteenth century, tried to 'clean its own house,' in response to the criticisms laid upon it by the Protestant reformers, had, of course, broad historical significance, far beyond the significance it had for the history of music. But it *did* have deep significance for the history of music and its philosophy; and that of course is what concerns us here.

The premier event in the Counter-Reformation was the Council of Trent, a deliberative council of the Roman Church, which met in Trento, Italy, between 1554 and 1563. Many important matters of Catholic liturgy, philosophy, and theology were discussed at this council, among them, the role of music in the Catholic service, and the form this music should take. What was principally at issue, in regard to the music, was the intelligibility of the *words*. The complaint was that the music had become overly complex and 'luxurious,' making the religious text that it was supposed to express impossible for the congregation to hear or (therefore) understand. Music, the churchmen insisted, was supposed to be servant to the text, not its master. In order to understand the nature of the complaint, and what resulted in consequence of it, we must know a little bit about the nature of the music itself.

From the late Middle Ages to the middle of the sixteenth century, which is to say, to the late Renaissance, liturgical music had become more and more *polyphonically* complex. I have already introduced the concepts of *monodic* as opposed to *polyphonic* music in Chapter 3. But I now need to remind the reader of these concepts, and to enlarge upon them briefly.

'Polyphony' has both a broad and a narrow sense. In the broad sense, polyphonic music is any music where there are more tones sounded simultaneously than simply those of the melody. A folk song, accompanied by simple chords on a guitar, say, would be an example of polyphonic music in this broad sense. Whereas the folk song sung by itself, without any accompaniment at all, would be an example of 'monodic' music, and would be even if someone accompanied the song by playing the very *same* melody on a flute or clarinet.

But, in the more narrow sense, 'polyphony' is music consisting of two, three, four, or even more separate melodies, sung or played (or both) *simultaneously*. Of course, the melodies must be so contrived that when they are played or sung together they will combine harmoniously with one another, and sound well. But they must *also* be interesting melodies in themselves. The art of composing music of this kind, constructed of simultaneously sounding melodies, is the art of 'polyphony' in the narrow sense, in contrast to a single melody, accompanied by chords, 'homophonic' music, and to single, unaccompanied melodies, 'monody.'

Now, if you understand that from the late Middle Ages to almost the end of the Renaissance, Catholic church music was polyphonic, in the narrow sense of the word, of ever increasing complexity, and thickening texture, you will understand why the clerics were having doctrinal difficulties with it. If you get five of your friends to recite, all at once, but at different speeds, Lincoln's *Gettysburg Address*, frequently repeating words and phrases before going on, and try to understand the text, you will have some idea of what the Council of Trent was objecting to in the sacred music of its time. Because the intertwining strands of melody, usually five at once, were all singing the text at once, each melody, at any one time, singing a different word of the text, and often prolonging a single syllable over many notes of music, the text being sung could simply not be understood by the listener. The religious message was being obliterated in the interest of musical pleasure. This, the Council of Trent told the composers, must be 'reformed.'

Of course, one way out of the dilemma would have been to abolish polyphony altogether. Before the advent of polyphonic music, the musical part of the Catholic service was monodic. A single melody was 'chanted' by a celebrant or by the choir. Part of the Catholic service has always been sung in this manner. It is known to us as Gregorian Chant, because tradition assigns a major role in its codification to Pope Gregory the First, who reigned at the end of the sixth century.

The abolition of polyphony was indeed seriously contemplated by the Council; but in the end the music-lovers prevailed and a compromise was reached. The composers were directed to simplify their polyphony, and be more faithful to the rhythm and pace of ordinary speech. In that way, the text would be understandable, while there would still remain an interesting enough musical structure to pleasure the musical taste. One way of putting this, I think, is to say that what the composers were essentially being told was to 'represent' human speech in musical tones, since speaking words, obviously, is the most effective way of making them understood.

What makes this way of looking at things even more plausible is that there were others besides the princes of the Church who were, at that time, or shortly afterwards, concerned with the problem of how to set words to music and still make the words understandable. We have met them before in the second chapter: the members of the Florentine *Camerata*, who were in the process of 'inventing' the music drama, or opera, which, you will recall, they thought of, really, as a revival of the way they thought Greek drama was performed in Classical times.

Like the Council of Trent, the *Camerata* was highly critical of complex polyphony, in the narrow sense. The members of the

Camerata were convinced, by the testimony of Plato, Aristotle, and other ancient authors, that Greek music (which, of course, they knew only through this written testimony) had had a profound emotional impact on its listeners. Complex polyphony—the music of their own times—had, they believed, no such emotive effect. The cause of this, they thought, was the combination of the different melodies, with which this music was constructed, and which tended, so to speak, to 'garble' the emotive message. Like the Council, but in far more explicit terms, they urged upon composers the task of representing the human speaking voice. But, where the Council stuck with a 'moderated' polyphony, in the narrow sense, the *Camerata* went for a very different sort of thing entirely: something close to monody; a harmonically accompanied musical 'declamation,' hardly a 'melody' at all, sung by a single performer, following closely the cadence and tone of emotional speech. Thus: a lone singer, a single melody, a completely intelligible emotive 'message' at any given point in the performance.

What the *Camerata* developed, then, was essentially the representation, in music, of human conversation. And this musical conversation was to form the basic structure of the first music dramas, which they sometimes called *dramma per musica*, and which became what we know as 'opera.'

Now opera, the theatrical staging of musical drama, was, from the start, a controversial artistic endeavor, and continues to be to this day. The attempt to fit music to words and stories, or, if you like it the other way round, the attempt to fit words and stories to music, is problematic just because, as I argued in the last chapter, absolute music is crucially different in form from the literary and dramatic arts. Opera is only the extreme case of the problem. Whether we are talking about setting the words of a simple poem or lyric, the setting of the Catholic mass, or the setting of unstaged drama, which is called oratorio, it is the *same* problem: making musical and literary aesthetics compatible when *inherently* they are not. But, because opera presents the problem in its most extreme, most visible, and most written-about form, in discussing *it* we will be discussing *all*, with the problem 'writ large.'

Well then, what *is* the problem? To understand it we must return to a point made *against* the fictional interpretation of absolute music in the preceding chapter.

You will recall the disanalogy I pointed out towards the end of Chapter 8 between the repetitiousness of music as opposed to the ongoing, directional character of fictional narrative. This disanalogy is the crux of the opera problem, and the problem, as well, of almost all music with text.

The repeating of musical material—both internally and externally—is what gives absolute music its shape. It is what gives it closure and inner structure. The so-called closed musical forms are constituted by the occurrence and subsequent reoccurrence of melodies, melody fragments, and whole sections. An example here would help.

The simplest and perhaps the most immediately satisfying closed musical form is the ABA pattern: in other words, a large self-contained section of music, a second contrasting, self-contained section, and the repeat, either literal or modified, of the first section. Many kinds of musical composition exhibit this pattern, from large symphonic movements to popular ballads. Other patterns feature a regular return of the first section: ABACADA . . . etc. And there are many more musical patterns that illustrate the basic fact that musical form is a function of musical repetition.

There's the rub, though. For narrative fiction, as we have seen, does not, for the most part, repeat itself. It is not cyclical, like musical form; rather, it is linear, one directional: it moves towards a goal, without doubling back on itself (although its movement towards the goal may be complicated by 'flashbacks' and by beginning in the middle of the story, *in medias res*, as the ancient writers described the procedure). And that directional flow is what causes the 'problem of opera,' and, to varying degrees, the problem of setting *any* text to music.

The very first operas, at the beginning of the seventeenth century, were constructed of just the kind of monody of which I have now been speaking. These operas were, in effect, 'conversations in tones': not so much music, but *musical*. The cadence and tone of emotional speech were represented with great faithfulness—the most successful project of its kind in the history of music.

Yet a heavy price was paid for making speech the master and music the slave. For just because language does not have musical form, the musical representation of it cannot either. The price the so-called *stile rappresentativo*, the 'representational style' of the early opera, paid for its faithfulness to human speech was its forfeiture of musical form: forfeiture of the 'closed' forms of music, with their necessary repetitions, which give us so much of the pleasure and satisfaction we call 'musical.' Of course, we are not dealing with 'absolutes' here. The operas of which I am speaking did possess some 'closed' musical movements: short songs, choruses, and movements for instruments. But the driving force, the altogether dominant feature, was the 'conversation in tones,' the *stile rappresentativo*. That being the case, whatever pleasures and satisfactions early opera could provide, and indeed still does provide, which are many and deep, true musical pleasures, the pleasures and satisfactions of absolute musical forms, it could not and cannot give, except in its 'peripheral' aspects.

The problem of opera was, and always has been, the problem of making some sort of accommodation between pure musical form, with all of its necessary repetitions in place, and fictional drama, given *its* non-repetitious, one-directional character. It is a problem, really, that *cannot* be solved, but that, at various times, has resulted in deeply satisfying if unstable solutions. And I think the problem itself can better be understood if we take a look at what two of the most satisfactory solutions have been.

It would be a good idea first to understand the time frame. The first operas, the kind in which speech was closely followed by the so-called *stile rappresentativo*, the representational style, were being composed at the beginning of the seventeenth century. The greatest practitioner of this art was the great Italian composer Claudio Monteverdi (1567–1643). He is credited with having composed the first operatic masterpiece, *Orfeo* (1607); and his only other surviving operas (he wrote approximately ten), *The Return of Ulysses to his Homeland* (1641) and *The Coronation of Poppea* (1642), are still, along with *Orfeo*, performed with great success. But, as great as these works for the musical stage are—and they *are* great works—they fail to provide the 'solution' to the 'opera problem' just because they fail to give musical form, with its internal and external repetitions, to the 'musical speech' that they largely consist in.

But, while the great Monteverdi continued reaping the harvest of early, *stile rappresentativo* music drama in the first forty years of the seventeenth century, a very different form of musical drama was developing, which reached its culmination in the first thirty years of the eighteenth century, in the operas of the great German composer Georg Frideric Handel, who occupied the seemingly paradoxical position of a German composer, writing Italian opera for an English audience. (He made his home, from 1710 to the end of his life, in London.) This form of opera, known as *opera seria*, was, unlike the music drama of the *stile rappresentativo*, a highly successful, as well as highly controversial, compromise between the demands of drama, and those of absolute music.

Opera seria, as can easily be inferred from its Italian name, was Italian opera, even though it flourished in many countries besides Italy, composed by non-Italians as well as Italians; and was always on *serious* subjects, usually drawn either from ancient history or from ancient and medieval legend. *Opera seria* is a form of 'number opera': that is to say, opera consisting of separate, self-contained musical movements, 'numbers,' connected by a very rapid musical speech, accompanied by the harpsichord, which pushed the plot forward. The musical movements, or numbers, in *opera seria* were almost exclusively arias, which is to say songs for a single singer, accompanied by an orchestra. The idea was that the opera could serve two masters at once. The rapid speechlike music, called *secco recitative*, literally 'dry' recitative, because of its lack of expressive character, as close to speech as music can get without ceasing to be music, provided a musical conversation that essentially told the audience what was happening, as dialogue and monologue would in spoken drama. The arias, on the other hand, occurred at points where it was logical for one of the characters to step forth and express his or her emotional reaction to what was happening: anger, fear, love, or whatever. But, unlike the *secco recitative*, the arias were perfect, closed musical forms, almost always in the ABA pattern. Thus, the *opera seria* provided a solution to the problems both of how musical drama could conform to the demands of linguistic expression and of how it could conform to the demands of pure musical form. It simply put them into separate compartments, and joined the compartments together in a temporal chain. It obviously must have been a deeply satisfying solution. It lasted more than a century, and operas in this form by Handel and Mozart are still performed today to enthusiastic audiences.

But the *opera seria* solution to the problem of opera was, I suggested earlier, an unstable solution. The instability lay in its most unstable part, the aria, about which I must now speak briefly.

The vast majority of arias in traditional *opera seria* are known as *da capo* arias. This is because their tripartite design, ABA, is achieved by literally repeating the first section of the aria after the second section has ended (although the singer was expected to add embellishments to her part the second time through, for variation). The end of the second section bears the instruction (in Italian) *da capo*, literally, 'from the head,' or, in other words, 'from the beginning.' A typical *da capo* aria, then, consists of a first section, in which a certain emotion, say love, is expressed by a character in the drama, a second section in which a contrasting but related emotion is expressed, say jealousy, and then a literal repeat of the first section, making a perfectly satisfying, unified ABA form. It is also satisfying from a dramatic point of view, from the point of view of verisimilitude, because the music is made to conform to the emotions being expressed by the character, by being expressive of those emotions itself: alternately, love, jealousy, and love again.

But the *da capo* aria, as satisfying as it was (and still is) from the purely musical point of view, eventually came to be seen as problematic from the dramatic side, from the side, that is, of dramatic realism. For, it was argued, people expressing their emotions or thoughts in life do not express them in ABA form. They do not, in other words, repeat themselves in musical form. There is seldom a *da capo* in human discourse. Nor are emotions, in life, experienced in the kind of static way that the *da capo* aria expresses them. The *da capo* aria dwells on emotions; in life emotions rush on unchecked.

In the heyday of *opera seria*, and, particularly, in the operas of Handel and his contemporaries, these criticisms were unfounded. For the *da capo* aria in the operas of Handel, during the first thirty or forty years of the eighteenth century, was, in its way, *both* perfectly suited to how the emotions were understood, philosophically, and, at the same time, perfectly suited to the kinds of characters that populated these operas. The theory of emotions was, at this time, as we have observed in Chapter 2, the Cartesian one: that is to say, the theory that René Descartes had put forward in 1649, in his *Passions of the Soul*. The emotions were seen as somewhat static, limited in number, and, therefore, well suited to expression in the somewhat static musical pace of the *da capo* aria. Furthermore, the characters in the operas, kings, queens, knights, ladies, magicians, temptresses, gods and goddesses, are all, as it were, larger than life and emotionally obsessive as well as 'overwrought.' In other words, they are just the kinds of characters that *would* express their emotions in static, stately form, and in an obsessively repetitive way. Their mode of expression is no more inappropriate to the *da capo* aria than verse is inappropriate to Shakespeare's kings.

But, after all, theories of the emotions change, as does musical taste. The last half of the eighteenth century saw a revolution in emotive theory and a revolution in opera along with it. A new solution to the problem of opera was called for, and forthcoming.

First, the new theory of the emotions. It emerged in Britain, out of a theory of psychology based on the 'association of ideas.' 'Associationism' was an attempt to understand how human consciousness works. The notion was that a person's consciousness is a train of ideas, and that it is possible to know how this train proceeds: that is, to know why one idea and not another has followed an idea currently present to the mind. An example will make plain what the associationist psychology was about.

When I think of Chinese food I frequently think right after that of my best friend in high school. That is because the first time I ever ate Chinese food was with her. Of course I don't *always* think of her. Often, when I think of Chinese food, I think right after that of jury duty. That is because in Manhattan, where I live, the court houses are right next to China Town; and when one has jury duty, one tends to have Chinese food for lunch. Thus, the idea of Chinese food has become 'associated' in my mind with the idea of my best friend in high school, and with jury duty. And these associations explain why just now I thought of my friend or thought of jury duty. It is because just before that I happened to think of Chinese food, and these associations were in place. You, of course, will probably have different associations from mine with the idea of Chinese food, so your train of ideas, in that respect, will be different from mine. Nevertheless, the associationist psychologist will tell us, every idea that you or I get is the result of a previous idea, and an 'association' with it.

Emotions, on the associationist view, are very different from the Cartesian emotions in four important respects that are the result of how the associationist thinks the emotions are acquired. Indeed, *that* the associationist thinks the emotions are acquired, rather than innate, is the first difference. For, on the Cartesian view, we are hard-wired, as we would say, with basic emotions—six, according to Descartes—whereas the associationist thinks we are hard-wired only to feel pleasure and pain, and the emotions are the result of our associating various things with pleasure or pain.

Envy, to take an example, is a feeling of pain at the accomplishments or good fortune of someone else. But I am capable of envy, possess it as part of my emotive 'repertoire,' only if at some time someone's accomplishments or good fortune caused me pain: for example, that person won a tennis tournament I very much wanted to win myself. If that happens, then whenever he, or someone else, accomplishes something that I want to accomplish, that is associated in my mental train with pain, and pain is what I will feel upon viewing the accomplishments of other people, if I am an envious person. On the associationist's view, envy is just, by definition, pain felt at the prospect of other people's accomplishments or good fortune.

The story just told about envy can be told, the associationist insists, for any of the other emotions. Each is a propensity to feel pain, or pleasure, in some determining situation that makes it the emotion it is; and each is acquired by association with the feeling either of pleasure or of pain.

But, just as associations are many, varied, and highly personal— your associations are *yours*, mine are *mine*—the associationist's emotions are not, like the Cartesian's, hard-edged and discrete. Rather, they are vague, blurry around the edges, and fade into one another. Furthermore, they are constantly changing, not static, innate, set pieces, like the Cartesian ones. That is because we never cease to acquire new associations, so our emotions, being built up of associations, are in continual flux. Finally, the whole associationist picture suggests an emotive life of rapid change, of fleeting, evanescent emotional states, as opposed to the Cartesian model of sluggish, stable emotions that must run their course before others can take their place.

One can readily see that the *da capo* aria, with its stately, deliberate ABA pattern, was ideally suited to represent in music the emotive set pieces of the Cartesian psychology. An emotion runs its course in the first section, and comes to a full close. A second, related emotion runs *its* musical course in the second section and comes to a full close. And then the first section, with its emotion, returns to close the circle. A perfect match between emotional reality, as the Cartesian saw it, and musical form has been achieved in the *da capo* aria, and the *opera seria* in which it is the major player. Opera at its best, in its ideal form, is what I like to call 'drama-made-music.' The *opera seria* and the *da capo* aria, in the age of the Cartesian psychology, achieved that ideal state.

But the gradual change in people's ideas about what emotions and the emotive life are like made *opera seria*, and the *da capo* aria, seem very remote from life—a poor musical representation. It is this fact, I think, more than the so-called absurdity of a character repeating what she had already said when the A section of the *da capo* aria returns, that made the *opera seria* obsolete, and urged composers on to other operatic forms. As long as we have *music*, after all, we will have *repetition*. The challenge is to make the repetition congruent with dramatic, which in opera usually means emotive, similitude.

Who knows whether the new direction opera took was an example of art imitating life or life imitating art? In either case, a musical form emerged in the second half of the eighteenth century that matched the new associationist psychology as neatly as the *da capo* aria had matched the Cartesian. It was what is called 'sonata form,' and we have spoken of it a little early on.

Sonata form, which was the form that many if not most movements took in the major instrumental works of the late eighteenth century, and the nineteenth century as well, was very different from *da capo* aria form in many respects: but in one in particular that is most relevant here. The sections of a *da capo* aria are almost always monothematic and, to coin a phrase, mono-emotive: the first section is based on one theme, expressive of one emotion, the second section again based on one theme, again, expressive of one emotion. But sonata form presents a broader canvas of themes and (therefore) emotions. To understand this let us first remind ourselves what the general outlines of sonata form are.

You will recall that a sonata-form movement consists of three sections: an *exposition*, in which the themes of the movement are presented; a *development*, in which these themes are varied, 'worked out,' in effect 'played with' by the composer, in whatever ways style dictates and his creative imagination suggests; and a *recapitulation*, in which the original themes are presented, usually (but not always) in the same order as in the exposition, but varied as to key, to make a proper close. For, whereas the exposition (usually) moves the music to the dominant key, the recapitulation must return to the tonic, the original key, to achieve a satisfying and *conclusive* musical resolution.

I hope the reader has not failed to notice that in one very obvious and important respect sonata form and *da capo* aria form are the same. They both exhibit a tripartite, ABA pattern, although in the *da capo* aria the return of A is literal, whereas in sonata form it is altered, in the way just now described. They are both closed forms, with clearly discernible patterns that completely satisfy our pure musical 'sense.'

But sonata form, as I have said, presents a broader and more varied musical canvas than the basically monothematic *da capo* aria. It is, therefore, capable of reflecting, musically, the broader, more varied emotive canvas of the associationist psychology. Sonata form can present, in its exposition, three or more themes, expressive of different emotions. The development can increase the expressive palette even further. The associationist picture of the emotive life is of a quickly changing, moving panorama of emotions. It is just this kind of dynamic emotive experience, not the stately, static Cartesian one that sonata form is ideally suited to represent in music.

The simultaneous presence of sonata form and the associationist psychology, then, pointed opera in a new direction, although with the same old purpose: to achieve staged drama in musical closed form: drama-made-music, as I have been calling it. But another circumstance came into play as well. And I turn to that now.

You will recall that the basic structure of the *opera seria* is a string of arias joined by the 'song-speech' called *secco recitative*, that is, 'dry' recitative. The arias are static points where the action stops and a character expresses his or her emotion in musical, ABA form. The arias are the real music of *opera seria*. The *secco recitative* is borderline music—'music' of little if any *musical* interest. The paradox is that where there is action there is no music, and where there is music there is no action. That, in essence, is *opera seria*'s solution to the 'problem of opera.'

But, the theoreticians and lovers of drama-made-music will ask (and did ask), cannot we have it both ways? Cannot we have music where there is no action *and* music where there *is* action as well? The answer is 'Yes.' And this gift was given to us by Wolfgang Amadeus Mozart (1756–91), in the form of what we call 'dramatic ensemble,' of which he is the universally acknowledged master.

The great American composer and conductor Leonard Bernstein once pointed out that in opera, unlike spoken drama, 'everybody can "talk" at the same time.' (His remark, as I recall, was directly aimed at Mozart.) This, of course, is the principle on which vocal polyphony (in the narrow sense) is based, and which the dramatic ensemble exploits. (There was no Council of Trent, in the eighteenth century, to forbid it!)

In Mozart's great comic operas—for it was in comedy that the dramatic ensemble first became a major player—large sections of the plot are played out in a continuous musical fabric in which three, four, five, or even more characters take part. This does not mean that they need all sing together all of the time. Characters can enter, exit, sing alone, or in twos and threes, and so forth. But the point is that the music is continuous, with no break for *secco recitative*, and can advance the plot by the musical dialogue, and the comings and goings within the ensemble.

The crowning achievement of this kind of operatic ensemble is, I think everyone would agree, the finale of Act II of Mozart's *Marriage of Figaro*, in which eight characters participate, and which consists of

939 measures—a good twenty minutes of continuous music without a break for *recitative*. And, although you will not find in it a strict adherence to sonata form (which you *will* find in other of Mozart's dramatic ensembles, such as the Trio in the first act of *Figaro*, and the Sextet in the third), you will recognize in it what Charles Rosen calls the 'sonata principle,' which is to say, the sense of a progression to the dominant key, and a sense of return, a 'feeling' of recapitulation, if not, literally, the thing itself. To sustain an operatic ensemble of this length and of this complexity and of this variety of emotional states, one required a psychology to make it seem a possible course of human events, and a musical form to 'represent' it. The former was provided by the associationist psychology, the latter by sonata form. Together they constituted the second 'perfect' solution to the 'problem of opera.'

I put 'perfect' in quotation marks, 'scare quotes,' as philosophers call them, to remind the reader of something I said a while ago about 'solutions'—there are those scare quotes again—to the opera problem. I said they were 'unstable.' Another way of saying that is to say there *is* no perfect solution to the problem of opera: to the problem of having something that is *both* music *and* staged drama, with all the things both of those art forms imply.

At this point I would like to introduce a somewhat artificial but useful distinction between what I shall call 'opera' and 'music drama.' It is not strictly observed in people's ordinary talk about such things, or the talk of the experts either. But it *is*, I think, informally observed, and will serve a good purpose.

By 'opera' I shall mean those kinds of musical theater in which an attempt is made to preserve the closed musical forms and still maintain some acceptable degree of dramatic and (especially) emotive verisimilitude: dramatic and emotive 'realism.' (In a moment I will introduce the term 'music drama' for something else.) Handel's and Mozart's operas are examples of 'opera' in my sense of the word. For both composers tried to preserve the closed musical forms, *da capo* and sonata form, while contriving to make those forms 'fit' the prevailing psychologies of their day (whether they were consciously aware of the psychological theories or, as is more probable, were intuitively aware of them as part of their general intellectual and social backgrounds).

Opera, however, even in these 'perfect' solutions, remained a controversial art form. Many people could not (and still cannot) accept the 'absurdities,' so called, of a drama where characters sing to each other in closed, repetitive movements, and then revert to an equally 'absurd' song-speech, *secco recitative*, which is neither music nor speech, just to get out of the way, as it were, all of the events that there is no time to sing, or can't be sung, that motivate the plot.

For composers to whom these so-called 'absurdities' really were unacceptable, two courses lay open: one, to tinker with operatic form in the hope of ameliorating if not totally removing the 'absurdities'; the other, to reject the 'problem of opera' altogether and strike out in a different (not, as we shall see, totally new) direction. What the tinkerers came up with was, essentially, a halfway house between sung opera and spoken drama: it is called *Singspiel* in German, literally sing-talk, ballad opera in English, *opéra comique* in French. The compromise was that the closed musical forms, aria and ensemble, should remain intact, but that the dialogue, instead of being sung in *recitative*, would be spoken.

This kind of musical theater seemed particularly suited to the popular taste, witness the 'operettas' of Gilbert and Sullivan, as well as, in our own times, the 'Broadway musical.' But it also took the form of serious drama, of which Ludwig van Beethoven's *Fidelio* is the most famous and frequently performed example.

Whether, however, opera in which characters sometimes sing and sometimes speak is any less 'absurd' than those in which they sing throughout—if, that is, you think opera 'absurd' in the first place—is questionable. And those who do find opera an 'absurd' art form, either half-sung or all sung, are inclined to seek another solution entirely to the problem of musical drama than the operatic solution of closed musical forms interspersed with *recitative or* speech. It is for this solution that I have reserved the name 'music drama,' not without some precedent in ordinary speech and the history of music.

Two splendid 'experiments' in music drama were performed in the eighteenth century, one a failure, the other a notable success but without future progeny. The failure was an odd sort of work for the stage known as 'melodrama.' The aesthetic thinking behind it is something like this. The villain in opera—what makes it 'absurd'— is the spectacle of dramatic characters conversing in musical tones, instead of speech. So let's, instead, have the characters speak their lines, while accompanied by a background of music expressive of what is being spoken. Melodrama was invented in France, and flourished very briefly in Germany. It failed, though, to satisfy the craving for *real music* that, after all, is the driving force of all musical theater worthy of the name, and the music of melodrama was merely a kind of musical background noise. But melodrama did actually survive in two rather different ways. It survived as a technique in opera, to supplement *recitative* and the closed musical forms, and is used, for example, by Beethoven in one of the crucial scenes in *Fidelio*, to accentuate a dramatic moment.

But melodrama survives in our own day, really, in the most influential of twentieth-century art forms, the *movie*. For, both in the silents, and in talkies, movies have, with few exceptions, been accompanied by music. The reasons for this are not altogether clear, and cannot be gone into here. However, the failure of melodrama to satisfy the yearning for a truly musical drama is underlined by its success in the movies. Because, whatever its success in the movies amounts to does *not* make the movies musical theater, and no one perceives them as such.

The second splendid eighteenth-century 'experiment' in 'music drama' (as I am using that term) was executed by the German composer Christoph Willibald Gluck (1714–87). Gluck was frequently referred to, and still is, as the man who 'reformed' Italian *opera seria*.

The most famous of his so-called reform operas, *Orfeo ed Euridice*, is very popular, and still frequently performed. But the two most fully realized examples, *Iphigenia in Aulis* and *Iphigenia in Taurus*, both based on Greek myths surrounding the onset and aftermath of the Trojan War, are, unfortunately, seldom mounted. (They are, by the way, settings of French, not Italian texts.)

The two *Iphigenia*s are not 'revolutionary' works of art, in the way that melodrama is. Rather, they make use of all the resources of opera that were available to Gluck. But, by radically changing the dimension of opera's inner components, especially *recitative* and aria, Gluck produced something close to what I want to call music drama, without, in the process, giving up entirely the closed musical forms.

One of Gluck's major 'reforms' was the elimination of *secco recitative*: the rapid 'tone-talk' interposed between the arias, and accompanied by the harpsichord. What now did the work for it was what is known as 'accompanied recitative.' In traditional *opera seria* there was a kind of middle ground, which I have not mentioned before, between *secco recitative* and aria, accompanied by the full orchestra, and saved for moments of heightened emotional tension. It still maintained a speechlike musical declamation; but it was much closer to real song than the rapid 'parlando' of *secco recitative*. Also, the orchestral accompaniment was far more elaborate and responsive to the text than the simple chordal accompaniment of the harpsichord. Accompanied recitative, therefore, had real musical attractions, unlike the 'let's-get-it-over-with,' throwaway character of *secco recitative*.

There were, from the 'reformers' point of view, three advantages to the replacement of *secco* with accompanied recitative. First, it eliminated the discontinuity many people felt, and still feel, between the aria, accompanied by full orchestra, and the *secco recitative*, accompanied only by the harpsichord. For now, with accompanied recitative holding exclusive rights, the musical fabric is a continuous orchestral fabric: the orchestra has become the ever-present 'commentator' on the dramatic events; a kind of 'Greek chorus' without words.

Second, the more elaborate character that accompanied recitative took on, now that it had the full resources of the orchestra, rather than the thin support of the harpsichord, provided the composer with an additional, and powerful dramatic tool. The orchestra could be used to emphasize dramatic and emotional points in the recitative text in ways that the simple chordal accompaniment of the harpsichord could not possibly duplicate.

Finally, as accompanied recitative possesses real musical value and interest, its exclusive presence is a musical plus for musical theater. That is simple arithmetic, which applies even to works of art.

Gluck's second innovation in his 'reform' operas was the drastic curtailing of the aria's musical dimensions. The *da capo* aria, and other 'luxurious' aria forms, must inevitably slow the pace of the drama. By reducing the length of the arias to almost 'songlike' size, Gluck thereby increased the dramatic pace. No longer was there such a marked disparity between recitative and aria. In short, the musical fabric of Gluck's last operas began to follow the pace of ordinary conversation more closely than anything on the musical stage (with the exception of the short-lived melodrama) since the early operas of the *stile rappresentativo*.

What, in effect, Gluck's two *Iphigenia*s were approaching was what is sometimes called 'through-composed' music drama, which is to say, a musical setting of the text in which there are no external or internal repeats at all. As the text unfolds, new music unfolds along with it. There is never a pause for arias or other of the closed musical forms. The drama is a seamless musical web even to the extent of avoiding cadences—that is to say, musical resting places. The master of this form of writing for the musical stage, which is the most completely realized example of what I have been calling 'music drama,' was the great German composer Richard Wagner (1813–83).

It is an exaggeration to say that there are no internal repeats in Wagner's most imposing music drama, the *Ring of the Nibelungen*, which gave the phrase 'of Wagnerian length' its meaning in our language. It is, in fact, four separate music dramas; and Wagner knit them together, musically, with what are called 'leitmotifs': musical phrases and fragments associated with particular characters, ideas, and events in the plot, which occur and reoccur, periodically, to represent or emphasize dramatic events. These leitmotifs do, indeed, lend a kind of continuous symphonic texture to the work. Nevertheless, the leitmotifs never literally repeat themselves, as Wagner has endlessly ingenious ways of altering the harmonies that accompany them, to suit the dramatic situation. And the overall impression is of a musical fabric that faithfully follows the meaning and emotive import of the words and events. It is a seamless musical fabric in which the *orchestra*—a giant one by the standards of Wagner's day—is the principal player. Needless to say, closed musical forms such as aria or dramatic ensemble are totally rejected.

In an obvious way Wagner's idea of music drama was not new, but, in effect, a return to the earliest conception of musical theater, as envisioned by the Florentine *Camerata*. It was opera, as I am using that term, with its attempt to reconcile drama with closed musical form, and with internal and external repetition, that was the innovation. However that may be, the division between opera and music drama is remarkable in its propensity for generating dispute, not just among theoreticians, composers, critics, and even philosophers, but among the public of music-lovers as well. There are music-lovers who can't abide the 'absurdities' of the musical theater at all, in particular, the 'spectacle' of conversation in music. But even among those who can accept that premise, there is a remarkable difference in tastes that seems irreconcilable and even, at times, violent. Wagner's music, in particular, has a tendency to generate either frenzied devotion or outright disgust. And, on the other side, there is no more fanatically committed audience than that for 'grand opera,' as well as no other art form so consistently lampooned, ridiculed, satirized, and generally just plain laughed at.

The source of these passions lies, I am convinced, in the deep divide that separates the literary and visual arts, on the one hand, from absolute music on the other, of which I spoke in the previous chapter. As great a 'pure' musical mind as Wagner possessed, and even his enemies cannot deny him that, the *Ring*, for many music-lovers, does not satisfy the 'pure' musical craving. And, as for the two universally acknowledged masters of opera, as I use that term, Mozart and Giuseppe Verdi (1813–1901), they, for their part, do not fully satisfy the 'pure' dramatic craving of the sophisticated theater-goer. Even for someone who can accept drama in verse, the step to drama in closed musical forms is a difficult one and, for many, impossible.

But these brief, summary remarks on the problems of opera and music drama do not yet, for our purposes, close the book on either the question of 'literary' music in general, or musical theater in particular. And, in order for that book to be closed, we must go on to talk about another attempt to bridge the gap between the arts of content and the art of absolute music. That will occupy us in the next chapter.

CHAPTER 10

Narration and Representation

I have emphasized in the previous chapter the role of music's expressive properties in the setting of operatic texts. There is good reason, I think, why the expressiveness of music has been such a major player in opera, and in other forms of music, in the modern Western tradition, where words are sung. The reason is this.

The expressive properties of music, within a certain narrow range, as we have seen, are clearly discernible to all listeners. (I am speaking here, of course, only of Western music, and listeners practiced in listening to it.) Because of that, they—the expressive properties—provide the most dependable, the most reliable, material for a composer trying to make her music appropriate to her text. For, because the emotive properties of music *are* so readily, so universally, recognized by even the most naive listeners, the composer can be sure that the appropriateness of music to text will be recognized. Just as long as the text expresses one of the emotions that music can be expressive of, then, if the composer makes the music expressive of that emotion, all listeners in our culture will recognize the emotion in the music and so recognize the music's appropriateness to that text.

But this is not to say that composers have restricted themselves only to the emotive properties of music in setting texts, nor that the expression of emotions is the only thing the texts they set do. Far from it. An example here will help.

Mozart's *Marriage of Figaro* is about estranged couples who, in the end, resolve their differences, and come together. The resolution of their differences occurs in the last few measures of the opera. And Mozart 'represents' this resolution by, at nearly the very end, taking the music from the key of G major to the key in which the opera began, D major. As a musician might say, Mozart 'resolves' finally to the key of D. So, in a fairly obvious sense, it at least seems as if Mozart has used his music in this place as a representational art. But is that really so? *Can* music really be a 'representational' art in the true sense of that word? And what *is* the true sense, anyway.

Let us begin by distinguishing two kinds of representation. I shall call them 'pictorial representation' and, for want of a better term, 'structural representation.' An example of pictorial representation is the *Mona Lisa*: an example of structural representation is the resolution to D major in *The Marriage of Figaro*. What's the difference?

In pictorial representation, I shall say, following the concept and terminology of the British philosopher Richard Wollheim, that we 'see in' the picture the lady's face. The analogous concept in music would be 'hearing in.' But we don't 'hear in' Mozart's resolution to D major the three couples resolving their differences and coming together. People resolving their differences doesn't *sound*, and can't be *heard* in the music. What happens here is that we hear and perceive in the music a structural analogy to the resolving of differences among the couples: hence my term 'structural representation.' And there is no doubt that without words and dramatic setting we would not, and certainly would not be entitled to, construe the resolution to D major as a representation of the couples resolving their differences (or a representation of anything else, for that matter).

This latter point suggests a second distinction: that between pictorial representations where what is 'seen in' the picture can be seen in without the aid of words and what can be seen in only if we have a hint from some accompanying text or title. Anyone can see the woman's face in the *Mona Lisa* without being told that it is a portrait of a lady. But there is a beautiful painting by the British artist J. M. W. Turner (1775–1851) in which we can see a sunset in the painting only if we know the title: *Sunset over Lake*. We really *do* 'see in' the picture the sunset over the lake—only, however, when we know the title. Without the words there would be no 'seeing in': only the impression of a non-representational color composition. For obvious reasons, then, I shall distinguish between what I call 'aided' and 'unaided' pictorial representations: those that require words for 'seeing in' and those that do not.

Here two interesting questions arise. Is music capable of pictorial representations at all, and, if so, is it capable of unaided as well as aided ones? We have seen already that it seems capable of structural representation. And I am going to assume that structural representation, at least in music, is always *aided*. That is to say, we can never determine that there is structural representation in music without a text or title—without words—to make us perceive the structural analogy.

Now visual pictorial representations represent what is *seen*: we *see* the woman *in* the *Mona Lisa*. Likewise, pictorial representations in music, if indeed there are any, represent what is *heard*: we *hear in* the music whatever it pictorially represents. So it seems clear that pictorial representations, if any, in music, must be representations of *sounds*. This does not mean music cannot represent other things besides sounds, or paintings things other than sights. But they can't represent them *pictorially*.

Not very much sober reflection is required to conclude that, if music is capable of pictorial representation at all, of the unaided kind, it must be a very limited capability indeed. For it is very hard to come up with any real, incontestable examples. Bird calls, like the cuckoo's, come to mind. Beethoven represented bird calls in his Sixth Symphony, the *Pastoral*. But we know from the title of the work and the titles of its movements to expect such things; and the composer even writes the names of the birds whose calls he is representing in the score.

The twentieth-century French composer Arthur Honegger (1892–1955) wrote a famous piece for orchestra called *Pacific 231*. A 'Pacific' is a kind of steam railway locomotive, and Honegger's composition represents the sound of the engine starting up, barrelling along at top speed, slowing down, and finally coming to rest. It is as close to an example of unaided pictorial representation as I have ever encountered in music. People who remember what a railway steam locomotive sounds like usually, in my experience, recognize without textual help what the music represents. But even they at least need to be told they are hearing a representation of *something*. And, anyway, such examples are so hard to come up with that it is probably best to give up the point and admit that unaided pictorial representation in music is, if possible at all, too rare a phenomenon to be counted as belonging to music's repertoire of aesthetic possibilities.

Aided pictorial representations, however, are another matter entirely. They seem to abound. Here are some examples, drawn from fairly well-known compositions. They are of two kinds: pictorial representations of natural or man-made sounds, and pictorial representations of musical sounds; that is, musical representations of music.

Some pictorial representations of natural sound events I have already adduced: Beethoven's representations of birdsongs—quail, cuckoo, nightingale—in his *Pastoral* Symphony. Other examples from that work are the pictorial representations of a thunderstorm, with loud musical crashes and drum rolls, and the pictorial representation of a gently meandering stream with a continuous 'flowing' melody in the strings. As for man-made sound events, there is, for example, Schubert's pictorial representation of a spinning wheel's whirring sound, in the piano accompaniment of his song 'Gretchen at the Spinning Wheel,' and, in Beethoven's opera *Fidelio*, the representation of a stone cover being rolled off the top of a cistern, with a low, 'grumbling' motive in the bass instruments of the orchestra. Such examples could be multiplied indefinitely; there is no dearth of them.

But composers also do something that seems to be best described as representing music with music. Here is an example. The opening scene of Wagner's opera *The Mastersingers of Nuremberg*, the plot of which revolves around the life of the poet-singer Hans Sachs (1494–1575), takes place during a church service. In the scene the congregation sings a Lutheran hymn. Wagner, we might want to say, 'represents' the hymn, which is music, with *his*, Wagner's, music.

These examples of aided pictorial representation seem straightforward enough to me. But others have not found that to be the case. In fact, two basic objections have been raised against such examples, based on what are perceived by most of us to be necessary conditions for pictorial representation: a distinction between representation and the thing represented, and that we be able to 'see in' or (in this case) 'hear in' the pictorial representation what is represented there.

The British philosopher Roger Scruton has argued that the first condition is not fulfilled in what I have been calling pictorial representations in music. He argues that, in the case of music's representing non-musical sounds, the music does not so much 'represent' as 'reproduce' the sounds; it is sound imitation. And, in the case of music's representing music, there is no representation either, because the music just *is* what it is (mistakenly) described as representing. Wagner's so-called representation of the Lutheran hymn just *is* a Lutheran hymn.

As for 'hearing in,' the American philosopher Jenefer Robinson has simply claimed that we *don't*. We just don't experience in music the kind of thing that we experience in painting, for example. There is not that sense of perceiving in the musical representation what is represented there, as there is of seeing, in the *Mona Lisa*, what is represented *there*.

With regard to Scruton's claim that when music represents music it just is what it represents, it suffices to observe that his own example belies that claim if the example is described in enough detail. The hymn that the congregation sings in *The Mastersingers* is a sixteenth-century hymn; for the sixteenth century is when the events are represented as taking place. But the music that we hear is not *really* a sixteenth-century hymn. It is a hymn accompanied by a huge orchestra, interrupted by orchestral interludes, and in distinctively nineteenth-century harmonies. There is no way one could mistake this music for a sixteenth-century hymn. And the most reasonable way I can think to express what is going on here is to say that a sixteenth-century hymn is being represented in a nineteenth-century musical style, as we would say that a vase of flowers is being represented in a nineteenth-century painterly style. A sixteenth-century hymn is the object of the representation, nineteenth-century Wagnerian harmonies are the medium.

Moving on to where non-musical sound is the object of pictorial representation in music, there seems even less reason to think that object and medium coalesce. Musical representations of music *are* music. But musical representations of thunderstorms, birdsongs, and the sound of spinning wheels certainly are *not* those sound events. The medium is music, and there is little temptation to mistake the medium for the object of representation, even though *both* are *sounds*. There is a big difference between an imitation of a birdsong—there *are* people and gadgets that do that sort of thing—and a musical representation of one, played with expression and musicianship on an oboe or clarinet.

In sum, then, there seems no reason to think that, in pictorial representations in music, medium cannot clearly be distinguished from the object represented. It appears that Scruton's objection does not hold up. What about Robinson's?

I think the best way to counter the notion that there is no genuine 'hearing in' in musical representation, significantly like 'seeing in' in the visual arts, is to be very careful in distinguishing, to begin with, between 'seeing in' and illusions. When we say that we 'see in' the *Mona Lisa* a woman, we do *not* mean to say that we really think we see a woman in the canvas, or even that we are momentarily tricked, as we are in the kind of painting called *trompe l'œil* painting, painting that, literally, 'deceives the eye.' We are aware that we are in the presence of a representation of a woman, and aware that there is a *medium* of representation, oil paint.

'Hearing in' should be thought of no differently. In particular, we should not set a 'standard,' so to speak, of 'hearing in' any higher than that for 'seeing in.' Of course we are not fooled by the accompaniment of Schumbert's song into thinking we are really hearing a spinning wheel, in the sense either of an illusion, or of *trompe l'œil*. But nor are we fooled into thinking we are in the presence of a real woman, in the sense either of an illusion, or of *trompe l'œil*, when we look at the *Mona Lisa*. Nevertheless we 'see in' the *Mona Lisa* a woman. Why should it not be the case that we 'hear in' Schubert's song the sound of the spinning wheel?

Perhaps it might be replied that the 'seeing in' of the woman in the painting is more 'vivid' than the 'hearing in' of the spinning wheel's whirring in the song. Well, however you measure 'vividness,' I guess the vividness of 'seeing in' varies from work to work; and I guess the vividness of 'hearing in' must vary from work to work as well. I also guess that, where vividness declines 'enough,' however 'enough' is measured, people won't be able to 'see in' and pictorial representation will fail. But, even if it should be the case (and I have no reason to think it is) that the most vivid cases of 'hearing in' never exceed in vividness the least vivid cases of 'seeing in,' there is no reason whatever to think that 'hearing in' consistently falls below the level of vividness necessary for successful pictorial representation in music (always to be understood as the *aided* kind). Indeed the readiness with which people recognize such pictorial representations as the whirring of the spinning wheel in Schubert's song, or the babbling brook in the *Pastoral*, strongly suggests that 'hearing in' occurs vividly enough and frequently enough—assuming, of course, that there is a text present to facilitate it. For that *is* the real difference between 'seeing in' and 'hearing in.' 'Seeing in' is usually unaided. 'Hearing in' probably never is.

So I think it is fair to conclude that neither the objection of Scruton's, nor that of Robinson's, is successful in convincing us that aided pictorial representation in music does not occur where we think it does. Let us, then, consider that case closed. We must now spend a moment considering structural representation.

Representing things other than sounds and sound events in music is a very old tradition in Western music. It was a going concern in the Renaissance. But it perhaps reached its peak in the music of the Baroque period, roughly between 1600 and 1750, and had its most ardent devotee in Johann Sebastian Bach. The point of Bach's 'tone painting,' as it is sometimes called, was to 'reflect' or 'illustrate' in his music concepts or images in the religious texts that he set. (He held, for the major part of his creative life, the post of Cantor in St Thomas Church, Leipzig, which meant that he was employed to compose music for the service of that church, as well as to rehearse the choir and orchestra, and to serve as the church organist.)

Of course the texts that Bach set, both from Scripture, and by religious poets of his day, were filled with Christian concepts and symbolism, as well as allusions to events in Scripture. These frequently elicited tonal 'images' from Bach. Thus, for example, in a text that mentions the Ten Commandments, the music is based on *ten* repetitions of what one might well describe as a very 'commanding' theme. Bach represents the faithful Christian following the precepts of Christ with two themes that 'follow' one another: each thing that one melody does the other repeats right after. (This is called a musical 'canon.' 'Canon' means 'rule'; and the 'rule' here is: the second melody does just what the first one does, or something like that.)

Or, again, when Bach sets a text that mentions Christ descending from heaven, the theme descends, and when it mentions his ascending to heaven, the theme ascends. And music to the text 'the rich he has sent away empty' Bach ends with a single, 'empty' chord on the keyboard, all of the accompanying instruments having dropped out the measure before, in such an obvious, conspicuous way that it is clear Bach has 'emptied' the piece of its accompaniment. Such examples abound, in Bach particularly, but in the music of other composers of the period as well, and it would be pointless to continue enumerating them.

But with some of these examples before us it can be seen why I call this kind of musical representation 'structural' representation. For the common characteristic is that, in each, some structural element in the music corresponds with something in the text that the structure, so to say, analogizes. The tenfold repeating structure corresponds to the Ten Commandments; the following structure of the two themes—the canon—corresponds to the Christian metaphorically following Jesus; the empty concluding chord corresponds to the rich sent away empty; the descending and ascending structure of the melodies corresponds to the descending and risen Christ.

Of course there can be no question with structural representation of 'hearing in.' There is nothing to 'hear in' the music, because the music, in these instances, does not represent sound, or sound events, but abstract concepts and things seen but not heard. One hears the musical structure, understands the text, and perceives, cognizes, the structural analogy.

But there is a very important thing that pictorial and structural representation in music have in common, at least on my view. They are both *aided* representations. They cannot be heard or perceived without the aid of a sung or read or implicitly understood text. They require the resources of language. And that is why, in previous chapters, I have objected so vigorously to literary and philosophical interpretations of absolute music. (This is a point I shall return to, once again, at the close of the present chapter.)

Taking stock, now, we can see that music has (at least) three ways of being perceived as *appropriate* to a text it sets or accompanies. It can be expressively appropriate: that is, it can be expressive of the same emotions the text expresses. It can be representationally appropriate in a pictorial way if it paints a sound picture of a sound event mentioned or described or implied in the text. And it can be representationally appropriate in a structural way if it analogizes in its structure some event or image or concept that the text contains.

Opera has harvested all three of these ways in which music can be appropriate to its text, but the expressiveness of music most especially, as I have said before. However, in the nineteenth century two other musical forms were exploited, and, if not invented (which they were not), at least developed more fully, explored more thoroughly, than heretofore. They are the programmatic symphony and the tone poem. They are worth—perhaps even demand—a look from the philosopher.

There is some marked ideological tension between the musical impulse and the literary impulse in nineteenth-century musical thought. On the one hand, it was in the nineteenth century that the concept of absolute music became solidified. The nineteenth century has been called the Romantic century and music *the Romantic art*. And a famous nineteenth-century art historian and critic, Walter Pater, remarked that *all* of the arts 'aspire' to music—*absolute* music obviously meant. Yet, on the other hand, the nineteenth century saw the rise for the first time of the 'literary' composer— the composer as person of 'arts and letters.' Indeed, three of the greatest composers of the century, Robert Schumann (1810–56), Hector Berlioz (1803–69), and Richard Wagner, each left behind a literary legacy as well as a musical one: music criticism in the case of Schumann and Berlioz, philosophical speculation on music in the case of Wagner, not to mention that Wagner wrote his own opera texts, and Berlioz wrote one of the most readable and fascinating autobiographies of the century. Furthermore, and most importantly, the century that gave us the concept of absolute music tried as hard as it could, nevertheless, to give instrumental music a literary content.

The major, most powerful impulse, in the nineteenth century, to make instrumental music a literary art is not, in my view, very difficult to trace to its philosophical source. It is, it seems certain, G. W. F. Hegel (1770–1831), whose philosophical presence was felt throughout nineteenth-century philosophical thought in general, thought on the philosophy of the fine arts in particular, and who decreed, at the time the status of music as a fine art was being debated, that absolute music could not be a fine art without a content and could not have a content without a text. It is this ukase that, either consciously or unconsciously, drove the century that invented the concept of absolute music to go on to subvert it with a music that was both instrumental and 'literary.'

As well, if sung conversations bothered you, and you thought opera and music drama 'absurd' on that account, 'literary' instrumental music solved that problem for you, as melodrama was supposed to do, but, in addition, did what melodrama never could: gave you *real music* to chew on. I do not say that this was ever fully stated as an aesthetic agenda by the supporters of 'literary' music. But I do say that it was at least an undertext.

Two musical forms, both generally referred to as 'program music,' and not always very easy to distinguish from one another, developed in the nineteenth century as attempts to give literary content to instrumental music. These are the 'symphonic tone poem' and the programmatic symphony. What, in general, they have in common is some 'extramusical' idea, or some set of such ideas that works in these genres are supposed to contain or, if you will, present, and a written text making this extramusical content explicit. Tone poems are generally in one movement, program symphonies multi-movement works. And the text, the 'program,' can range in complexity from a mere title to a fully worked-out story.

Let us suppose the limiting case: a single movement with the title *Tragic Overture*, but no other textual baggage at all. It is by Johannes Brahms (1833–97) and is in clearly recognizable sonata form. What are we to make of it?

Now, once the composer gives his work a title, even one as vague as *Tragic Overture*, it licenses us to search the work for representational aspects. My own take on Brahms's overture is minimalist. I merely infer from the title that Brahms wishes to make explicit that his work is expressive of tragic emotions rather than other kinds of dark emotions it might suggest to the listener. But, if someone were to hear *King Lear* in the music, there is certainly no reason to rule such a reading out of court without a trial. By giving the work that title Brahms has invited us to look for representational content if we like, and the search for *Lear* in it is not excluded, as it would be, in my view, if the work had no title at all.

What would the defender of a *Lear* interpretation have to bring to the table in her defense of it? Obviously she would want to point out musical aspects of the work that represent, pictorially or structurally, events and characters in the play and emotive properties in the work that might be expressive of the emotive tone of the play at various points.

When we are confronted with something more elaborate than a single movement with a title as its only accompanying text, let us say a program symphony with an accompanying story-text, then, of course, we have more to go on: a far more definite correspondence between events and characters in the story and expressive or representational features in the music. A real musical example I think would help here, so let us consider one: Hector Berlioz's *Symphonie fantastique*, perhaps the most famous (and controversial) work of program music in the repertoire.

Symphonie fantastique—the *Fantastic Symphony*—is in five contrasting movements, each with a title: Reveries-Passions; A Ball; Scene in the Country; March to the Scaffold; Dream of a Witches'

Sabbath. Each movement also has attached to it from one to two paragraphs describing what happens therein.

Briefly, the story is as follows. A young musician falls in love, at first sight, with a woman who excites in his musical imagination a melody that Berlioz calls an *idée fixe*, and that occurs periodically throughout the symphony (Reveries-Passions). The musician is at a ball, where the image of the beloved appears to him (A Ball). He wanders in the country and hears shepherds playing their pipes; but his tranquility is disturbed by thoughts of his beloved's possible infidelity (Scene in the Country). He takes opium in an attempt to kill himself, but instead of dying he has a ghastly opium dream in which he is led to the guillotine and executed (March to the Scaffold). The dream continues with visions of witches dancing in a devilish orgy, which ends in the musician's own funeral, accompanied by the Gregorian funeral chant: *Dies irae* (Dream of a Witches' Sabbath).

As might be expected, all of the kinds of representation I have enumerated, as well as the emotive properties of music, are utilized by Berlioz in 'telling' his story in music. There is pictorial representation of music: a waltz at the ball, the piping of the shepherds, the funeral music. There is pictorial representation of non-musical sounds such as the guillotine's fall. There is structural representation of the witches' orgy. And, of course, the emotional tone of the music at all times reflects the emotional tone of the events in the narrative.

But does the music actually *tell* the story? Not really, which is why, of course, I put 'telling' in scare quotes in the preceding paragraph. We know *music* can't tell a story for reasons I have already gone over thoroughly in previous chapters. What, then, *is* the music doing? It seems to me that the best way to answer this question is by analogy with the silent movies.

Berlioz's *Symphonie fantastique*, and program music like it, is, I want to suggest, the sound analogue of the silents in these respects. The music is 'moving' sound images, the film is 'moving' visual images. (I put 'moving' in scare quotes because neither the sound images nor the visual images *literally* move: that is an illusion.) The written text of the symphony is to the music what the titles of the silent movies are to the pictures on the screen. The music does not tell the story. It is the text that tells. (An illustrated novel might be another analogue.)

Of course program music is *music*, after all. And being music, it must fulfill the 'syntactical' and formal requirements of its period and style. The *Symphonie fantastique* is a symphony—although it has five movements rather than the usual four (as does Beethoven's *Pastoral*). And most of its movements are in familiar symphonic form. The first movement, for example, is in somewhat eccentric but recognizable sonata form. One way to put this is to say that, even without the written text, program music, at least of the 'better' kind, can be musically appreciated in its own right, purely as music, without the text—in fact, without knowledge of the text. This fact has suggested a philosophical objection to the whole concept of program music.

Roger Scruton, whom we have mentioned before, in a similar context, argues that, *since* program music or representational music in general can be fully appreciated, musically, without knowledge of what story it tells, or what it is supposed to represent, then it can't truly be described as narrative or representational at all. For in true representational arts it would be absurd to claim that someone could fully appreciate it without knowing what it represented. (Recall my example of the guy who said he loved Renaissance painting but was unable to perceive what was represented in it!)

The problem here rests on the word 'fully.' For when I said that program music of the better sort can stand on its own as music alone, I was *not* allowing it could be *fully* enjoyed as music alone. That is because there are always (or at least usually) musical features of it that 'don't make sense,' or at least don't make *as much* sense, if you don't know what the program is.

For instance, Richard Strauss (1864–1949) describes his tone poem *Till Eulenspiegel's Merry Pranks* as in 'rondo form.' And, like all rondos, it is tied together by a recurring, easily recognizable theme: the theme that 'represents' Till. But many of the contrasting themes are very 'odd'; and there seems no real musical reason why they are as they are, or why they come when they do. So as a rondo it doesn't totally 'hang together' until you know what these other themes represent in the story, and what the storyline is, all of which explains their 'oddness,' and why they come when they do.

Or, to return to our previous example, *Symphonie fantastique*, in spite of its clearly recognizable symphonic form, still is oddly 'disjointed' in many respects as compared, for example, to the tightly organized symphonies of Beethoven, Haydn, or Berlioz's great contemporary, Felix Mendelssohn (1809–47). The *idée fixe* theme keeps recurring, throughout the symphony, as an 'organizational' theme might, in a work of absolute music. But it enters in odd, awkward, at times musically 'unprepared' ways, which often have no particularly *musical* explanation. As well, the entrance of the Gregorian chant *Dies irae*, towards the close of the symphony, seems quite inexplicable on musical grounds. Why *this*? Why *here*? These kinds of musical peculiarities abound in Berlioz's *Symphonie fantastique*; and they don't make sense—musical sense—until they make narrative sense. And they don't make narrative sense, obviously, until you can fit the program to the music. The program is the major organizing principle of the symphony, as musical as it nevertheless is on its own.

Thus it is certainly true that *Symphonie fantastique* can be appreciated as absolute music, in ignorance of its program (and later in his life Berlioz expressed the wish that it be appreciated just that way). But it is certainly not true that it can be *fully* appreciated just that way. There are, however, two ways in which this claim can be understood, and they should be carefully distinguished.

If we mean that the *Symphonie fantastique* cannot be fully appreciated *as a work of art*, that is to say, *as the work of art that it is*, without knowing the program, that of course is trivially true. *Symphonie fantastique* is a work of art, and its programmatic text is part of that work of art. So, if you are not aware of that part, you are not fully appreciating that work of art. Something in your appreciation is lacking.

But what could you mean by saying that *Symphonie fantastique* cannot be fully appreciated as absolute music unless the program is known? Because, when you know the program, you can't, by definition, be appreciating, any more, a piece of absolute music at all. Music with a program isn't pure, absolute music.

There is, however, another way to construe 'appreciate fully' that can make better sense, non-trivial sense of the claim that you cannot appreciate the *Symphonie fantastique* fully as pure instrumental music. For, if you compare it, without the program, as absolute music, to pure instrumental music by other composers of Berlioz's stature, like Beethoven or Mendelssohn, you will see that it has gaps and defects, *as absolute music*—just those gaps and defects that the program makes good. So *Symphonie fantastique* is not fully rewarding, *as absolute music*, in comparison to those works, by the acknowledged masters, meant to be heard as pure music. Another way of saying this is that it cannot be as fully rewarding as those other works: or, in other words, it cannot be *fully appreciated* that way.

However, Scruton is certainly right in his insight that there is a very big difference between, let us say, representational painting and representational or program music. Certainly it *would* be nonsense to say that we could appreciate a Renaissance painting (say) *at all* if we had no idea whatever what it represents. Whereas it does make sense to say that we could appreciate (at least to a substantial degree) *Symphonie fantastique* without having the least idea what *it* represents.

Nevertheless, the above is a very misleading observation. For the fact is we *can't* perceive a Renaissance painting without perceiving what it represents. We seem to be 'hard-wired' in that respect. But that is exactly what we *can* do with representational music because, unlike representation in most painting, representation in music is, of necessity, *aided*, not unaided representation. And, if you accept the concept of aided representation in music, then the disparity Scruton points out, between representational painting and representational or program music, has no purchase. It is simply irrelevant as an objection. The defender of representation accepts the premise of the objection.

I have, in this chapter and the previous one, outlined some of the ways, in opera, music drama, and program music, that music can be appropriate to a text. It can be emotively appropriate, the music being expressive of those emotions mentioned or implied in the text or dramatic situation. It can represent, pictorially, what the text mentions or implies, if what it mentions or implies is a musical, or man-made or natural sound event. And it can structurally represent almost anything mentioned or implied in a text just as long as what it mentions or implies can be structurally reflected in the music.

With these possibilities before us I can now suggest a way of looking at absolute music that explains a lot about why fictional interpretations at least *seem* to work so well, and are so *easy* to come up with. Absolute music always possesses the *potential* for being used to underlie a text or dramatic situation. One could, for example, write a program for a work of absolute music just because it is an expressive structure that *could* fit numerous programs or dramatic plots. Not only could one do it; it *was* done in the nineteenth century. But, when one does that, one is, of course, creating a *new* work of art: a program symphony using someone else's music; it is a collaboration. It is something similar to what a choreographer does when she creates a dance with a plot, performed with the accompaniment of a piece of absolute music.

Absolute music is, in a way, like pure mathematics. For example, non-Euclidean genometries were discovered (or invented, if you prefer) as pure mathematical structures. They didn't represent anything. Indeed it was generally believed that the real world, *our* space, was Euclidean. *It* was represented by Euclidean genometry—the kind of geometry you learned in high school. But, when physicists came to a different view of the world, non-Euclidean geometries were waiting there for them to use. *They* were then given the role of representing the real world, *our* space.

Musical structure is like that. It is there waiting to be used, by composers like Berlioz and Richard Strauss, to illustrate and represent. If it didn't have the structures it did, it couldn't be so used. But it does have them; and it has them when they are fashioned into works of absolute music. And that is why it is so easy to put fictional stories to absolute music. All you need do is fit *your* fictions to that music. Whatever that is, however, it is not interpretation. Interpretation tells us what is there, not what we can put there with little more effort than we exert in seeing things in clouds. To show that absolute music 'means' requires more than merely showing that it 'could have meant,' since its structures are expressive and capable of pictorial and structural representation. What must be shown is that absolute music exists as a representational or linguistic system. And that, so far as I know, has never been shown by any of those who practice the fictional or representational interpretation of the absolute music repertoire.

There is one further, and important, point to make before we go on to other matters: a point that is valid both for opera, and for the kind of music with text we have been looking at in the present chapter, although perhaps in varying degrees. It is that when text is added to music, particularly if it results in fictional narrative, the arguments against the musical work's potential for arousing the garden-variety emotions goes completely by the board. Once the conceptual apparatus of language is added to music, the work becomes *as* capable of arousing 'real-life' emotions as any other literary work of art.

Of course, as we saw earlier, there *is* a problem of how *any* fictional story can arouse the life emotions in its audience. For the emotions in 'real life' are aroused, in part, by our beliefs that things are really happening to real people. And in fictional works that is not so.

But the problem of how, or whether, fictional works can arouse real emotions—how, or whether, we *really* feel sorry for Anna Karenina, are *really* afraid that the Frankenstein monster will kill the little girl—is a problem not for the philosophy of music particularly; rather, for the philosophy of art as a whole. My own opinion on this matter is that we really *do* feel sorry for Anna, *are* afraid for the little girl, and, similarly, really *are* sorry and afraid for operatic heroes and heroines. It is not my place, however, to argue for that point of view here. What *is* relevant for me to do is to remind the reader that he or she should be very careful to distinguish between the question of whether absolute music can arouse the garden-variety emotions from that of whether texted music can. My answer to the first question has been an emphatic *No*, and I have presented detailed arguments for that negative opinion. My answer to the second question is at least a tentative *Yes*, and I give no arguments for that positive opinion here as it is not in my province as philosopher of music to do so.

At this point in our proceedings we have reached the end of a long story that has gone from theories about music and the emotions, to an outline of the doctrine known as formalism, the version of that doctrine I have called enhanced formalism, which I have defended, the critique of that doctrine and my answer to it, and the use to which music has been put in the setting of dramas and texts. But now we must turn to other things; and first to the difficult problem of what we are really talking *about* when we talk about *music*, in particular, musical *works*. Here is what I mean.

I have, throughout the preceding chapters, referred quite freely to 'works' of music, without any explanation or excuse. Probably you all knew what was meant. For it is just the ordinary way we talk about music. There are 'works' of music; and, of course, there are 'performances' of those works. Music is a performing art.

Yet, when one tries to dig beneath the surface of such perfectly ordinary talk, some quite extraordinary and puzzling difficulties become apparent, and one begins to realize that what one thought was perfectly clear about what a work is, and what a performance of it is, are not so clear after all. In the next two chapters I will examine some of these difficulties, and present what *I* think works and performances are. But I should emphasize that what I have said in the preceding chapters is perfectly consistent with various other views about the work–performance thing. You can reject what I say in the next two chapters, and accept the rest, though I hope, of course, that you will accept it all.

CHAPTER II

The Work

Like many philosophical problems, the problem of the musical work—what kind of a 'thing' it is—can initially be raised, very simply, by looking at how we ordinarily speak.

Suppose you picked up your morning paper and saw the headline: 'Da Vinci's *Mona Lisa* stolen. Culprits sought by police.' You would, no doubt, be shocked by the audacity of such an act. But you would not have difficulty imagining what had taken place. Thieves somehow got into the Louvre, evaded the guards, lifted the canvas off the wall, and spirited it away to their hideout.

But suppose you picked up your morning paper and read: 'Beethoven's Fifth Symphony stolen. Culprits sought by police.' Surely your reaction would not be shock but profound puzzlement. You would *not* be able to imagine what had taken place. Where did the thieves find Beethoven's Fifth Symphony? What did they do when they found it? How can you 'pick up' Beethoven's Fifth Symphony? How can you take it to your hideout? What would be the 'it' you were taking there?

Of course thieves could make away with the late Leonard Bernstein's personal score of Beethoven's Fifth Symphony, with all of the great conductor's markings and comments written in it: *that* would be a collector's item and fetch a handsome price. They might even pilfer Beethoven's original manuscript, an absolutely priceless artifact. But in neither case, clearly, would they have stolen Beethoven's Fifth Symphony. For we could still go on enjoying its beauty. There would remain other scores, and lots of recordings. This is very unlike the case of the stolen *Mona Lisa*. As long as the thieves have it hidden away, only *they* can enjoy *its* beauty.

At this point the reader will surely have come to the conclusion that the reason one can steal the *Mona Lisa* and not Beethoven's Fifth Symphony is that the *Mona Lisa* is a *physical object* and Beethoven's Fifth Symphony is a . . . Is a *what*? That's the problem.

Certainly we talk all the time about musical 'works,' even when we don't use the word. You say that you heard a symphony by Beethoven, or that your daughter sang a song in the school play, or that Sousa's marches are okay for parades but not much good for listening to. *What* are you talking about? 'Things.' But the growing suspicion that these 'things' are not physical things, like paintings and statues, is troubling. Like paintings and statues, musical works are 'works of art.' Yet they are not objects you can pick up or steal or even locate anywhere. They *aren't* anywhere, it would seem. They're not situated in space and time; not, apparently, situated *in our world*. They are beginning to look like very mysterious things or objects indeed: ghostly apparitions that common sense, which we all are proud of having, recoils from with quite understandable aversion.

Perhaps, though, things are not as desperate as they seem. There *are* two kinds of 'physical object,' at least if we stretch that concept a bit, closely associated with musical works. And it might be the case that they together offer us a way to avoid the threatening invasion of the non-physical into our musical space. I have reference here to musical scores and musical performances. Let's take a brief look at them now, for starters. We will take a longer look later on (in the next chapter).

It is an obvious but important truth that music is a performing art. And ever since there has been musical notation in Western music there has been a distinction between the performance and the thing performed. In the very early period of musical notation, in Medieval times, a good deal of the music may have been 'made up' on the spot, in performance: what we would call 'improvising.' There was also a good deal that was preserved not by the notation but by memory and tradition, with the notation more or less a 'reminder,' a jogger of the memory, rather than itself the preserver of the 'work.' At some point, however, in the history of notation, it began to make sense to say that 'something' was being repeated, from one performance to the next; and, however vaguely that something was determined by the notation, that was the 'work,' whether or not there was a word for it, and whether or not memory played a prominent role in the proceedings.

Now the history of Western musical notation is a fascinating study, and casts a good deal of light on the questions of what a work and a performance are. But this is, after all, an *introduction* to the subject; and we must therefore pick a place somewhere 'in the middle of things,' where the concepts of score, performance, and work are securely in place. The example I began with was Beethoven's Fifth Symphony, I guess the most famous piece of classical music there is. And I think it would be a good idea to stick with it. Beethoven completed the work in 1807, and there can be little doubt that the score/work scheme was, at that point in music history, firmly entrenched. Opinions may differ about how far back before that date one can still validly talk about the work/performance distinction. I tend to say *very far back*. Others may disagree. However, here would not be a good place to argue the point. For the time being, 1807, and Beethoven's Fifth Symphony, will suit our purposes very well. Let's begin with scores.

A musical score is a complex symbol system. From the performer's point of view it is a complex set of instructions for producing a performance of the musical work that it notates. In the case of a large orchestral work like Beethoven's Fifth Symphony, many performers are required; and they do not all read from a score. Rather, each reads from his or her 'part'—the oboists from theirs, the violinists from theirs, and so on. Those parts are extracted from the score for purposes of performance; and they themselves are individual 'instructions' for the oboists and violinists and the rest. The score is the master instruction, so to speak, from which all the other instructions are derived. It is like a recipe for a complicated dish from which the chef extracts a recipe for roasting the meat, a recipe for sautéing the truffles, a recipe for preparing the sauce, and then assigns them to his associates.

I will, from now on, speak of the score of Beethoven's Fifth Symphony as, from the performers' point of view, a set of instructions for realizing a performance. But you will understand from what I have just said that that is an abbreviated way of describing what really takes place in a performance, when it involves many performers following many subsidiary instructions in their parts that, when put together, make a performance of the whole work. Let's turn now to the performance itself for a moment.

The word 'performance' is ambiguous. If I refer to a 'performance' I may be taken either to be referring to the *act* or to the *product*: that is to say, the act of playing a piece, or the sounds that that act produces. In what follows, when I use the word 'performance,' I will always mean the product, not the act.

Now when the performers correctly follow the score of Beethoven's Fifth Symphony, they together produce a performance of it. When they do, we will say that they have 'complied' with the score's instructions, as we would say that, in driving on the left side of the road in Great Britain, I have complied with the traffic regulations of that country.

What, then is the performance? It is a very complex sound event, composed of many different musical sounds, occurring over a certain extended period of time. But there is nothing mysterious about this big sound event. Sounds are vibrations of the air, a physical medium; and, without bending the concept of 'physical object' too far out of shape, we might say that a performance is a complex physical object. Or, perhaps we want to say that it is a complex sound event. In any case, there is nothing mysterious about its *existence*. It can be located in time and space, much like any other physical object. Just as my car was in the garage from 5.00 p.m. on Monday until 10.00 a.m. on Tuesday, a performance of Beethoven's Fifth Symphony took place in Carnegie Hall Monday from 8.00 p.m. until 8.30 p.m.

Returning now to the score for a moment, we can see that there is nothing mysterious about *it* either. It is a physical object—paper with ink marks on it—locatable in space and time. Of course there are a lot of scores of Beethoven's Fifth Symphony, and of many other works. But that need not bother us, at least for our purposes.

So, now, when Leonard Bernstein and the members of the New York Philharmonic Orchestra performed Beethoven's Fifth Symphony, there does not seem to have been any mysterious, ghostly object involved. The score is a physical object; the performance is a physical object: a complex sound event in compliance with the score. So, if we could say what the work is by merely talking about score and performance, there would be no mystery.

The great twentieth-century American philosopher Nelson Goodman thought he could do just that. Goodman had a very strong aversion to 'mysterious objects' in all areas of philosophy. And he thought he could avoid the conclusion that the musical work is a kind of mysterious, ghostly apparition by defining the musical work as follows: *the compliants of a score are performances and the compliance class is a work*. What did Goodman mean by this?

We already know what it means for a performance to be a compliant of a score. But what does Goodman mean by the compliance class?

A 'class' of objects is simply a specified collection or group: specified or collected in accordance with some rule or 'fact.' Thus, you and I are members of the class of human beings, human beings are members of the class of primates, the number two is a member of the class of even numbers, and so on. The class of compliants with the score of Beethoven's Fifth Symphony, then, is the class of *all* performances of Beethoven's Fifth Symphony. And by 'all' is meant *all*: all performances past, present, and to come. So what Goodman is telling us is that Beethoven's Fifth Symphony, *the work*, just is the class that comprises all of its performances: the ones that have been, the ones that are now taking place, and the ones that will take place in the future. In short, any musical work is the class of its perform-ances; the class of compliants with its score.

The work that is Beethoven's Fifth Symphony, then, if Goodman is right, turns out not to be a weird, non-physical object, although it certainly turns out to be a pretty unwieldy one: a class of who knows how many members, yet to be, and unknown to us. But, after all, the classes of human beings and of presidents of the United States are both classes with who knows how many members, yet to be and unknown to us; and we don't find these classes difficult to live with. The question is: Will Goodman's idea of the musical work *work*. Will it do what we require of it? Well, what *do* we require of it?

It is generally agreed upon that the kind of philosophical ana-lysis Goodman is proposing must allow us to talk about the object of analysis in just the old ways we are accustomed to, given that the analysis is true. Thus, in the given case, we want to say that a musical work, unlike a painting, say, cannot be stolen or damaged or replaced with a fake. And Goodman's analysis does allow us to talk that way about musical works if they are, as he claimed, classes. Because certainly it makes no sense to assert that a compliant of a score has been stolen or damaged or faked. How *could* you do these things to the class compliant with the score of Beethoven's Fifth Symphony? How can you steal or damage or fake a performance, let alone a class of performances that contains members yet to be? So far so good for Goodman.

But we also want to say, for example, of Beethoven's Fifth Symphony—indeed I have already said it—that it was completed in

1807. However, we *can't* say that if it—the work—is the score compliance class: the class of all performances of the symphony. For that class is not yet complete—there will be future performances. And it certainly wasn't complete in 1807, since it has had many performances since then.

Furthermore, we want to allow the possibility of there being musical works that never have been, and never will be, performed because, perhaps, their scores were lost before they had even one performance. Imagine the score of a symphony forever hidden in some inaccessible, unknown place, doomed never to be performed. There is no class of its performances, no compliance class. On Goodman's analysis we would have to say that the symphony does not exist. But that seems absurd. Of course it exists; what never has or will exist is a performance of it, not *it*.

As well, it is generally agreed that there are things true of a work but not of its performances, and vice versa. I might say that a performance of Beethoven's Fifth Symphony was unexpressive; I would hardly say that the symphony itself is unexpressive. Likewise, I might say that every performance of Beethoven's Fifth Symphony in the first ten years of its existence was unexpressive. In that case I would be saying that a whole class of its performances was unexpressive, and not the work.

Imagine now a very expressive twentieth-century work, but a work so difficult to perform that it is destined, through all time, *never* to receive a truly expressive performance. In that case the compliance class of its score is unexpressive, and the compliance class of its score, according to Goodman, *is* the work. So the *work* is unexpressive. However, we have already assumed that the work *is* expressive: so we have a palpable contradiction. The problem is that we want to preserve the possibility that a work might be expressive, and that the class of all its performances might not be. This possibility apparently cannot be preserved if the work is identical with the class of its performances, the score's compliance class, as Goodman suggests.

It appears, then, that the strategy of identifying the musical work with its performances is not going to pan out. We just can't say all of the things we want to say about the work by merely talking about its performances, even the class of *all* of them. Where do we go from here?

Let's return to 'ordinary language' again. In the wonderfully imaginative television series for children, *Sesame Street*, a character appears during one of the skits and tries to sell *the* number two to an unsuspecting sucker. He opens his trench coat, revealing underneath a large, garishly colored number two, for the inspection of his prospective buyer, the way a street vendor with (probably stolen) watches displays his wares to the unwary.

The skit, of course, is supposed to give children some insight into what *the* number two is, and what it isn't; and it is supposed to give children the idea that there is a big difference between *the* number two and *a* number two. It is *a* number two that the sharpster is offering for sale, falsely advertised as *the* number two. *The* number two is not the kind of 'thing' that can be sold, any more than Beethoven's Fifth Symphony is the kind of 'thing' that can be stolen.

Furthermore, the number two, like Beethoven's Fifth Symphony, is not the sort of thing that can be stolen either. Does the rest of the analogy hold? Is Beethoven's Fifth Symphony not the kind of thing that can be sold?

Surely here the analogy breaks down, you would reply, if you knew anything about the great composer's way of life. For didn't Beethoven make part of his living selling his works? As a matter of historical fact, he sold the Fifth Symphony to the music publishers Breitkoph and Härtel, under whose imprint it appeared in 1809. So there it is: a symphony bought and paid for.

But we should be careful about this. There is a big difference between selling a symphony and selling a painting. When Leonardo sold his *Mona Lisa*, it was wrapped, delivered, and no longer in the possession of the artist. When Beethoven sold his Fifth Symphony, a *manuscript* was wrapped, delivered, and no longer in the possession of the composer. It should be obvious, however, that the Fifth Symphony was not wrapped or delivered, and still was in the possession of the composer, in the obvious senses that he also had a score, could play it on the piano, and probably had it committed to memory as well. You cannot sell a symphony, any more than you can sell the number two. What Beethoven sold to Breitkopf and Härtel we would describe today as the 'rights' to his symphony: the exclusive legal right to publish the score. Thus, when we understand what it does and does not mean to 'sell' a symphony, we see that the analogy between Beethoven's Fifth and the number two holds perfectly, at least as far as we have taken it: neither can be stolen and neither can be sold; and, of course, there are a great many other things we can't do to the number two and Beethoven's Fifth Symphony, all apparently due to the fact that neither is a physical object, locatable in space and time.

Now here is the big question I have been leading up to: given that there is this striking analogy between the number two and Beethoven's Fifth Symphony, or, to generalize from the individual case, a striking analogy between numbers and musical works, could it be that Beethoven's Fifth and the number two, musical works and numbers, are *the same kind of things*?

Well, what kind of thing *is* the number two. I wish I could tell you with confidence. But that is one of the hardest questions that philosophers have ever asked, and one of the oldest. It goes back to Plato; and it remains a hotly debated point among mathematicians and philosophers of mathematics.

I am not a philosopher of mathematics, so I cannot give you an educated opinion as to what *I* think numbers are. But I can give you one philosophical answer to the question that I incline to: it is sometimes called 'realism' with regard to the numbers, and to other mathematical objects; and it is sometimes called 'Platonism,' because the answer originates with Plato (as indeed does the whole question). And the reason I am giving you *this* answer—realism or Platonism—is because it is *this* take on numbers and other mathematical objects that I suggest can be applied to musical works as well. So, first, what is mathematical realism or Platonism?

I shall say, following the terminology of the great American philosopher Charles Sanders Peirce (1839–1914), that numbers are 'types,' and their instances are 'tokens.' Here is an example to illustrate what types and tokens are. The 'two' that the man on *Sesame Street* was trying to sell was a token of the type 'two' (although he was claiming that it was the type). *The* number two, like all other numbers, is a type; and all of the written, printed, engraved, sculpted, and otherwise inscripted 'twos' are tokens. The tokens are easy to pin down: they are physical objects. It's the type that's hard to fathom. What is *it*?

According to the realist, the type, two, is a real, existent thing. (That is why such a philosopher is called a 'realist.') But it is not a *physical* thing. It is not locatable in space and time: indeed, it is 'timeless.' It did not come to be; it cannot cease to be. And, not being a physical object but a spaceless, timeless entity, it is clear that it cannot causally interact with our world of space and time. It is causally inert. It cannot do or be done to. A strange 'thing' indeed. Some people, like Nelson Goodman, have found, and find, it, and its many companions, so strange that they cannot lend credence to their existence. On the other hand, defenders of realism in mathematics claim that, as strange as these objects are, the way we do mathematics, and the way we talk about what we do, simply imply that such objects must exist. We will, they insist, just have to acknowledge that there *are* such strange objects, and to learn to live with them, to try to understand them as best we can.

One very important aspect of the realist's position in mathematics, and elsewhere, demands our particular attention. It has deep implications for the application of realism to the work/performance concept, and it is the work/performance application that is, of course, the aim of this exercise.

In ordinary life we distinguish sharply between the activities of making and discovering. We say that Columbus discovered America, not that he made it, and that Edison made the first electric light, not that he discovered it. (When we want to pay 'making' a big compliment we call it 'creating.') America was already there. Columbus had the perseverance and imagination to find it. The electric light was not already there. Edison had the perseverance and imagination to bring it into being.

Now one of the things that gives realism in mathematics its initial appeal, many would say, is that, if realism is true, mathematics turns out to be a process of discovery, not making. For the 'objects' about which mathematicians discourse, numbers and so forth, according to the realist, *exist*—always have, always will. Like America, they are 'out there,' waiting to be discovered (although, unlike it, they do not 'come to be' or 'pass away.') And, when you try talking about mathematics, you see right away that 'discovery talk' sounds right, 'creation talk' doesn't. For example, it sounds right to say that Pythagoras discovered the famous theorem that bears his name, not that he made or created it. As well, we say about unproven conjectures in mathematics, that is, statements in mathematics that seem as if they might be true, but whose proofs we don't yet know, that these proofs have not yet been 'found.'

Furthermore, it does appear reasonable to think that what the skit in *Sesame Street* does, for children, if it is successful, is to get them to discover for themselves the existence of the number two, by seeing the difference between it and the thing being offered up 'for sale.' Would it be too much to claim that this skit, if kids 'get it,' suggests kids are 'natural Platonists' with regard to numbers?

As we shall see in a little while, the fact that types are discovered, not created, causes some difficulty for those who wish to construe musical works as types. But before we get to that, let us see why it is tempting to make this move.

What is most enticing about the type/token distinction is that it seems to map very well onto the work/performance one. Performances of Beethoven's Fifth Symphony are particular, spatio-temporal 'things,' Beethoven's Fifth Symphony one 'thing,'

apparently not spatio-temporally located, of which the performances are 'instances.' This is just the way we talk about the relation
between type and token. *The* number two is an object, not spatio-
temporally located, of which all the physical 'twos,' written Arabic
and Roman numerals and so forth, are instances, obviously locatable in space and time.

Furthermore, the tokens of the type differ from one another
within given limits, even while being recognizable as tokens of that
type. This is certainly true of the token 'twos'; and certainly true, as
well, of musical performances. Indeed, some of the differences among
performances are much valued, as we shall see in the next chapter,
where the nature of musical performance will be taken up. But, of
course, the range and degree of difference among performances are
under the strict control of the score. For, although there are ways
in which performances can, and are supposed to, differ from one
another, they must all be in compliance with the score, or fail to *be*
performances of the work—fail to be tokens of that type. A 'performance' with 'too many' mistakes and wrong notes, or a performance
in which the player willfully departs from the score in impermis-
sible ways, is *no* performance *of that work*, whatever else it may be.

Two marginal notes at this point. I will call the view that musical
works are types of the kind the realist in mathematics says numbers
are 'extreme Platonism.' And I shall assume, as I already implicitly
have, that all performances of the work are instances of the work:
tokens of the type. But it would be advisable, as we shall see, to hold
out the possibility that there are instances of the work that are not
performances. In short, all performances are tokens of the type; but
not all tokens of the type are performances.

There are many problems raised by the view that musical works
are types, like the number two; and, given the limitations on space,
and on your patience, that an introduction to a subject naturally
imposes, I intend to deal only with four of them here, none, certainly, with the thoroughness it deserves. These problems are, first,
that types are discovered and, most would say, musical works are

made; second, that musical works, if types, would appear to be, so to speak, pure sonic structures, whereas most would say that how works are performed, that is to say, by what instruments, is essential to their nature; third, that the discovery of types seems an 'impersonal' thing, whereas the musical work, like all works of art, bears the personal stamp, is the personal 'expression' of the artist; and, fourth, that types are timeless, and cannot be destroyed, whereas it seems easy enough to imagine destroying, completely obliterating, a musical work—a fate, alas, that many of Bach's works have suffered, much to the sorrow of music-lovers all over the world.

The notion that composing music might be a process of discovery rather than of making, or, to pay it the compliment we usually do, *creating*, is going to seem strange to many of my readers. But it appears to me that trying to see composition as a process of discovering sound structures is not a counterintuitive idea at all, and might be a new, refreshing, and insightful way to see what composers really are doing. One way to see this is to consider the compositional process Beethoven went through in bringing forth his great masterpieces.

Beethoven left behind a large number of so-called sketchbooks when he died, which reveal the compositional struggle he went through to achieve the final results with which the musical world is so familiar. Many of the sketches in these books—all but indecipherable to the lay person—have been made available to us by scholars; and when one perceives the gradual progress the great composer makes towards getting the themes, and modulations, and structures he is finally satisfied with, one is very tempted to say, at least I am, that what we are seeing here is a struggle to 'find' the right theme, the right modulation, the right musical structure. Beethoven has left behind, in other words, the gradual steps he took in discovering what he was after.

One might object that what Beethoven did in his sketches can *equally well* be described as a struggle to *create* his themes, modulations, and larger structures by trial and error. What the sketchbooks contain are the rejected 'creations.' The final 'creation' is the work. I think it is a fair point. But all the defender of the musical work as type needs is the concession that describing what is going on in composition as 'discovery' works *as well as* describing it as creation. He can then go on to point out that, since the type/token distinction maps nicely onto the work/performance distinction, we can adopt it as an analysis of the work without worrying that it is unacceptable *because* it implies works are discovered and not created.

Nor need the extreme Platonist with regard to musical works deny that there *is* a very important act of creation involved in the compositional process. It is what the contemporary American philosopher of mathematics and language Jerrold Katz calls 'first-tokening'— which is to say, creating the first concrete object to make it possible for us to appreciate the abstract type the composer has discovered.

One might want to say that the first token of the musical type, when we are talking about composers of the stature of a Beethoven or a Mozart or a Bach, is 'in the head,' in the mind or imagination of the composer, perhaps as a mental 'performance.' But of course the first-tokening that makes the discovered work available to the rest of us is the writing-down of the score, or, to a limited few, the playing of the work by the composer. However you want to put it, what Katz wants to say is that we can pack into the first-tokening everything we would like to say about the creation part of musical composition.

Composing, then, turns out to be a dual process of discovery and creation, on Katz's view. The work, which is a type, is discovered. But the first-tokening, which reveals the work, the discovery to the world, is creation. And what Katz is suggesting is that the first-tokening, being creation, can bear the weight of those things, originality, for example, that the notion of composition as discovery might seem to preclude. Originality, for Katz, is first-tokening of the type.

There is much much more that would have to be said about discovery as a way of describing what composers do to begin to convince the skeptical that it is a plausible option. But I must leave that for a more suitable occasion. I only hope I have said enough to make it seem to the reader at least a *possible* option. And I pass on now to the second problem for extreme Platonism: the problem of performance means.

It is tempting for the extreme Platonist to fall into the position (as I have in the past) that, just so long as the sonic structure of the work is sounded, that counts as a performance of the work. The work type is a sonic-structure type, the performance a sonic-structure instance of the type. But suppose four woodwind players were to perform a piece specifically written for four string instruments; and suppose, further, that they played all of the notes correctly. In other words, they presented the sound structure completely intact, as envisioned by the composer and notated in her score. Would that be a performance—and instance—of *the work*? It would seem that the extreme Platonist would have to say 'yes,' whereas the ordinary, theoretically uncommitted person *might* perhaps be inclined to say 'no' (although I am not sure he would). But, if 'no' is the right answer, then, clearly, extreme Platonism must be a false theory.

Actually the answer to the question cannot be a simple 'no' or a simple 'yes' because composers' attitudes towards performance means have not been the same throughout the history of Western music. In certain periods the attitude was fairly lax: in other words, what mattered most was the sound structure; means of performance, at least within certain wide limits, was left more or less up to the performers themselves. Music, in this *laissez-faire* period, clearly poses no problem for extreme Platonism in the present regard.

In the modern era, however, from perhaps the middle of the seventeenth century to the present, the attitude of the composer has become more and more intransigent towards his or her stipulations with regard to instrumentation, and, as well, the music has become less and less possible to realize with instruments other than those the composer has stipulated. Nevertheless, I think that extreme Platonism can still be maintained with regard to such music.

To see this let us recall that 'formalism,' as I have construed it, encompasses not merely musical form, narrowly conceived, but various other aspects as well. Among these I count 'tone color.' Thus, where a particular instrument is specified by the composer to play a particular passage, the particular tone color of that particular instrument is stipulated as part of the sound structure that is the work. Thus it is that sound structure, tone color and all, belong to the type the composer discovers and first tokens.

That being said, it must be said as well that specified instrumentation, in the modern era, although frequently essential to the preservation of work identity, is by no means always so. And that is why rescoring works for different instruments does not always induce us to say we now no longer have 'the work,' whereas changing the notes, or at least, enough of them, does drive us to that conclusion.

What this strongly suggests is that sound structure, unspecified as to instrumentation, which is to say, timbre or tone color, lies far closer than anything else to our deepest intuitions about what makes the musical work the type that it is. That fact notwithstanding, however, there *is* a large body of Western music for which timbre or tone color is an integral part: part, one wants to say, at least I want to say, of its sonic structure. But, as I have pointed out, *because* timbre or tone color can be construed as part of the discovered type, this causes no problem for extreme Platonism.

What does seem to pose a problem for extreme Platonism is what might be described as the artificial production of timbre or tone color. This obviously never would have been thought of before the advent of late-twentieth-century technology. For the entire history of Western music, until very recently, the only way to make the sound an oboe makes was to blow on an oboe, the only way to make the sound of a violin was to play one, and so on. But one can now synthesize these sounds on an electronic gadget, and, in fact, 'construct' a 'sounding' of Beethoven's Fifth Symphony, with the structure, timbre or tone color included, completely intact. Is it a performance? Is it an instance of the work?

Of course the synthesized sounding of the Fifth Symphony is not a performance *act*, so not a performance in *that* sense of the word.

And I stipulated from the start of this chapter that I would mean the *product* when I used the word 'performance,' in other words, the sounds produced by the act. But the synthesized sounding of Beethoven's Fifth Symphony is *not* a product of the performance act at all, so not, therefore, a 'performance' of the work in either the act or product sense.

At this point it seems advisable to say that, although all performances of a work are instances of it, there can be instances that are not performances, synthesized sound occurrences being a case in point. To some this may seem an entirely reasonable solution. But others might have intuitions pointing in a different direction. They might want to say that, unless the sounding is produced in something like the customary way, by means of musicians and instruments, a sounding not only cannot be a performance but cannot be an instance either. What can we say to them?

We might just dig in our heels, pit our intuitions against theirs, and add that there is nothing in musical scores, as we know them, that rules out the possibility of an instance being produced by something other than a performance act, and, hence, at the same time, being an instance but *not* a performance. Another, more daring, suggestion is that we construe a musical performance, product, that is, as not merely a sound occurrence but a visual occurrence as well. An opera, in a concert performance, without costumes, stage setting, and the rest, is not an instance of the work, which is constituted of visual as well as sonic components. A work written as part of a liturgical service, a mass, let us say, has, like an opera, a visual component, a stage setting, if you will, namely the service of which it is a part. So a concert performance of *it*, like the concert performance of an opera, would not be an instance of the work. But wasn't Beethoven's Fifth Symphony written to be performed in public concerts, Mozart's wind divertimenti and serenades at social functions, with all of *their* visual components in place? (I am not, of course, suggesting that the participants must wear period costumes!) If a visual performance is an essential component of a musical work, then a true instance of the work must have a visible performance, and the type must reflect that necessity. It would be an aspect of what the composer discovers and first tokens.

I do not think intuitions or philosophy can take us further than this, at least within the confines of this introduction. I will simply conclude that, with regard to instrumentation, extreme Platonism is at least still in the running.

The third problem for the extreme Platonist, it will be recalled, is that musical works, like all works of art, one would presume, bear the unmistakable personal mark of the artist: they are the artist's 'personal expression.' Whereas a discovery is an 'impersonal' sort of thing. As Jerrold Levinson forcefully poses the objection, America is out there waiting for Columbus to discover it, whereas a composer's symphony is irrevocably and exclusively his.

The discovery of America, as opposed to the composition of a symphony, certainly makes a stark contrast. But it does seem like stacking the cards against extreme Platonism. Perhaps a contrast more friendly to the Platonist would be that between Beethoven's composing his Fifth Symphony and Newton's discoveries of the laws of motion as expressed in his great *Principia mathematica* (1687). For the *Principia* certainly bears the personal stamp of Newton, as the Fifth Symphony does of Beethoven. (Mathematicians and mathematical physicists, I am told by the experts, have clearly discernible *personal styles*, some better than others.)

The contrast between Beethoven's Fifth and Newton's *Principia* suggests at least a partial answer to Levinson's problem. The answer is, as Jerrold Katz has it, that the personal stamp is borne by the first-tokening. The artist's creative achievement, then, on Katz's view, her special, personal relation to the work, lies in her being able to make it possible for *us* to hear what *she* has heard, which is to say, our being able to hear what she has discovered.

This way of looking at composition is well illustrated by an old, very Romantic film about the life of Beethoven, called *Eroica*. (Beethoven titled his great Third Symphony *Eroica*—the heroic symphony; and he was himself seen as a hero, as heroic, by the nine-teenth century.) There is a memorable scene in the film in which Beethoven first fully realizes that he is becoming deaf—that he will be a *deaf* composer. He is in despair. But his friend Amenda, a priest, tries to console him with the thought that God has closed up his ears so that he can hear what only can be heard when worldly clamor has been subdued; so that he can hear in his mind's ear, as it were, totally new, other-worldly sounds that he can then enable *us* to hear as he has. The sounds are *there*; only Beethoven, the *deaf* composer, can hear them; we cannot. It is *his* special gift, his special genius to discover them to us. They are his special sounds; only *he* can dis-cover them because only he can 'hear' them.

We tend to think of artistic *creation* as a peculiarly Romantic notion. It would be a useful corrective to this notion to be reminded, as the film *Eroica* reminds us, how imbued with 'discovery language' Romantic discourse about the arts really is.

I do not want to leave the impression, in concluding this point, that I think Katz's suggestion has fully answered Levinson's worry. There is far more that must and can be said. This is just a beginning. But beginnings after all are all that an introduction can be expected to give. The reader will have to find her own endings if she is motiv-ated to go further with the question.

This leaves remaining the fourth difficulty for extreme Platonism: that works, being types, as they cannot be created, cannot be destroyed, whereas it does seem that works of music can perish, and have done. I will set this difficulty aside for the moment, and intro-duce at this point an alternative to extreme Platonism that Jerrold Levinson calls 'qualified Platonism,' and that is the view that he him-self holds. At the end of the chapter I will return to it.

I shall state Levinson's view very briefly and simply. Levinson, like the rest of us, would have his cake and eat it too. He is attracted, as am I, by how well the type/token distinction maps onto the work/performance one. But, unlike defenders of what I have been calling extreme Platonism, like Katz and like me, he finds the notion of musical works as discoveries, and the implications of that notion, unacceptable. How can we have the one without the other?

Well, if you want to preserve the type/token distinction as an analysis of the work/performance distinction and block the implication that works are discovered rather than created, why not simply hold that musical works are *created* types? That is precisely what Levinson suggests. Musical works, in his terminology, are 'initiated types.' They are not discovered but made. They begin to exist only when initiated by intentional human acts. The Lincoln penny is such a type, as is the Ford Thunderbird and Beethoven's Fifth Symphony, according to Levinson. The penny in my pocket is a token, *the* Lincoln penny is the type. Your red Thunderbird is a token, *the* Ford Thunderbird is the type. The performance of Beethoven's Fifth Symphony we heard last night is a token, *the* Fifth Symphony is the type. All of these types, however, were created at some point in human history, not already in existence and discovered; and there could be no tokens of them, no pennies, no Thunderbirds, no performances of the Fifth Symphony, until the creation, the initiation, of the respective types.

Musical works, then, being initiated types, come into being. Can they pass away? Once initiated, can they be terminated? For the extreme Platonist, musical works, like the number two, are neither created nor destroyed. They have no beginning in time, and can have no end. What *can* happen to them is that they can be permanently removed from human consciousness and memory: all of the means of performing or otherwise making instances of them available to us can be destroyed; all of the scores, recordings, memories in the minds of musicians can crumble to dust. In that sense, Beethoven's Fifth Symphony can be destroyed. It can become nothing *to us*. But it cannot cease to be. *Could* it cease to be if it were an initiated type?

Levinson's answer to this question is interesting. He thinks the most defensible view, as he puts it, is that a musical work can, indeed, be destroyed, if it should come to pass, and there is no reason to think it could not, that no one knows of the work or ever will again. But he nevertheless feels strongly drawn to the more extreme Platonic intuition that a type cannot be destroyed; that even an *initiated* type, a type that has come to be, cannot, once created, cease to be, but must remain forever in the strange world occupied by the number two and the rest of the extreme Platonist's menagerie. Like Dr Frankenstein, the composer creates a monster that thenceforth cannot be subdued.

But the entertaining of extreme Platonism, even at one end, so to speak, the denial of mortality, suggests at least a serious worry about the whole notion of an initiated type. Can we create *anything* that cannot be destroyed? Furthermore, whether or not an initiated type can cease to be, it is, after all, an abstract object that occupies a spaceless, timeless realm *with which we cannot causally interact*; that is to say, a world of objects that neither we nor anything else in the physical world of time and space can do anything to, as well as a world of objects that cannot do anything to us or our world. This may well suggest to you, as it seems to to Katz, that such an object *cannot* be brought into existence through the agency of human action. For what else could that creation by human agency be but causal intervention in that realm of spaceless timeless objects with which we have already agreed we cannot causally interact? The notion of an initiated *type*, in other words, is simply incoherent; if it is initiated, it cannot be a type; if it is a type, it cannot be initiated.

Here I must let the matter stand. All I can do for present purposes is to present the reader with three options, 'on offer,' as philosophers are fond of saying. Perhaps the reader will feel, after seeing the difficulties that extreme and qualified Platonism raise, that the notion of the musical work as the compliance class may not be so hopeless after all, and worth some reconsideration. If, on the other hand, the reader thinks, as I do, that that view is a non-starter, he or she may want to accept extreme Platonism, with all of its seemingly counterintuitive implications, and try to understand them and to live with them. Or, finally, the reader may want to go with qualified

Platonism and work out some way of understanding an initiated type that can accommodate its existence as a type with the fact that composers, flesh-and-blood creatures, can create spaceless timeless entities with which we cannot causally interact. As they say in the market, 'You pays your money and you makes your choice.'

My choice is extreme Platonism. It is, of the three, the most startlingly counterintuitive. But it is also, it appears to me, the most philosophically interesting. And the notion of composition as discovery, when you get over the shock, I think casts much needed light on the so-called creative process, over which so much mystery seems to hover. As well, it thereby draws an analogy between at least *some* of the arts, and the scientific enterprise, thus helping to close a conceptual gap many have found disturbing.

But, whichever of these three choices you, the reader, will make, it will be consistent with everything that has been said about the philosophy of music *prior* to this chapter. In addition, it will be consistent with everything I say about the closely related concept of *performance* in the chapter that now directly follows.

CHAPTER 12

And the Performance thereof

I said at the end of the previous chapter that what I have to say about musical performance in this one will be consistent with any of the three theories put forth there about what the musical work is. The reason for this is that the question of what a musical performance is assumes as its first principle only that a musical performance must be compliant with a score. That is the basic necessary condition for being a performance of a musical work and not something else. But all three analyses of what a musical work is, previously examined, make that assumption as well. That is to say, whether you think the work of music is the score compliance class, or a created type, or an uncreated, discovered type, you will, as well, think that a performance of the work must be compliant with the score. On this, the anti-Platonist, the extreme Platonist, and the qualified Platonist agree. Thus, the examination of what a musical performance is starts out with a minimal definition of it, namely, a compliant with the score, common to all three analyses, and hence consistent with them all. Whatever else we say about performance beyond this minimal definition will make no further, deeper assumptions that have anything to do with the nature of the musical work.

I do not say that the analysis of musical performance that I am about to give is consistent with *every* possible analysis of what the musical work is. I cannot say that, because I cannot be acquainted with every possible way the musical work might be construed. All I can affirm with any certainty is that what I am going to say about musical performance here is consistent with what I have already said about the musical work. That, I trust, will suffice for present purposes.

The consideration of what a musical performance is will break down, in this chapter, into two subsidiary questions. Since we have already seen that, to begin with, a musical performance is compliant with a score, the first question obviously must be: What is it to be compliant with a score? How, in what way, does a musical performance 'comply'?

But, once we know what it might mean for a complex 'sound object' to comply with a score, and, hence, fulfill the minimal requirement for being a performance of the work, we will then want to know what *else* it is. After all, a house is a compliant with the architect's blueprint, a game of chess is compliant with the rules of chess. But a house and a game of chess, although both compliant in something like the sense in which a performance is compliant, are very different things from one another. What kind of a compliant 'thing' is a musical performance? Is it like a house to its blueprint, like a game of chess to the rules, or some other kind of thing entirely? That is our second question.

But, first things first. So let us begin by asking what it might mean to comply with a musical score.

The most obvious thing to say is that a compliant with a score or notation is a sound object produced in accordance with the instructions for performing that are embodied in the score or notation.

That is what I will say, and all that I will say, as a 'definition,' if you will, of what score compliance is. What further I will do to amplify this rather empty abstraction is to put forward four concrete examples of musical notation, and discuss some of the ways in which they differ. In doing that I hope to give the reader a more definite idea of what complying with a score or notation really involves from the practical point of view. This will not result in a logically airtight definition of score compliance. For that you will have to turn to minds of a different stamp from mine. What it will accomplish, I hope, is to give a general understanding of what score compliance involves, no matter what the ultimate fine points of the logic turn out to be. With that general understanding to hand I can then go on to say something about what kind of a 'thing' a performance is and what kind of agent produces it.

Let us say that, from the performer's point of view, complying with a score means 'simply playing the notes as written.' For if, it would seem, you do anything more or anything less, if you add notes or if you omit notes, you are not following instructions. And if you are not following instructions then you are not, by definition, in compliance with the score.

But to the injunction 'simply play the notes as written,' any sensible performer will retort that, if you only did *that*, you would produce a very unmusical, which is to say a very bad, performance. The performer, the good, the musical performer, must add something beyond the merely as written, must she not? That certainly sounds right. However, before we get to such considerations, it would be a good idea to see if we can first get a handle on what it means 'simply to play the notes as written.' It may mean more than meets the eye. So let us now look at the four examples of musical notation I said that I would produce for discussion.

Figure 1 is an example from a very early period of musical notation in the West; Figure 2 produces an example from the first half of the eighteenth century, the period of the 'figured bass' (which I shall explain in a moment); Figure 3 is an example of what might fairly be

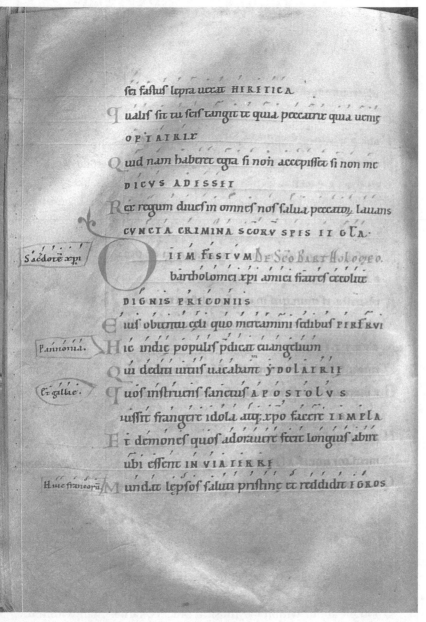

figure 1. Example of early Medieval chant notation

called musical notation in its present form, although it is from the early nineteenth century; and Figure 4 is a modern performing edition of the example presented in Figure 2.

Now at this point those of you who do not know how to read music are beginning to get nervous. *Don't!* Whatever I say about these musical notations will be quite understandable to *anyone*, whether musically 'literate' or not.

The first example will look strange to anyone who has even the most minimal acquaintance with modern musical notation. If you simply know what modern musical notation looks like, without knowing anything more, you will not even recognize this example of early musical writing, from the Medieval period, as musical notation at all; it will look merely like a text with what appear to be accents over the letters. But these marks are really instructions to the singer to sing higher here, lower there: in other words, they are the notation of a melody; a liturgical chant.

Now one's first reaction to this musical notation is to think it a primitive vehicle indeed for conveying musical thought. For example, modern notation tells us what pitch a melody starts on, and exactly how much higher or lower the next pitch of the melody is supposed to be. But these 'chicken scratches' merely say 'go higher here,' 'go lower here.' How much higher, how much lower; and higher or lower than *what*? Surely, it might be concluded, this notation does not tell us in any determinate way what compliance with it would be. It needs improvement, one might insist, before the concept of score compliance can validly be applied to it at all.

This reaction, I think, would be a mistake. For it overlooks the fact that this notation, like any notation from any period, exists within a musical practice. No musical notation can be interpreted outside the background knowledge required for its interpretation. And the so-called primitive notation being examined here seems uninterpretable to us, on first reflection, simply because it is being thought about within *our* musical practice rather than within the one of which it was a part: a practice that the great Medievalist and musicologist Leo Treitler tells us was one in which a good deal depended upon the memory of the performer, for which the notation provided reminders rather than instructions. In short, compliance with this notation *is* fully determined by it, given what the performer was supposed to bring to it in the musical period and practice of which it was a part. So, if compliance with it seems to produce a wider range of pitch possibilities than compliance with a modern notation would countenance, that does not mean there was not a class of compliants with that notation. It merely means that that wide range of pitch possibilities *was* compliant with that notation, although a similar range of pitch possibilities would not be in compliance with a modern one.

To nail this point down let us jump some hundreds of years to a notation that looks for all intents and purposes to be a modern one, except for one slight anomaly (Figure 2). To the person only vaguely familiar with what musical notation looks like, this example, the beginning of a sonata for flute and harpsichord by Johann Sebastian

Figure 2. Opening measures of Johann Sebastian Bach's Sonata for Flute and Harpsichord (BWV1034) in figured bass notation

Bach (1685–1750), will look just like what he or she would expect. Unlike the previous example, of early Medieval notation, it is unmistakably musical notation, not chicken scratches. But there *is* something funny about it, which you will see if you look closely. Above the second part, the bass accompaniment, there are little numbers. What are these little numbers doing in a musical notation? More obvious though, I said that this was a sonata for flute and harpsichord. But all Bach seems to have given the harpsichordist to do is to play the bass part with his left hand. What was he supposed to do with his right hand? Stick it in his pocket? Did harpsichord players only use their left hands in Bach's day?

To see what I am driving at, here (in Figure 3) is what the beginning of a sonata for oboe and piano looks like, by the nineteenth-century composer Gaetano Donizetti (1797–1848). Just as one would expect, there is a part for the oboe, and notes to play for both the pianist's right *and* left hands. Notice too that there are no little numbers over the bass notes in Donizetti's piece.

So what is going on in Bach's sonata? The experienced musician will know that the little numbers in Bach's score tell the harpsichordist what chords to play with his right hand. This is called 'figured bass.' And, when the harpsichord player follows the instructions that the numbers in the figured bass give him, he will get something like the result you see in Figure 4, which now *does* look like a sonata for flute and harpsichord, not merely a sonata for flute and a one-handed harpsichordist.

But, again, as in the case of the Medieval notation, the reaction of the reader may be that Bach's notation does not fully determine what the performer, in this case the harpsichord-player, is meant to do, so the concept of score compliance cannot apply to this notational system. Donizetti tells the pianist exactly what to play in both the right and left hands. Bach, however, merely stipulates what chords the harpsichordist is meant to play with his right hand. And the harpsichordist has great leeway in how he plays those basic chords. He can play all sorts of other notes, at his own discretion,

Figure 3. Opening measures of Gaetano Donizzeti's Sonata for Oboe and Piano

just so long as he does not disobey the 'numbers' and the general rules of musical 'grammar' that Bach's period mandates. One accompanist's rendition will, therefore, sound very different from another's. The very notes they play will be different. That cannot happen in performances of Donizetti's sonata. If two pianists play different notes with their right hands, one, or both, are not in compliance with the score. 'Play only the notes I have written,' Donizetti's notation commands us.

Again, however, as in the case of the Medieval notation, the belief that Bach's score has not fully determined compliance with it arises from the mistake of thinking about it in terms of a more recent musical practice rather than in terms of the musical practice of Bach's time, of which figured bass, in particular, was an integral part. It may seem sensible to say that the difference between Bach's notation and Donizetti's is that Donizetti's has fully designated the conditions of score compliance for the right hand of the keyboard part whereas Bach's notation has not done that. Bach's notation is, so to speak, 'vague,' because it does not determine 'exactly' what notes the right hand is to play, as Donizetti's notation does, but merely gives fuzzy boundaries within which a wide range of individual realizations is possible. But that is the wrong way to look at things. Compliance with Bach's score *is* fully determined. What the right hand of the harpsichordist plays, in performing the flute sonata, is in full compliance with Bach's score if it just follows correctly the instructions embodied in the numbers of the figured bass. And these instructions *include* whatever freedom the figured bass not only allows but in a very real sense *commands*. This freedom is part of score compliance in the case of Bach's notation as it is not, for instance, in the case of Donizetti's. Appearances to the contrary notwithstanding, then, Bach's notation determines score compliance just as fully as does Donizetti's.

With this in mind, we can turn to Figure 4, which has something more to tell us about what full compliance with Bach's score really amounts to. The notes in the right hand of the keyboard are part of what is called a modern 'realization' of Bach's figured bass. In Bach's time the right hand of the harpsichord was improvised, in other words, realized on the spot, in performance. It was part of the harpsichordist's training to enable him to read the numbers of the figured bass 'at sight.' It was considered part of the musical performer's 'art.' But many accompanists today do not possess that skill, so 'performing editions' of music with figured bass supply for the contemporary player a written-out version of what he or she is

Figure 4. Opening measures of Johann Sebastian Bach's Sonata for Flute and Harpsichord (BWV 1034) in a modern performing edition

to play with the right hand. The point I want to make with regard to this is that using a modern edition, with a written-out realization of the figured bass, cannot produce a performance in full compliance with the score. And that is because the score calls for an *improvised* performance of the notes in the right hand. An improvised performance produces a sense of spontaneity, and variety among performances of the same work that a prepared, written-out figured bass lacks.

One way of looking at the keyboard accompanist in Bach's day, then, is as a kind of composer himself. The right hand notes in the performance are *his* 'composition.' To realize a figured bass is, in a very real sense, to engage in an act of musical composition. The person who does that is a composer. So what we see here is that at least one kind of musical performance is a form of musical composing. This provides the key to determining just what kind of thing a musical performance is. And that determination is my next task in this chapter.

We know that a performance is, *at least*, a compliance with the score. As well, we now have some idea, in a very practical but informal way, what compliance with a score amounts to, even though we do not have, and will not get in this book, a logical definition or analysis of score compliance. The next problem is how to characterize the musical performance beyond the mere minimal condition of compliance with the score.

Why not begin with the obvious fact that musical performers, in the classical music tradition, at least, are called performing 'artists'? For, if they, as performers, are artists, then what they produce, performances, it would seem to follow, are works of art.

Of course we call lots of people artists without really meaning it. If I say that my plumber is a real 'artist' with blowtorch and monkey wrench, I mean to pay him a compliment; but I hardly mean to say that the pipes and faucets he installs are literally works of art and he of the company of Rembrandt and Shakespeare. I am using 'artist' in what is sometimes called its 'honorific' sense. I am trading on the high value we place on art and artists to bestow extravagant praise on a craftsman. So perhaps that is all I am doing when I call a violinist or pianist a performing 'artist.'

I do not believe so. I do not believe the cases are the same. Think of how odd it would be to say of someone: 'She is a real artist with the violin.' What *else* would she be with a violin? 'He is a real artist with a monkey wrench' makes sense, because a plumber is not an artist and a monkey wrench not customarily a tool of the artistic trade. Contrariwise, it makes no sense to say 'She is a real artist with the violin' just because classical performers are agreed on all hands to be artists and violins *are* some of the tools of the performing artist's trade.

So musical performers appear to be artists, and their performances consequently works of art. But what kind of works? The obvious answer is musical works. And that answer poses yet another question. The work the performer is performing, in most instances, was composed by someone else. Bach composed the flute sonata. Samuel Baron played it. There does not seem to be room in the equation for another work and another composer. There *is* though; and, if we go back for a moment to figured-bass notation, we will see why.

Remember that, when a harpsichordist realizes the figured bass in his right hand, he is really, *literally*, composing; putting notes where none was there before. Not only that, *his* composition will be different from another accompanist's. If he is good enough, there may even be a recognizable style to his figured-bass realization, different from another accompanist's style, if *she* is good enough. If you need an obvious example, Bach's style of realizing the figured bass would be very different from that of his great contemporary's, Georg Frideric Handel. His would be recognizably Bachian; Handel's Handelian.

Suppose, now, that two very good harpsichordists should each improvise in performance the figured bass of the Bach flute sonata quoted from in Figure 2. What would each have produced? Well each has produced a performance of the work. But they are very different performances, even to the extent that the notes in Ralph's performance are different from the notes in Sylvia's. They are different compositions; but yet they are the same composition: Bach's Sonata for Flute (BWV1034). One way to describe their performances is to say that they are two different versions of the same work.

Compare this example to the following. Johannes Brahms composed a set of variations on a theme of Joseph Haydn's (Op. 56B) for two pianos. He later scored it for full orchestra (Op. 56A). We do not think they are two different works, and Brahms did not think so either: that is why he gave them the same 'opus number'—*opus* is Latin for 'work.' But they are different even to the extent of having some different notes, and, of course, very different 'sounds': two pianos sound very different from a symphony orchestra.

The proper musical term for what Brahms did when he made the orchestral variations from the two-piano ones is 'arranging' (or sometimes 'transcribing'). And the result of his labors was not two works but two 'versions' of the same work.

Arranging is a non-trivial enterprise. It requires at its best considerable skill and *artistry*. It is, in reality, a branch of the composer's art; and there are some practitioners who have gained considerable fame for doing it well, at least in musical circles. Good arrangements are 'works of art' themselves, apart from their being arrangements *of* works of art.

So I want to put it to you now that what Ralph and Sylvia have produced, in their accompaniments to Bach's flute sonata, are their 'arrangements' of it: their 'versions.' They have produced instances of the work, compliant with the score, that are, at the same time their particular arrangements of it: their versions. And I want to put it to you, as well, that this is true of all performing, in the classical music tradition. Performing classical music is most akin to, though not, of course, literally, arranging music. The kind of artist the performing artist is is akin to an arranger; and the kind of work of art he or she produces is akin to, but not literally, an arrangement.

Furthermore, to the extent that musical arranging is a branch of the composer's art, musical performers are akin to, but not literally, composers.

Now at this stage of my argument I imagine the reader might be having the following problem. Figured-bass notation is, of course, very favorable to the point I am trying to make. For there is a very clear sense in which realizing a figured bass is, quite literally, composing, and a very clear sense in which Ralph's and Sylvia's performances are different versions of Bach's work: after all, they literally play different notes in their respective right hands. But it is quite another matter with Donizetti's sonata. Two pianists who correctly execute the accompaniment will of necessity be playing the *same* notes. What *they* do is just play the notes that Donizetti has written for them: no more, no less. So whereas Bach's figured-bass notation allows the freedom for the performer to 'compose,' modern notation, of which Donizetti's is an example, does not.

But when we look more closely at what, in the case of modern notation, it means 'just to play the notes as written, no more, no less,' we see that it is in the nature of music as a performing art to allow the performer a large degree of freedom as regards *how*, in what manner he or she is to obey the injunction just to play the notes as written. For the notes, as written, allow for very different interpretations. That is why we can recognize and appreciate the very different styles that different performers evince in their playing.

Performers get diverse tones from their instruments. They make delicate gradations in how long they hold a given note, within allowable limits. They phrase the notes differently. They group them differently, placing emphases on different ones, and de-emphasizing different ones. Some performers play with machine-like precision, others with Romantic abandon. Some play very expressively, others with understated restraint.

Because of these considerable differences in manner of performance, we can clearly recognize performance styles of various kinds. French, German, Italian, English, and American performers may have identifiable national characteristics. Diverse individuals have become world famous for the particular way that they play. And they have produced students who have emulated them, thus establishing a variety of 'schools' of piano playing, violin playing, clarinet playing, and so forth.

Perhaps all of this can best be illustrated by reference to a gadget known as the Melograph. This machine can measure the exact length of time each note of a melody is held, and the exact interval of silence between notes, in any individual's performance, and record them on a visual display. And when you look at the differences that the Melograph records, between two performances of the *same* melody, you will see that performers play different notes, even while obeying the injunction just to play the notes as written, no more, no less. Thus, although figured-bass notation may be a more obvious example of how different performers play different notes, the Melograph shows us that, even where the composer has written out all and only those notes that the performer is to play, as in Donizetti's notation, what results is: different performers, different notes.

As long as music remains a performing art in this tradition, performances of the same work will differ markedly. That is part of the 'contract' between performers and composers in any period in the history of Western art music for which the notation survives and the tradition is recoverable. The composer, in other words, expects the performer to be an artist in his or her own right, at least from the time in Western music history where there *is* an identifiable composer and a clearly discernible performance practice. The performer's art is, I have argued, most akin to arranging, the performer's product, the performance, a work of art in its own right, most akin to an 'arrangement': a 'version' of the work. In music, as in all the performing arts, you get two works of art for the price of one.

Now against this analysis of performer and performance that I have been giving, some inroads have been made in our own times, owing mainly to the efforts of historical musicologists, and a movement they have spawned that I shall call, as some others do, the 'historically authentic performance' movement. I shall conclude this chapter with a discussion of the movement so named, and of the further light it may cast on the nature of musical performance, or, rather, how the nature of musical performance might change under its influence.

I said that there is a kind of contract between the composer and the performer. It might be stated this way. The performer is under contract to play *what* the composer has written. But the contract also enjoins the performer to exercise his or her artistry as to the manner in which what the composer has written is played. And I use the word 'enjoins' rather than the weaker 'allows' or 'permits' quite intentionally to emphasize that being an artist in his or her own right, a performing artist and not merely the 'composer's machine', is not the performer's option to choose or not to choose but the performer's obligation under the contract. The relation between composer and performer has traditionally been one in which the performer is not merely permitted freedom to exercise his or her artistry but required to do so, and admired for doing so well. The composer, under this dispensation, expects the performer to produce a 'performance work of art.' This is what music's being a performance art amounts to.

But it is not so easy to separate what the composer has written from the manner in which what is written is to be played. For the composer writes not only notes but performance instructions as well: indications as to *how*, in what manner, he or she wishes the notes to be played. Thus, as the reader can see in referring back to Figures 2 and 3, Bach has written, in Italian, at the beginning of the first movement of his flute sonata, Adagio ma non tanto, which means, slow, but not too slow. Of course, 'slow, but not too slow' leaves the performers some considerable leeway in regard to the tempo at which they can play this movement. How slow is 'slow' and how slow is 'not too slow'? Nevertheless, it seems clear that performers who might play it Presto, which means very fast, would be disobeying the composer's instructions. It seems equally clear that in this case they would not be playing what the composer has written, would not be playing the composer's notes. For a note is not merely a pitch but a pitch with a certain duration. So to play notes in a very fast tempo that Bach wanted played in a more or less slow tempo would not be to play Bach's notes, nor, needless to say, to achieve the musical effects Bach wanted to achieve. (The 'same notes' played Presto will have a very different character from what they would have if played Adagio ma non tanto.)

The instructions composers put in their scores as to the manner in which they want their notes performed are usually described as expressing their 'performance intentions.' 'Intention' is probably not the best word: 'wishes,' 'suggestions,' and perhaps 'commands' would do better, in my opinion, because they connote the degrees of influence such instructions were meant to have, and ought to have, on the performer. It is one thing for the performer to ignore the composer's command: Adagio ma non tanto, quite another to ignore his suggestion, forte (i.e. loud), when, in the particular circumstances in which she finds herself, she decides mezzo forte (i.e. half-loud) might work better. But I am afraid that 'intention' is too firmly entrenched to be dislodged from the vocabulary of music aesthetics at this late date, so for the remainder of what I have to say in this chapter 'intention' will have to do.

Now I don't think it is a matter of dispute that Adagio ma non tanto is an expression of Bach's performing intention for his flute sonata (BWV1034) that is as much a part of that musical composition as the notes he has written for the flute. Even though there may be a range of speeds that would fall under the instruction Adagio ma non tanto, playing it Allegro (fast), or Presto (very fast) would just be plain wrong—as wrong as playing the first note of the flute part E instead of B.

From the time of Bach to the present, composers have tended to put more and more detailed instructions into their scores with regard to how they intend their music to be performed. Nevertheless, there are always decisions that the performer must make for herself. How are they to be made?

Let me begin to answer that question with an example. The tempo indication Bach put at the beginning of his flute sonata's first movement tells us in no uncertain terms what his performing intention was in that regard. But such tempo indications are very frequently lacking in the musical scores of Bach's time. When they are lacking, how is the performer to decide at what tempo to play? Well, shouldn't it then just be up to the performer? Isn't the composer saying: 'this one *you* decide'? Not necessarily.

Staying with the example of Bach's flute sonata, we may observe that it has four movements that Bach has marked: Adagio ma non tanto (slow but not too slow); Allegro (fast); Andante (moderately slow); and Allegro again. This work is an example of the form called the church sonata. It is always in four movements: slow, fast, slow, fast. The other kind of sonata cultivated in Bach's time, known as the chamber sonata, is in three movements: fast, slow, fast.

Suppose now that you find a manuscript from Bach's time of a four-movement work entitled Sonata for Flute and Figured Bass, with no tempo indications at all at the beginnings of the movements. Should you play the movements at any speeds you like just because the composer has not left written instructions in his score? Of course not. The composer's intentions as to the tempi at which these movements are to be played are easily inferred from the fact that the piece is a sonata in four movements, therefore a church sonata, and the historical knowledge that such sonatas, in Bach's time, always alternate slow, fast, slow, fast. So, if the performers of this sonata were to play the movements (say) fast, slow, fast, slow, this would be as retrograde to the composer's intentions as if they did the same with the Bach sonata, where the tempi are clearly marked. It would clearly be a case of not playing the correct notes.

This, of course, is but one example of the ways in which composers' intentions can be inferred by means of historical knowledge applied to the interpretations of scores that may lack specific instructions in this regard. Let me adduce two others preparatory to making an important general point.

Modern musicians play with what is called vibrato—literally 'vibrations.' It is a technique by which the instrumentalist slightly varies the pitch of a sustained note to give it a liveliness and intensity it would not otherwise have. On string instruments this is accomplished by the performer's shaking his left hand as he holds his finger on the string. (You have probably observed this yourselves at concerts.) Players of woodwinds and brass instruments achieve the same effect by vibrating the diaphragm—the organ below the lungs that helps us in breathing.

Historical evidence strongly suggests that vibrato, although it was known in the eighteenth century, was used seldom, and sparingly. So, it appears, one can confidently infer that Bach and his contemporaries did *not* intend their music to be played with vibrato to anywhere near the extent to which the contemporary instrumentalist employs it. To play this music in the modern way, with regard to vibrato, is to play it incorrectly. If you are playing Bach with a lot of vibrato, in other words, you are not playing the right notes.

It is a historical fact, as well, that musical instruments have undergone significant changes over the past three centuries. This is readily apparent with regard to wind instruments even to the inexpert eye and ear. The modern flute is made of silver, or gold, or platinum, the eighteenth- and nineteenth-century instrument of wood. And, although clarinets, oboes, and bassoons continue to be made of wood, the kind of wood used and, particularly with regard to the oboe, the shape and bore are quite different from their seventeenth- and eighteenth-century ancestors. In addition, the modern woodwinds display an elaborate system of keys and levers almost entirely absent from the seventeenth- and eighteenth-century versions, which have been added to improve intonation and extend the instruments' technical capabilities.

Although not as noticeable to the lay person, violins, violas, cellos, and brass instruments have also undergone significant alterations.

Fiddles have longer necks and different bows. Trumpets and French horns have valves or 'pistons' that enable them to play notes they could not play prior to the nineteenth century. The long and short of it is that the sound of the orchestral ensemble has changed markedly since the time of Bach. The string and woodwind sound is brighter now, the brass sound not as bright. In general, everything is louder, and pitch is higher.

But, with these historical facts of instrumental evolution in mind, we can reach the obvious conclusion that Bach and his contemporaries intended their music to be played on their instruments, not on modern ones, which may have the same names, but sound very different. And, if we do not comply with these intentions in this regard, we are playing their music incorrectly: in other words, we are not playing the right notes.

The performance practices of past musical periods are now the subject of intense scrutiny by historians of music. And the history of performance practice has been pursued not merely out of pure intellectual curiosity, but as a guide to the contemporary performer. What I see as a whole new aesthetic, if you will, of musical performance has arisen from this historical research. In a way, what I shall call the historically authentic performance movement has urged on the performer a different 'contract' with the composer from the traditional one I spoke of earlier. Let me try to explain what I mean.

Consider the case of vibrato. Under the old contract, the performer is free to choose how much or how little vibrato to use, or none at all, for that matter, in this place or that place, on the basis of her own aesthetic judgment and interpretation of the work she is performing. It is part of her 'artistry.' But under the new contract she must use only as much or as little vibrato as was customary during the historical period in which the piece was composed. Another way of putting this is to say that what was part of the manner in which the notes were played has now become part of the notes themselves: part of the work itself. To use vibrato under this new contract is to play the wrong notes, which *neither* contract allows.

Ideally, under the new contract, we could, through historical research, completely determine manner of performance in every detail for any given work in any given period. Just as long as you assume, or prove, that what the composer's performing intentions are constitute part of the work, and that the performance practice of the composer's time, as well as his specific instructions, constitute his intentions, it seems to follow logically that under the new contract the performer ceases to be an artist in her own right and becomes something else. Her performance is not, so to speak, her work of art but a kind of archaeological reconstruction of the composer's optimal performance. The two works, the musical work and the performance work, have coalesced into one work: the one and only authentic performance of the work, which is nothing more nor less than the work itself, since the composer's performing intentions thoroughly determine the manner of performance and constitute part of the work, as surely as do the rhythms and pitches.

Now, of course, no one really thinks that we ever could have perfect historical knowledge of performance practice and the composer's performing intentions for any work in any period. Thus, if the performer's contract is to play only in accordance with them, and have them completely determine her product, it is a contract impossible, in practice, to fulfill. Under the new dispensation, the historically authentic performance movement, there will always be a gap in our knowledge, hence a gap where the performer's own decisions will prevail—decisions dictated by her own taste, judgment, and artistry.

However, it must be observed that, even though both under the old contract and the new there is ample room for the performer's taste and musical judgment to operate in, the aesthetic significance of that taste and judgment is very different. For, whereas, under the former, the gap between performance and work in which taste and judgment are exercised is a cherished, positive aspect of the composer–performer relationship, in the latter it is an unwanted lacuna in our knowledge where taste and judgment prevail by default, as it were, because the composer's intentions are not present to guide. In the original contract the performer's decisions are valued, in the new contract they are grudgingly tolerated. If one has signed on with the historically authentic crew, the assertion that it sounds nice played this way is always overridden by the assertion that it was intended to be played that way.

Are there any arguments to guide us here in determining which of these philosophies of performance is the correct one? One argument that proponents of the historically authentic performance offer is that it is the performer's role, on everyone's philosophy of performance, to execute the composer's *work*, and, since all of the composer's performing intentions, and the musical practice of his times, are part of the work, it follows that to perform the work in the manner of the historically authentic performance is the only way to fulfill that role. To do otherwise is not to play the notes.

I think the problem with this argument is that it simply begs the question in favor of the historically authentic performance. After all, no one really possesses a supportable 'definition' of the musical work that makes all of the composer's performing intentions, expressed and implied, or the performance practice of his times, part of the work. So anyone who defends the traditional contract between composer and performer will simply deny that the work is so constituted. She may with perfect consistency maintain that such explicitly expressed, strong intentions as that a piece be played Adagio ma non tanto are part of the work, whereas whether or not one plays with vibrato, or on modern instruments, or plays with Romantic abandon rather than Classical restraint are the prerogatives of the performer, relative to her judgment and taste, not mandated by the score.

Another argument in favor of the historically authentic performance, offered more often by musicians and musicologists than philosophers, perhaps, is that playing a work as exactly as possible in accordance with the composer's performing intentions and performance practice of his times will of necessity result in the *best* performance. That is because, so it is insisted, the composer is the best judge of how his work is to be performed. He has made it, and is more intimately involved with it than anyone else could possibly be. He has composed it with exactly those performance means and practices in mind that exist in his own time and place. He has carefully adjusted it to those and just those conditions. It is in a sort of delicate balance vis-à-vis those performing intentions and conditions that must be upset by any change in either: no change in either can be a change for the better but only a change for the worse.

Against this argument it can be urged that there is no convincing reason to believe its basic assumptions; for assumptions, really, is all they are. Performers may well find ways of rendering a composer's work that are better than the ways he had in mind. And, as for the notion that there is such an intricate, delicate adjustment of the work to the prevailing conditions under which it was first performed, there is no evidence to support it, only the insistence of its defenders. It has all the appearance of an article of faith that exists for the purpose of justifying the historically authentic performance rather than a principle established on independent grounds. The only possible evidence for its truth would be the finding, over time, that historically authentic performances are better than other kinds of performance. But that, of course, is exactly the point at issue.

It is also important to notice that there are certain questionable aspects to the whole agenda of the historically authentic performance movement. It is frequently asserted by defenders of the movement that its goals are (1) to perform music as closely as possible in accordance with the composer's performing intentions for the purpose of (2) producing a musical sound just like the musical sound the composer's contemporaries would have heard. Both goals are highly problematic.

For one thing, composers' intentions, as the American philosopher Randall Dipert has pointed out, may be at different 'levels,' so to speak. A composer may wish a passage to be played on a certain instrument, in a certain way, to achieve a certain musical effect. He has two intentions, then: what Dipert calls a 'high-order' intention to achieve the musical effect he wants, and a 'low-order' intention to achieve the effect with a certain means. But suppose, in the circumstances we find ourselves in today, the composer's high-order intention can no longer be achieved by following his low-order intention. Should we find our own means to achieve his high-order intention? Or should we doggedly adhere to his low-order intention? Common sense suggests the former. But in practice the proponents of the historically authentic performance seem to stick with the composer's low-order intentions come what may: hence the almost obsessive attempt to reproduce a performance as close as possible to what it would have been, *physically*, in the composer's own time and place.

Furthermore, what it means to carry out someone's intentions is not at all as obvious as defenders of the historically authentic performance make out. What they fail, in general, to take into account are what are called 'counterfactual intentions.' We must ask, in other words, not just 'How *did* Bach intend this piece to be played?' but 'How *would* Bach want his piece to be played today?' Obviously Bach did not intend his music to be played on twentieth-century instruments any more than the framers of the US Constitution intended private citizens of the United States to be allowed the possession of assault weapons. Modern instruments were not known to Bach, or assault weapons to Franklin, Jefferson, and the rest. But what we mean to ask, when we ask what the framers intended about the right to bear arms, is what they would have intended now, today, given the existence of modern weaponry, and what they wrote in the Constitution. And what we *ought* to be asking about Bach's intentions is how he would want his music to be played, now, today, given that he had a choice between his instruments and ours. The assumption of the historically authentic performance proponents that we are necessarily carrying out Bach's 'real' intentions by playing his music on *his* instruments is completely unjustified. What we should be asking about Bach, with regard to *all* aspects of performance, is not only what he intended but what he *would have intended if*. . . .

Finally, let us consider for a moment what might be taken for the ultimate result of the historically authentic performance if it is successful: what, in other words, it is meant to achieve. It is, one supposes, the production of the musical sounds the composer's own audience would have heard: if you will, the 'historical sound.' What it would mean to achieve that is not altogether clear.

A historically authentic performance of a work by Bach, for example, will typically be designed to reproduce the 'Bach sound' by using only those physical means at Bach's disposal: a relatively small orchestra, say, fifteen string players altogether, and the appropriate winds and brass instruments. The instruments would all be replicas of the instruments employed in Bach's time, and the manner of performance as much like Bach's as historical research, at its present stage, can determine. Would such a performance produce the 'Bach sound'?

If you mean by the 'Bach sound' the physical vibrations of air—call it the 'physical sound'—that a performance in Bach's day, under Bach's direction, would have produced, then the historically authentic performance would, more or less, produce it. But if you mean by the 'Bach sound' the musical 'object' as heard by the listener, then it is quite another matter. For instance, a Bach-sized orchestra sounds very small and intimate to us. For we are used to orchestras of 100 players and more. And we hear historically authentic performances as reconstructions of a past tradition, whereas Bach's audiences, obviously, did not hear them that way at all, but as the sounds of their times. Let us call this other sound 'musical sound.'

Now which sound is the 'historical sound'? Is it the physical sound or the musical sound? If you answer the physical sound, then the historically authentic performance method does produce it, or at least something like it. But if your answer is the musical sound, then it does not. And it is hard to find aesthetic reasons for wanting to produce the physical sound rather than the musical sound. For it's the musical sound, after all, that matters: that is the bearer of the music's aesthetic and artistic properties. Thus we arrive at the somewhat paradoxical conclusion that the best way to produce the historically authentic Bach sound may be not on Bach's instruments in Bach's manner but on our instruments in our manner.

I have presented in this chapter what might be called two 'philosophies of musical performance.' Which one is the right one?

When two philosophies of something contradict one another, it is generally agreed upon that they can't both be right. For the philosophy of something is supposed to tell us what the nature of that something is, and either that philosophy has got it right or it hasn't.

Now, if the two philosophies of musical performance I have just presented to you are philosophies in the sense of telling us what the nature of performance *is*, what it *really is*, then only one of them can be right, although perhaps both of them may be wrong. But there is another way of looking at them, namely, as examples, if you will, of 'practical philosophy.' Looked at in this way, one purports to tell us what its proponents think is the 'best' way to do something, that is to say, the best way to perform Western art music. And I do not think there *is* a 'best' way to perform all classical music. There are only better and worse ways to perform individual works. Furthermore, it is your taste and my taste, your musical ear and mine, that constitute the final court of appeal.

But the good news is that, with regard to musical performance, we can have it both ways. The so-called historically authentic manner of performance is now flourishing alongside what is sometimes called 'mainstream' performance practice. You can hear your Bach on modern instruments, with vibrato, and on 'antique' instruments without. There are, of course, the zealots who will have it only one way or the other. For most of us, though, pluralism is to be preferred.

With the discussion of musical performance I draw to the end of my story. There are, of course, many more questions of musical philosophy than those I have raised in these pages, and many more aspects to the questions I *have* raised that I have not been able to explore. But there is *one* question outstanding that for me has always been paramount.

Most of the music in the world, past and present, as I have had occasion to mention before, is sung music: music with a meaningful text. Pure instrumental music, associated so closely with the Western musical tradition, is neither the most common nor the most popular. And there is something about it that is profoundly puzzling. It is sound, of course: sound intentionally produced for people to listen to in rapt attention. But it is sound that, unlike speech, does not convey any readily apparent message or meaning. That being the case, why in the world do we listen to it (at least those of us who *do*)? What does it have to offer us if not communicated meaning? That question perplexes me mightily, as it does others. And I can think of no better way to end this introductory exploration of musical philosophy than by raising and, I hope, at least *beginning* to answer it.

CHAPTER 13

Why should you Listen?

Why should you listen to symphonies, sonatas, string quartets, and the rest of what constitute the absolute music repertoire? On first reflection that sounds like a pretty silly question (as do so many other questions that we think of as the peculiar domain of philosophy). Such music has given pleasure for centuries to generations of listeners of all kinds. It is very likely it will give pleasure to you if you are willing to take the trouble to listen in an appropriate way. *That's* why you should listen. Do you need a better reason?

But that would be to misconstrue the real significance of the question, Why should you listen? Of course the question already assumes that you know absolute music gives pleasure or satisfaction or whatever else you think best describes your experience. The question really is, rather, Why should you want *this* kind of pleasure or satisfaction instead of some other kind? And *that* question has some depth to it, because of what we think absolute music *is* and because of what some of us, anyway, think it *isn't*.

What we all think absolute music *is*, needless to say, is fine art, along with painting, sculpture, the poem, the play, the novel, and, in our own times, the moving picture. What many of us think it *isn't*

—which all of those other things so predominantly *are*—is representational or imbued with linguistic content. These two, what absolute music is, and what it isn't, have been, since the eighteenth century, in continual conflict with one another. We all feel this conflict. And it is this conflict that lies at the heart of the perplexity I have tried to express in the question, Why should you listen?

The thinker who first understood and expressed clearly the perplexity about absolute music of which I have been speaking is Schopenhauer. He also had the glimmering, although confusedly, of what I think is at least part of the right answer. So it is to Schopenhauer's philosophy of music that we must now return.

But before we do that, I want to make it clear that there isn't *one* answer to the question, Why should you listen? There are many answers, and some of them have already been given in earlier chapters of this book. For, wherever I have tried to explain what the elements of enhanced formalism are, wherever I have tried to reveal what I think are the things in absolute music that we enjoy, and how we enjoy them, I have been giving answers to the question, Why should you listen? However, there is , I want to suggest, a more general answer to our question, Why should you listen?, to which the other answers, so to speak, contribute. And *that* is the answer I want to pursue here, in my final chapter, with Schopenhauer's help.

Schopenhauer thought that all of us organize our world, *the* world, under the categories that comprise what he called the Fourfold Root of the Principle of Sufficient Reason. The Principle of Sufficient Reason, which was put forward by the great German philosopher Gottfried Wilhelm von Leibniz (1646–1716), simply states that *nothing happens without a reason*, there is a sufficient reason for everything there is and everything that happens. That doesn't sound very controversial, and I imagine all of my readers would agree to it. It merely says that nothing exists or happens without there being a reason or cause or explanation for it, whether or not we know what the reason or cause or explanation is.

Schopenhauer called Leibniz's Principle of Sufficient Reason the Fourfold Root of the Principle of Sufficient Reason—let's just call it the Principle, for short—because he thought the reasons for things and events were framed in four different ways: in terms of cause and effect, premise and conclusion, motive and action, space and time. Thus, the Chicago fire was caused by Mrs O'Leary's cow kicking over a lantern, the conclusion that Socrates is mortal follows from the premises that all men are mortal and that Socrates is a man, Orestes killed Clytaemestra from the motive of revenge, and, finally, all that we perceive and encounter occurs within the confines (if you will) of space and time, the conditions of our experience. These categories, which comprise the Principle, rule, indeed dominate, our practical and theoretical lives: our lives as doers and thinkers.

With the Principle in hand, I go on to Schopenhauer's theory of the fine arts. We are, as Schopenhauer saw it, rather like slaves to the Principle. It gives us no rest, but drives us relentlessly on to reason from effect to cause, action to motive, inference to conclusion, in a never-ending quest for a finality we can never achieve, always under the domination of space and time, the conditions under which we are compelled to perceive our world. Schopenhauer compares the human condition to the Wheel of Ixion, in the Greek myth. Ixion, in the myth, made amorous advances to Hera, the wife of Zeus. As his punishment for this outrage, Zeus bound Ixion to a wheel that is forever whirled through the air. Like Ixion, we are bound to a wheel, the wheel of the Principle, around which we revolve in a never-ending dance of unmitigated striving.

Unlike Ixion in the myth, however, we have a means of at least temporary escape: a temporary exit from the wheel of life, the wheel of the Principle. It is the fine arts. For it is the gift of the artist to be able to liberate himself from the thraldom of the Principle, at least for intermittent periods of time. In other words, the artist is able to see the world, or, in a sense, *see through* it, free of the Principle. He is able, in something like a mystical illumination, to experience things outside cause and effect, premise and conclusion, motive and action, space and time. When he does this, he perceives, through the veil of appearances, the eternal ideas that lie behind. These ideas he can represent in works of art that *we* can perceive and that, while we do, liberate *us* from Ixion's wheel, allowing us to see what the artist saw. Art is *our* liberation from the Wheel of Ixion, the wheel of life, the Principle.

But, among the arts, music, on Schopenhauer's view, is very special, as we saw in an earlier chapter. The other arts reveal the ideas behind the appearances. But *music* reveals what is behind the ideas: the basis of all reality, the striving metaphysical will. (Just why Schopenhauer thought *will* is somehow the most basic reality of the world is an obscure question that there is no need for us to grapple with here.)

Now I do not expect readers of this book to put much credence in these views of Schopenhauer's, which must seem to them, as they do to me, extremely bizarre in many ways. But there are two ideas here that it seems to me do have value for us if we alter them appropriately to our purposes. They are the ideas of liberation, and of music's special, unique status among the fine arts. Let us look at music's uniqueness first.

Schopenhauer realized that absolute music is very different from the other fine arts. Unlike many of his predecessors, however, he did not think that it is *so* different from them that that difference disqualifies music as a fine art. He argued that our experience of music is very much like our experience of the other arts, and that, since our experience of the other arts depends so heavily on their representational character, it must follow that music is representational too. What makes it unique is not that it fails to represent but the uniqueness of *what* it represents. All the other arts represent the ideas. Music alone represents the will.

Now Schopenhauer was certainly right that absolute music is unique among the fine arts (although that does require some qualifications to come). He was quite wrong, however, about where that uniqueness lies. It lies not in the uniqueness of what music represents but in the fact, as I have argued throughout this book, that absolute music does not represent at all: it is simply not a representational art.

This brings us to Schopenhauer's second idea: that the fine arts are *liberating*. Again, I think there is some truth here, but a different truth from the one that Schopenhauer sees. For what makes music unique among the fine arts is not only the negative fact that it does not represent (or in any other way possess 'content'). There is also the positive fact that, *unlike* the other fine arts, music alone *is* the liberating one. The two facts are closely related.

If we are to salvage from Schopenhauer's reflections on the fine arts anything of value for ourselves, we must, I think it is obvious, dismiss straightaway his way of structuring the world into appearance, idea, and will. I cannot believe that this world-structure can form any part of our world view, which, I take it, is that of modern science, at least in so far as the lay person can comprehend it (although I am not ruling out the possibility that, for many people, the scientific world view exists side by side with a religious world view as well). And, if we reinterpret Schopenhauer as saying that the fine arts liberate us from thinking about the world we experience every day of our lives, the world in which we live and die, or, in his way of describing it, the world of cause and effect, motive and action, inference and conclusion, space and time, then I think he is seriously mistaken.

Leaving aside for the moment the art of absolute music, it seems clear that all of the other fine arts, painting, sculpture, drama, the movies, and literary fiction in general, have, for most of their history, had the 'real world' as their subject matter. I will call these arts, when they do have real-world content, the arts of content or, for short, the 'contentful arts.'

To be sure, various works of the contentful arts differ a great deal as regards their involvement with the 'real world.' Works of fantasy distort it considerably, so-called escapist art makes it better for us than it really is , and another way of describing that kind of art is as 'wish-fulfillment' art. But even such genres of the contentful arts that greatly distort 'reality' are in touch with it. More important, much of the art we consider truly great or profound is just that art—particularly literary art and dramatic art—that raises for us the profoundly difficult, disturbing moral, political, social, and philosophical problems of the real world: just the world of cause and effect, premise and conclusion, motive and action, space and time, from which Schopenhauer thought it rescues us. In short, Schopenhauer to the contrary notwithstanding, the fine arts, absolute music excepted, have been, for most of their history, the contentful arts; and as such they have been knee deep in reality.

But there remains the art of absolute music to consider. And it is here, it seems obvious to me, that Schopenhauer's dream of an art that liberates from the Wheel of Ixion is fully realized. Music, alone of the fine arts, makes us free of the world of our everyday lives. Thus Schopenhauer turns out to have been right. Music *is* unique. Its uniqueness, however, does not lie in its unique object of representation; rather, in the fact that it does not represent, does not possess content at all. Hence it is unique in the fact that it alone of the fine arts is the 'liberating' art. Furthermore, Schopenhauer turns out to have been right, too, that fine art frees us from the world of the Principle—from the world of our practical, philosophical, political, existential *angst*. He was surely wrong, though, in his ascribing this to fine art across the board. For the contentful arts, at least in many, if not most, of their most admired and valued instances, do just the opposite: they plunge us into our world with a vengeance, and compel us to think deeply about it. Only music, music alone, is the true art of liberation. And it is important enough that Schopenhauer had an inkling that there must be some point at which fine art and liberation from the Principle intersect: that point is absolute music. Let us look at the nature of 'musical liberation' (if I may so call it) a bit more closely.

It seems appropriate to describe contentful works of art, at least those of the more important or elaborate kind, as presenting us with 'worlds' to inhabit imaginatively or, perhaps, to observe: 'art worlds,' so to speak. Different works present, of course, different worlds. But each world is a version of our own. They may be greatly altered worlds, as in the case of fantasy or science fiction. They may be close relations of our world, as in the case of 'realistic' film, novel, and drama.

It is, of course, part of the charm, the attraction of contentful works of art that they afford us exit from our world and entrance, at least as observers, into theirs; and sometimes that is all we want or require. But even so, many, if not most, of the contentful works of art we place the highest value on present us with versions of our world that reflect back on it in ways that, far from being 'escapist,' compel us to think of our own world and its—which is to say, *our*—problems. Perhaps an example might help.

In his wonderful film trilogy, *Marius*, *Fanny*, and *César*, Marcel Pagnol presents us with what can best be described as a 'world': a cinematic 'art world,' if you will. Anyway, that is the way I, and most of the people I know who have seen these movies, think of them. In this world, full of richly developed and generally lovable characters, the young people, Fanny and Marius, fall passionately in love. But Marius has the *Wanderlust*. He wants to sail away on a ship, experience the sea, and go to exotic places. He definitely does not want to remain in Marseilles and live his father's César's, settled, middle-class life as a café-owner whose greatest pleasure is to sit around with his friends, arguing and drinking pastice.

Marius finally gets a berth on a sailing vessel. Should Fanny tell him that she is carrying his child? If she does, he will certainly 'do the right thing' by her, marry, settle down, and eventually go into his father's business. She decides not to reveal her secret because she feels Marius will forever resent the loss of his chance for adventure. He sails away, leaving poor Fanny in her (to him unknown) predicament, from which she is rescued by marriage to the elderly Panisse, a kind widower who provides a home for Fanny, becomes father to her son, and saves her the disgrace of having her child out of wedlock.

Marius, however, has second thoughts, returns to Marseilles, only to find his beloved Fanny married to Panisse. The young people fall into each other's arms in a passionate embrace only to be confronted by César, who lectures them on their duty to renounce their love rather than hurt the good Panisse, who has been both a devoted husband to Fanny and a loving father to her child, even though he is not his biological son. The lovers acquiesce in César's moral assessment of their situation, and Marius departs once again, this time to a town some few miles from Marseilles, where he opens a car repair shop. From here he watches his son grow into early adolescence without ever revealing to him his true identity, even after, by accident, they meet and become friends.

When the boy is about 15 years old, Panisse dies. And finally, after these years of renunciation, Fanny and Marius marry and, we hope, 'live happily ever after.'

The world of Pagnol's trilogy is, needless to say, not my world, nor yours (unless, of course, you are the son of a café-owner, or the daughter of a fishmonger, in Marseilles, France). It is, nevertheless, certainly a world that we are meant not only to observe, but to think about. Did Fanny do the right thing in not telling Marius that she was pregnant? (Consider the chain of unhappy events her decision initiated.) Did César give Fanny and Marius wise counsel in convincing them to renounce their love so as to avoid hurting Panisse and violating César's code of middle-class morality? (Think of the hurt done to Marius's son, who was to grow into adolescence without having or benefiting from the companionship of his biological father, not to mention the unhappiness caused to Fanny and Marius.) Pagnol leaves no doubt in the viewer's mind about what his (Pagnol's) answers to these questions are. But it seems clear as well that part of the experience we are meant to have in viewing these films is the experience of questioning *for ourselves* whether Fanny, Marius, César, and the rest acted wisely or well in the circumstances. And, because these characters are, after all, not so unlike us, their circumstances possible circumstances for us, when we think about their problems, we are thinking about *our* problems too. Far from giving us respite from our world and the Principle, such works of art as Marcel Pagnol's trilogy, which form so large a part of the art of the West, our art, plunge us into our own lives and our own problems in the most intense way.

Absolute music too presents us with worlds of art into which we enter or, if you prefer, that we observe. Beethoven's Fifth Symphony, like Pagnol's trilogy, is an art world of its own: a sound world. But, unlike *Marius*, *Fanny*, and *César*, it is not a version of our world: it is a world unto itself, as are all the art worlds of music alone. Beethoven's Fifth Symphony is truly a world full of sound and fury, signifying nothing. That is not a defect in it. To be 'senseless'—to lack semantic or representational content—is not, as we have seen earlier, something 'missing' from an artifact that was never meant to possess it in the first place.

To be sure, we do use words of our ordinary, workaday world to describe absolute music. We say that Beethoven's Fifth Symphony has the qualities of conflict, and resolution, struggle, and, in the end, triumph. But they are the struggle, drama, conflict, and triumph of no one. They are the phenomenal, heard properties of the music itself. And it is worthy of note that absolute music, unlike any other art of the West that I know of, can be described in a purely technical language that has no application at all to anything external to music itself: a symptom, I think, of its self-contained character.

Thus absolute music is truly the liberating art that Schopenhauer sought, wrongly, in all of the arts. And this liberating function is, so to speak, absolute music's overarching, comprehensive charm. Other charms it has as well, and we have become acquainted with them in previous chapters. But the joy of liberation it is always ready to give us, along with the rest, if we are receptive.

Here one may begin to wonder about just what kind of 'charm' this liberating charm of absolute music might really amount to. It sounds more like, as it were, a negative rather than a positive one: that is to say, the removal of something unpleasant rather than the imparting of a real, captivating satisfaction—the kind of hedonic 'rush' that music-lovers get when they listen to the great masterpieces of the absolute music repertoire.

I think this negative view of music's liberating power can be dispelled if we give a little attention to just what the cessation of pain or discomfort, at least in certain circumstances, really amounts to. In Plato's famous dialogue, the *Phaedo*, which purports to give an account of Socrates' last day, before his execution by the Athenian state, Socrates is represented as maintaining that the experience of ceasing to be in pain is itself a positive pleasure. And I think that if you recall your own experience of intense pain giving way to release from it you will see what Socrates was getting at. Freedom from pain itself, particularly when experienced for protracted periods of time, is not particularly noted. To put it directly, you just get used to it. What Socrates was talking about is the *process* of going *from* a state of pain to a state of its absence. It is that experience, the process of liberation from pain, that, Socrates was telling us, is a positive pleasure. And my own experience is that he was right: it is one of the most intense pleasures possible, particularly, I think, when you are reflecting on it while it is happening. Whether it is your experience as well you must decide for yourselves (although I hope your pains will be few and far between).

I am arguing, then, that listening to absolute music is, among other things, the experience of going from our world, with all of its trials, tribulations, and ambiguities, to *another* world, a world of pure sonic structure, that, because it need not be interpreted as a representation or description of our world, but can be appreciated on its own terms alone, gives us the sense of liberation that I have found appropriate to analogize with the pleasurable experience we get in the process of going from a state of intense pain to its cessation. I have emphasized that this feeling of liberation, like the liberation from pain, is a positive rather than a negative feeling: that it is a palpable pleasure or satisfaction rather than simply a release from something bad. And I am emboldened to think that this is perhaps what Schopenhauer had in mind when he wrote of the arts as giving us release from the Wheel of Ixion.

I should add, by the by, that one needn't share Schopenhauer's generally pessimistic view of human existence to appreciate the liberation from the affairs of 'real life as we know it' that absolute music, so I am arguing, provides. You don't have to be downcast or miserable to feel the liberating uplift upon entering the world of music alone: in other words, you don't have to wait until you need 'therapy' to go to a concert. I think there is always some burden to be lifted by the musical experience. But nor am I denying that this liberating effect is *particularly* potent when one *is* downcast or miserable: weighed down by the petty or powerful aggravations of the human condition. Again, I ask the reader to determine for him- or herself whether my experience in this regard is shared.

Many of my readers will, I am sure, have found the foregoing reflections on the liberating power of absolute music too speculative and highfalutin for their taste. For those who do, I suggest that the other charms of absolute music described in previous chapters as constituting what I called 'enhanced formalism' will suffice as an account of *why you should listen*. But, for those who are willing to follow me a bit further in this speculative venture, I will continue in this vein for just a little while longer.

Unlike Schopenhauer, I have maintained that music is unique in possessing the liberating power of which I have just now been speaking. But I also added the warning that the uniqueness claim would need to be somewhat qualified. Now is the time to do so. For, strictly speaking, neither is music totally unique among the fine arts in this power of liberation, nor is this power confined to the fine arts alone. There are other human works and activities that also, as part of *their* charm, possess the power to transport us to pure structural worlds.

Among the fine arts in the Western tradition, what is sometimes called 'non-objective,' sometimes 'abstract,' visual art is, at least on first reflection, art of pure aesthetic structure. And such non-artistic activities as chess, or, even more obviously, the contemplation of pure mathematics provide, it has seemed to many participants in these endeavors, just that kind of experience of pure aesthetic structure that I have been ascribing here to absolute music. Furthermore, if the experience of pure sonic structure, in absolute music, provides liberation, there is no reason to believe that the contemplation of pure visual structure, pure mathematical structure, or an elegant game of chess does not do so as well.

Pure mathematics—that is to say, mathematics not being used as part of the scientific representation of nature—is a particularly interesting case in this regard, just because it is so typically described by mathematicians in aesthetic terms. One proof is frequently preferred to another because it is more elegant or more beautiful or, in general, more aesthetically satisfying. Philosophers have argued over the significance of aesthetic considerations in pure mathematics. But few have denied their presence.

What, then, is left of the 'uniqueness' claim for absolute music, given these considerations? Perhaps this: that among the fine arts in the Western tradition, absolute music has completely overshadowed the rest as *the* pure abstract art *überhaupt*. Apparently, the sense of hearing and not the sense of sight is by far the most amenable to being pleased and intrigued by pure formal structure, in the absence of representational or semantic content. *Why* this should be so is a matter of speculation and debate. And for present purposes we will have to leave it at that.

With these considerations of what I have called music's 'liberating power' I have reached a reasonable place, I think, to conclude my introduction to a philosophy of music. It is *my* end but not *the* end. There are many topics I could go on from here to discuss, and they are no less worthy of discussion than the ones I have already discussed. However, a book must end somewhere, and for this book here, with the question of Why should you listen?, seems as good a place as any.

But before I close I want to give my reader an important bit of prudential advice. *Don't believe anything I have written*. This is an introduction to *my* philosophy of music. There is probably no view I have put forward here that enjoys universal assent. I have tried to give a fair account of the opposition in the appropriate places, but I am certain that the opposition will not think so. So beware! You had better give the opposition a separate hearing.

The point of an introduction to any branch of philosophy ought to be not to convey information but to get the reader to think about the relevant questions as an independent agent. It was to make this point that I employed, in my epigraph, the quotation from Plato's *Phaedo* in which Socrates adjures his disciples to think for themselves, after he is gone. It is the only quotation in this book. I could think of no better way of beginning it than with Socrates' admonition. And I can think of no better way of ending it. 'If you think that what I say is true, agree with me; if not, oppose it with every argument and take care that in my eagerness I do not deceive myself and you and, like a bee, leave my sting in you when I go.'

READINGS
AND REFERENCES

Chapter 1   *Philosophy of . . .*

There are many short introductions to philosophy meant for the novice and beginning student. Some of them are good, some indifferent. But two stand out head and shoulders above the rest. First, there is Bertrand Russell's enduring classic, *The Problems of Philosophy*, originally published in 1912, and still going strong. And for a more recent take on what philosophy is, for beginners, one cannot recommend too highly *What Philosophy Is: A Guide to the Elements* (1968), by the distinguished American philosopher Arthur C. Danto.

The philosophy of music being a branch of the philosophy of art, the beginning student may also find useful a general introduction to the latter subject. As with general introductions to philosophy, there are many, and some that are good. A perennial favorite is Richard Wollheim, *Art and its Objects: An Introduction to Aesthetics* (1968). Also highly recommended is the more recent *Philosophy of Art: A Contemporary Introduction* (1999), by Noel Carroll.

A word about 'Wee Willie' Keeler. He was born William Henry Keeler, in 1872, in Brooklyn, New York. He was one of the smallest men ever to play Major League Baseball, being a scant 5′4″, 140 pounds. Among his many astounding statistics, his lifetime batting average was 341, which any baseball fan will tell you is pretty darn great. In 1939 he was one of the first two dozen players named to the Baseball Hall of Fame. Actually, his complete 'philosophy of baseball was': 'Keep a clear eye, and hit 'em where they ain't.' (I am grateful for all of this information, and much more, to Ted Cohen.)

Chapter 2 *A Little History*

Plato's reflections on music and the other arts are to be found largely in the *Republic*, books III and X. There are many good translations available. Book VIII, chapter 5, of the *Politics* is the source of Aristotle's reflections on the musical emotions. But the *Poetics* is also to be consulted for further illumination. Both the *Politics* and the *Poetics* are available in English translation.

The relevant writings of the *Camerata*, on musical expression and other related matters, can be found, in English, in the historical anthology *Source Readings in Music History* (1950), edited by Oliver Strunk. They are contained in section VIII.

Those interested in Descartes's theory of the emotions will find that there is at least one complete translation into English of *The Passions of the Soul* (1966), as well as extracts from it in various anthologies of Descartes's writings.

The most important and influential musical treatise outlining a theory of the musical emotions on Cartesian principles is by the eighteenth-century composer and theorist Johann Mattheson (1681–1764). It is called, in German, *Der vollkommene Capellmeister*, and has been translated into English, in its entirety, by Ernest C. Harriss (1981). It is not for the faint of heart and should be consulted only by those most devoted to the history of the subject. The core of Mattheson's account of the emotions in music can be found in part I, chapter III, and part II, chapter XIV. These portions have been excerpted and translated by Hans Lenneberg in the *Journal of Music Theory*, 2/1–2 (1958).

Those interested in a full account of Schopenhauer's theory of music, and its place in his theory of the fine arts should consult vol. I, book III, of *The World as Will and Idea* (1819), as well as vol. II, chapters XXIX–XXXIX. Volume II was published many years after the first volume (1844) as a supplement to it. The complete work, in two volumes, exists in two English translations. The older is by R. B. Haldane and J. Kemp (1896); the more recent by E. F. J. Payne, under the title *The World as Will and Representation* (1958).

Susanne Langer's account of music is to be found in chapter 8 of *Philosophy in a New Key* (1942). But it will be more readily understandable if the previous seven chapters are read as well. Those interested in pursuing further Langer's aesthetic philosophy will want to consult, as well, her later work, *Feeling and Form* (1953).

Carroll C. Pratt's *The Meaning of Music* (1931) is a pioneer work in twentieth-century music aesthetics, and is still well worth consulting by the interested reader.

Chapter 3   *Emotions in the Music*

For Charles Hartshorne's complete discussion of expressive qualities the reader is enthusiastically urged to read his unjustly neglected book *The Philosophy and Psychology of Sensation* (1934). It is not readily available, but was reprinted once, and, of course, can be found in libraries. It is philosophy that is intriguing; and, for all of its currently unpalatable theorizing, it is full of useful philosophical insights. Anyway, for anyone with a taste for philosophy, it is extremely enjoyable to read.

O. K. Bouwsma's *bon mot*, that the sadness in the music is more like the redness to the apple than the burp to the cider, occurs in his essay 'The Expression Theory of Art,' originally published in *Philosophical Analysis: A Collection of Essays* (1950), edited by Max Black. Bouwsma later reprinted it in a collection of his work called *Philosophical Essays* (1969), and it has also appeared in a number of anthologies. It is a ground-breaking essay, written in a lively and engaging style. It is well worth the trouble to hunt it down.

My book *The Corded Shell: Reflections on Musical Expression* (1980) contains the complete version of the 'contour theory' that is outlined in this chapter. The book was later reprinted, with an extensive supplement, as *Sound Sentiment: An Essay on the Musical Emotions* (1989). The last-named is still available in a paperback edition.

Stephen Davies has, recently, presented another version of what I call the contour theory in his book *Musical Meaning and Expression* (1994). You will also find there an account of just about every theory of music and the emotions there is. Davies's book also contains the most complete bibliography of the literature that I know of, and is, therefore, extremely useful as a reference work.

Chapter 4   *A Little More History*

For those readers interested in getting a full dose of Kant's theory of art and beauty, there are three English translations of his *Critique of Judgment* (1790), of which two are readily available in paperback editions. The oldest translation is by J. H. Bernard (1892). But the two most popular ones, at present, are by James Creed Meredith (1911), and, more recently, Werner S. Pluhar (1987), both currently in print. Many people think the Pluhar translation a big improvement over its predecessors. I myself am partial to Meredith's. All three are readable.

The story I have told of the rise of instrumental music, the rise of formalism, and Kant's role in the enterprise is told more thoroughly in chapter 1 of my book *Philosophies of Arts: An Essay in Differences* (1997), which is currently in print in a paperback edition.

Chapter 5 *Formalism*

The first part of Leonard Meyer's book *Emotion and Meaning in Music* (1956) is the most relevant to the argument I have given. But the entire book can be read with profit. Also to be recommended in this regard are Meyer's essays, 'Meaning in Music and Information Theory,' 'Some Remarks on Value and Greatness in Music,' and 'On Rehearing Music,' all in his essay collection *Music, the Arts, and Ideas: Patterns and Predictions in Twentieth-Century Culture* (1967).

A comprehensive version of my view, as expressed here, will be found in my book *Music Alone: Philosophical Reflections on the Purely Musical Experience* (1990), chapters 3–7.

Chapter 6 *Enhanced Formalism*

I have written previously on the subject of emotive properties as 'syntactical' ones. For those who wish to pursue further my views on this subject I suggest that they look at my essay 'A New Music Criticism?,' which appears in my book of essays *The Fine Art of Repetition: Essays in the Philosophy of Music* (1993).

On the subject of expression and reference, the reader must go to the relevant portions of Nelson Goodman, *Languages of Art: An Approach to a Theory of Symbols* (1968), where the subject is discussed with logical rigor. (The book's index will help the reader locate the places to read.)

A vigorous defender of music's at least limited ability to 'say things' about emotions is Jerrold Levinson, in his essay 'Truth in Music.' The essay can be found in his collection *Music, Art, and Metaphysics: Essays in Philosophical Aesthetics* (1990).

Margaret Bent's essay from which I derived the example of how history can affect our perception of musical form is called 'Tonal Structure in Early Music,' and appears in *Criticism and Analysis of Early Music* (1998), edited by Christle Collins Judd.

On the advent of the public concert and the concert hall, and their influence on our perception of music, the reader can consult my book on musical performance, *Authenticities: Philosophical Reflections on Musical Performance* (1995), chapters 4 and 8. These same chapters are relevant for the discussion of absolute music's 'purity' (or lack of it).

Chapter 7 *The Emotions in you*

On the 'persona' theory of musical arousal, see Jerrold Levinson's essay 'Music and Negative Emotion,' in *Music, Art, and Metaphysics: Essays in Philosophical Aesthetics* (1990). Also of interest in this regard is Edward Cone's book *The Composer's Voice* (1974), where the musical 'persona' is discussed extensively.

The 'tendency' theory of musical arousal was first stated, as far as I know, by Colin Radford, in his article 'Emotions and Music: A Reply to the Cognitivists,' which appeared in the *Journal of Aesthetics and Art Criticism*, 47 (1989). Stephen Davies has defended it also in chapter 6 of his excellent book *Musical Meaning and Expression* (1994).

In my criticism of the 'tendency' theory I have benefited greatly from the thought-provoking article by T. S. Champlin published in *Proceedings of the Aristotelian Society*, NS 91 (1991). My more extensive reply to Radford and Davies can be found in my essay 'Auditor's Emotions: Contention, Concession and Compromise,' reprinted in *New Essays on Musical Understanding* (2001). This essay also has my response to Levinson's 'persona' theory.

The question of how the painful, 'negative' emotions might be valuable or enjoyable, if aroused by music, as some people believe, has been treated with great ingenuity by Jerrold Levinson, in his previously cited essay 'Music and Negative Emotion,' and, more recently, by Derek Matravers, in chapter 8 of his book *Art and Emotion* (1998). My response to Matravers is in 'The Arousal Theory of Musical Expression,' in *New Essays on Musical Understanding* (2001).

For those particularly interested in knowing more about the 'cognitive theory of emotions' as a philosophical doctrine, it was first stated, as far as I know, in a very readable little book by Anthony Kenny, *Action, Emotion and Will* (1969). The literature on the topic has grown quite large. But anyone who wants to go beyond Kenny, without becoming an expert, can go on to the collection of essays *Explaining Emotions* (1980), edited by Amélie Oksenberg Rorty.

The full statement of my own views concerning how music arouses emotion, in which I make use of the 'cognitive theory of emotions,' is in chapter 8 of my book *Music Alone: Philosophical Reflections on the Purely Musical Experience* (1990).

Chapter 8 *Foes of Formalism*

For those who may be interested in my views, and some of the contrary ones, on the knowledge claims of literary fiction, they are to be found, among other places, in chapter 5 of my book *Philosophies of Arts: An Essay in Differences* (1997).

The best exposition and defense I know of the concept of the plot archetype in music is by Anthony Newcomb, 'Once More "Between Absolute and Program Music": Schumann's Second Symphony,' *19th-Century Music*, 7 (1984). My argument against was first stated in 'A New Music Criticism?,' in *The Fine Art of Repetition: Essays in the Philosophy of Music* (1993).

Susan McClary's interpretation of Tchaikovsky's Fourth Symphony is to be found in her essay 'Sexual Politics in Classical Music.' It is published in her book *Feminine Endings: Music, Gender, and Sexuality* (1991). Other essays in this volume should be read by anyone who wants to get a fuller idea of 'the other side.'

David P. Schroeder's 'philosophical' interpretations of Haydn are laid out in his book *Haydn and the Enlightenment: The Late Symphonies and their Audience* (1990). There is a lot of documentation provided—the reader can decide if it is convincing.

The role of author's intention in criticism is one of the most vexed questions in contemporary philosophy of art. The reader will find a good selection of views on the question in *Intention and Interpretation* (1992), edited by Gary Iseminger.

A fuller account of the problem of repetition in music, if the reader is interested, can be found in my essay 'The Fine Art of Repetition,' which is the title essay of my essay collection *The Fine Art of Repetition: Essays in the Philosophy of Music* (1993). And the discussion of appreciating absolute music in contrast with appreciating pictures and poems without perceiving their 'content' is laid out in greater detail in 'Absolute Music and the New Musicology,' in *New Essays on Musical Understanding* (2001).

Chapter 9 *First the Words; Then the Music*

This chapter presents, in capsule form, my own 'philosophy of opera,' which is fully expounded in my book *Osmin's Rage: Philosophical Reflections on Opera, Drama and Text* (1988).

Those who wish to get deeper into the 'opera problem' are enthusiastically urged to read Joseph Kerman's classic *Opera as Drama* (1956), as well as Paul Robinson's splendid book *Opera and Ideas from Mozart to Strauss* (1985). Of all the books written on opera in the twentieth century, these are the ones I most admire.

My discussion of Mozart's dramatic ensembles, both here and in *Osmin's Rage*, was strongly influenced by the ideas of Charles Rosen, in chapter 3 of his well-known and admired book *The Classical Style: Haydn, Mozart, Beethoven* (1972). There is no better writer on music alive than Charles Rosen.

The presence of music in the movies is an intriguing and puzzling phenomenon. I have taken a stab at it, and suggested the relation of music in cinema to eighteenth-century melodrama in my essay 'Music in the Movies.' It is published in *Film Theory and Philosophy* (1997), edited by Richard Allen and Murray Smith, and contains a useful bibliography for anyone interested in pursuing the subject. The interested reader will also want to consult Noel Carroll, 'Notes on Movie Music,' in his essay collection *Theorizing the Moving Image* (1996).

Chapter 10 *Narration and Representation*

A full account of my position on musical representation and program music can be found in my book *Sound and Semblance: Reflections on Musical Representation* (1984).

The views of Roger Scruton that I criticize are in his article 'Representation in Music,' in the journal *Philosophy*, 51 (1976); and the views of Jenefer Robinson are to be found in her essay 'Music as a Representational Art,' published in *What Is Music?: An Introduction to the Philosophy of Music* (1987), edited by Philip Alperson. I have responded to Jenefer Robinson's views at greater length in the Afterword to the second edition of *Sound and Semblance* (1991).

A thorough discussion, both historical and aesthetic, of Berlioz's *Symphonie fantastique*, on which I have relied for various points, is that of Edward T. Cone, in the introduction to his edition of the score for Norton Critical Scores (1971).

Chapter 11 *The Work*

The statement of Goodman's view that the musical work is the class of compliants with the score is to be found in his *Languages of Art: An Approach to a Theory of Symbols* (1968), especially chapter V, sections 1 and 2.

Two of the criticisms I have aimed at Goodman's score-compliance analysis have their source in Richard Wollheim, *Art and its Objects: An Introduction to Aesthetics* (1968), although Wollheim does not aim them specifically at Goodman. (The two books appeared in the same year, so Wollheim could not possibly have known of Goodman's position.) Sections 1–39 of Wollheim's little book provide an excellent introduction to the problem of stating what a musical work is.

My own view, which I have described here as extreme Platonism, is put forward in a series of essays, 'Platonism in Music: A Kind of Defense,' 'Platonism in Music: Another Kind of Defense,' and 'Orchestrating Platonism,' all reprinted in my essay collection *The Fine Art of Repetition: Essays in the Philosophy of Music* (1993).

Those interested in pursuing further the example of Beethoven's sketches, which I adduced in putting forth my view, are recommended to read *Beethoven and the Creative Process* (1990), by Barry Cooper.

Jerrold Levinson puts forth his view, qualified Platonism, in 'What a Musical Work is,' and defends it against extreme Platonism, in 'What a Musical Work Is, Again.' Both essays are to be found in his *Music, Art and Metaphysics: Essays in Philosophical Aesthetics* (1990).

The concept of first-tokening can be found in chapter V of Jerrold Katz's *Realistic Rationalism* (1998). You must read the whole chapter (and perhaps the whole book) to get what Katz is saying, and it will be heavy going for the beginner in philosophy.

Finally, the interested reader will find a beautifully worked-out Platonic account of the musical work in part II of Nicholas Wolterstorff, *Works and Worlds of Art* (1980).

Chapter 12 *And the Performance thereof*

For those who seek initiation into the mysteries of early musical notation in the West, there is no better place to begin than with Leo Treitler, 'The "Unwritten" and "Written Transmission" of Medieval Chant and the Start-up of Musical Notation,' *Journal of Musicology*, 10 (1992), 131–91. I have relied on it heavily.

My own views on the significance of Treitler's article can be found in chapter 1 of my essay collection *New Essays on Musical Understanding* (2001).

Philosophers have only just become interested in musical performance as a subject of philosophical inquiry. My 'philosophy of musical perform-ance' is presented in its full form in *Authenticities: Philosophical Reflections on Musical Performance* (1995). A general work on performance well worth consulting is Paul Thom, *For an Audience: A Philosophy of the Performing Arts* (1993).

To get the musicologists' perspective on the historically authentic per-formance, the reader is directed to Nicholas Kenyon, *Authenticity and Early Music* (1988), and Peter Le Hurray, *Authenticity in Performance: Eighteenth-Century Case Studies* (1990).

Some articles by philosophers I have greatly benefited from are, Stephen Davies, 'Authenticity in Musical Performance,' *British Journal of Aesthetics*, 27 (1987), 39–50, and 'Transcription, Authenticity and Performance,' *British Journal of Aesthetics*, 28 (1988), 216–27, as well as Randall R. Dipert, 'The Composer's Intentions: An Evaluation of their Relevance for Perform-ance,' *Musical Quarterly*, 66 (1980), 205–18.

Chapter 13 *Why should you Listen?*

Schopenhauer's view of the 'liberating' power of the fine arts is laid out in book III of *The World as Will and Idea* (1819 / 1844), and you pretty much have to read the whole of book III to get the full import of what he is saying.

A more complete version of my own notion of music's 'liberating' power can be found in chapter 7 of my book *Philosophies of Arts: An Essay in Differences* (1997).

INDEX